MORE ZEAL THAN DISCRETION

Number Thirty-one: Elma Dill Russell Spencer
Series in the West and Southwest
Andrés Tijerina, General Editor

MORE ZEAL THAN DISCRETION

The Westward Adventures of Walter P. Lane

Jimmy L. Bryan Jr.

Texas A&M University Press
College Station

First edition

This paper meets the requirements of ANSI/NISO Z39.48-1992 (Permanence of Paper).
Binding materials have been chosen for durability.

Library of Congress Cataloging-in-Publication Data

Bryan, Jimmy L.
More zeal than discretion : the westward adventures of Walter P. Lane / Jimmy L. Bryan Jr. — 1st ed.
p. cm. — (Elma Dill Russell Spencer series in the West and Southwest ; no. 31)
Includes bibliographical references and index.
ISBN-13: 978-1-60344-070-7 (cloth : alk. paper)
ISBN-10: 1-60344-070-4 (cloth : alk. paper)
1. Lane, Walter P. (Walter Paye), 1817–1892. 2. Veterans—Texas—Biography. 3. Generals—Texas—Biography. 4. Texas—Militia—Biography. 5. Texas—History—Revolution, 1835–1836. 6. United States—History—War with Mexico, 1845–1848. 7. United States—History—Civil War, 1861–1865. I. Title. II. Series.
F390.L25B79 2008
976.4′05092—dc22
[B]

2008010755

For Liza, to whom I dedicate all my endeavors.

CONTENTS

LIST OF ILLUSTRATIONS

ACKNOWLEDGMENTS

I *have been working on* this biography of Walter Lane for more years than I wish to admit. I owe debts to a great many people who contributed to the several versions of this work and to my development as a scholar. Attempting to name them all will inevitably lead to gross omissions. To those I miss, my thanks and my apologies.

Sam Haynes, University of Texas at Arlington, deserves special mention. He was there at the very beginning. He, along with Richard Francaviglia and Gerald Saxon, served on my thesis committee, and their insistence on scholarly rigor has significantly influenced this biography. Also at UTA, Stephanie Cole first introduced me to the rich field of gender studies. Diana Hines and the staff at the UTA interlibrary loan office worked tirelessly to chase down obscure titles, and Katherine Goodwin, Sally Gross, Marcelle Hull, and the staff of the UTA Special Collections cheerfully assisted me in researching their rich archives. At Southern Methodist University, I enjoyed the opportunity to work with an impressive array of talent. I count Edward Countryman, Crista DeLuzio, Benjamin Johnson, Sherry Smith, and David Weber as mentors and friends. Without the generosity of Gov. William Clements, I could not have pursued an academic career. Thank you.

In the course of my research, I visited a number of libraries and archives. The staff at the Archives Division, Texas State Library, maintains an environment of professionalism, congeniality, and accessibility that never ceases to impress. Thanks to Melissa Essex of the Guernsey County District Public Library, Peggy Fox of the Col. Harold B. Simpson History Complex, and Lisa Struthers of the San Jacinto Museum of History. I am grateful for the assistance of the numerous staff members who I encountered of the Texas/Dallas History and Archives at the Dallas Public Library, the Harrison County

Museum, the New York State Library, and the archive formerly known as the Barker Texas History Center.

I would like to thank Mary Lenn Dixon of Texas A&M University Press for her patience and perseverance in bringing this unwieldy manuscript to publication. Thanks to Archie McDonald and the *East Texas Historical Journal* for publishing my article on the Surveyors' Fight, a modified version of which appears in chapter 3. James Crisp and Ralph Wooster read the over-long draft of the book, and I am grateful for their insightful encouragement.

My family and friends have been unwavering in their support of my academic endeavors. I have always counted on my mother Candance, my father, the original Jimmy Bryan, my lifelong friends James Solis and Christian Dovel, and most of all, my wife, Liza, to whom I dedicate this volume.

MORE ZEAL THAN DISCRETION

INTRODUCTION

In the middle of May 1847, somewhere in the chaparral near Monterrey, Mexico, Capt. Walter P. Lane and his company of Texas Rangers spent a frustrating day searching for local partisans. One evening, while the rangers attended to their camp, two local rancheros approached them. They had darkened their faces with gunpowder to conceal their identities—as much from the rangers as from Mexican authorities, who might charge them with treason for collaborating with the enemy. They informed Lane that they knew where the partisan captain lived. José Nicolás García, they claimed, was as much a threat to their lives and livelihood as he was to U.S. supply lines, and they offered to take the rangers to him.

Lane agreed and ordered his men to their horses. Closely guarding their guides, the rangers rode through the night and entered a small village near Cerralvo. The rancheros pointed to the largest dwelling, and Lane pounded on the door until an attendant finally opened it. As the captain rushed into the back room, a woman jumped from her bed, startled by the sudden intrusion. Even in this moment of danger and uncertainty, Antonia García's beauty was such that Lane would comment on it forty years later. He demanded the location of her husband, but she professed not to know. Lane bitterly recalled, "[A]s I had been atrociously lied to by *white* women, I did not give much credence to the assertions of the Mexican sister."[1] Indeed, the rangers found Nicolás García concealed beneath the blankets. They hauled him out of his home, his wife imploring for mercy. The next day, the court martial that Lane organized at Cerralvo found García guilty of guerrilla warfare and sentenced him to death. On May 29, after the local priest performed the sacred rites, García defiantly stared down the Texan rifles that, under Lane's command, took his life.[2]

According to his memoirs, Lane found himself in these circumstances because he repeatedly succumbed to his appetite for excitement. He viewed himself as an adventurer and indeed lived much of his life "on the wing," as he termed it, but as the episode near Cerralvo illustrated, adventurism not only placed Lane into situations of risk and violence but also into situations fraught with gendered and ethnic tensions.

The ranger captain was born in 1817, in County Cork, Ireland. In 1821, at the age of four, he crossed the Atlantic with his family, sailing for the United States and settling in rural Guernsey County, Ohio. Fourteen years later, filled with romantic images of Indians and far-off places, Lane left his parents' home and joined the embattled Anglo-Texans in their fight against what they perceived as Mexican tyranny. He fought at San Jacinto, served on a privateer, and assisted in the removal of Tejano and Indian communities in East Texas. Mexican lancers, gulf hurricanes, Kickapoo bullets, and Texas alligators did not diminish his enthusiasm for adventure, and he joined the Texas Rangers during the U.S. invasion of Mexico. In 1849, Lane crossed the Rocky Mountains and mined gold in California. He traveled to the Sonoran Desert and gambled with U.S. Army officers. With the outbreak of sectional hostilities, he joined the Confederate Army and actively served on the west side of the Mississippi River. When he retired from the adventurer's life, Lane settled in Marshall, Texas, and found only modest success at business and politics. During Reconstruction, he assisted in the so-called redemption of Harrison County from the black majority, reestablishing traditional white rule. He served the State of Texas in several minor offices, but he seemed most content when reconnecting with old comrades at various reunions.

Although Walter P. Lane neither fashioned the policies that directly influenced the course of events, nor commanded the decisive campaigns that executed them, he did participate in many important movements of the nineteenth century—adventurism, romanticism, expansion, secession, reconstruction, among others. An examination of Lane's experiences illustrates how larger movements influenced the life of one individual and reveals how Lane expressed and derived personal meaning from the social and cultural currents of his day.

To Lane, perhaps the most important movement was adventurism. It defined much of his life and informed the ways that he regarded gender and ethnicity, but few scholars have seriously examined the phenomenon and its historical manifestations.[3] For many historians, "adventure" and "adventurer" were throw-away—even derogatory—terms, used to dismiss those qualities in their subjects that they deemed unimportant or fleeting.[4]

As Lane's experiences demonstrated, adventurism was an important cultural phenomenon of the nineteenth-century United States.

Adventurism, however, was not new. The earliest stories, from Gilgamesh to Odysseus, described those who endured journeys of peril, but they were reluctant heroes who suffered the whims of capricious gods. The idea of deliberately seeking risk in far away places probably did not emerge until the twelfth century. In France, young men of noble families formed the *chevalerie,* joining military ventures, such as the Crusades, with the hope of obtaining titles and lands that primogeniture denied them. In the fifteenth century, during the closing decades of the Reconquista against Iberian Muslims, the *hidalgos* of Spain expressed similar ideas when an emerging merchant class threatened their status.[5]

In their time, the chevalerie and hidalgos came from the upper classes, but in the early nineteenth-century United States, the romantic emphasis on the individual and a belief in an egalitarian ethic presented male citizens of the United States opportunities that cut across class lines. These equalities were more imagined than real, but middle and lower class men, such as Walter Lane, did enjoy greater economic and political liberties than in generations past, and the expansion of the United States created accessible spaces for adventure.

Although no longer the exclusive privilege of the chevalerie and hidalgos of old, U.S. adventurers nevertheless viewed their perilous careers as opportunities to improve their economic and social status. Delving into Lane's life experiences, however, reveals that adventurers expected that their quests for wealth and fame would fundamentally transform them into vital, American men. Furthermore, they sought the companionship of like-minded men by joining expeditions to fight battles, survey the landscape, or encounter Native America. Throughout his life, Lane would turn to these enterprises, consistently turning away from a settled life.

These masculine relationships proved important to Lane. During the nineteenth century, men gauged their own manliness by the judgment of other men.[6] During the expedition, as in few other arenas, boys could quickly attain manhood, and men could achieve greater reputations by performing manly acts of risk-taking. The expedition created environments where men of Lane's generation could indulge in appropriate forms of violence. The idea of the quest focused the efforts of expedition members and fostered a spirit of teamwork, purpose, and camaraderie, forging masculine companionship and affection. The expedition also incorporated mechanisms of restraint to channel these manly passions. Formal command structures and informal codes of honor sought to curb the behavior of the more destructive members. Breaking these agreements could result in disciplinary measures but could also result in the censure from one's comrades. As Lane experienced in northeastern Mexico, however, this channeling was more effective in theory than in practice.

The image of the gentleman adventurer represented one of these mechanisms. Indeed, Lane did not see himself as a crude, unprincipled frontiersman. Instead, he viewed himself as a genteel champion of virtue. In his aptly titled autobiography, *The Adventures and Recollections of General Walter P. Lane . . .* (1887), he cultivated a self-image of a gentleman adventurer, who adhered to a code of honor like that expressed in Walter Scott's historical novels. He exhibited magnanimity to his enemies, a strict sense of duty, and a stark concept of right and wrong. He also displayed arrogance—or a certainty of his own ethical standing—which made him impatient with and self-righteous toward those who possessed lesser moral grit.[7]

Encountering different cultures on the frontiers of North America, however, challenged Lane's genteel and moralistic self-image, eliciting an ambiguous response from Lane. While he could admire individuals such as Mexican general Manuel F. Castrillón, balk at the needless slaughter of Mexican soldiers at San Jacinto, or seek to understand the plight of Texas Kickapoos, he also could order the execution of Nicolás García, see duplicity in the causes of East Texas Tejanos, and describe his Yankee enemies as "deluded bigots."[8] Reconstruction brought Lane into another frontier—a black and white one. He allied himself with the white minority of Harrison County, defended their cause with ethnically charged rhetoric, and warned the black majority of the county with threats of violence. All the while, Lane embraced a whiteness that formed a crucial part of his ideas regarding manliness.

Throughout his life, Lane consistently drew upon the notions of adventurous manhood. From 1835, at the age of eighteen, to the late 1850s, after he reached his fortieth birthday, he lived a life of prolonged adolescence, during which he joined numerous expeditions of various forms. In his early forties, he settled near his brother, George, in Marshall, Texas and sought to establish community ties. Adventurism, however, was an anathema to community and family. Marriage would have solved that problem, but Lane jealously guarded his bachelorhood—his adventurer personae. Gaining membership into this mixed-gender society required a compromise with domesticity, and he did so by establishing a home with his niece, Mary Jane Lane, as housekeeper.

When civil war seized the nation, family and community ties helped determine on which side Lane would fight. He joined the Confederate Army, claiming that he followed no cause other than an old adventuristic impulse. The absence of ideology might have been exceptional among Civil War soldiers, but adventurism may also have sustained Lane's morale when so many others became disillusioned.[9] During the war, however, Lane was no longer a youthful risk-taker, and he assumed the role of a paternal adventurer with the men under his command—a role that manifested itself as both the caring father and the strict disciplinarian. After the Civil War, he turned to veterans' reunions to fill the void that age created. Meeting with his old comrades provided retired adventurers such as Lane with the opportunity to recreate the all-male associations of the expedition, and swapping stories about their exploits testified to their manhood when they were too old to perform feats of manliness.

Adventurism, however, represented a specific manifestation of a larger cultural movement. The romantic ethic not only influenced Lane's attitudes and the decisions he made; it also shaped the world around him. As an intellectual movement, romanticism was a reaction to the Enlightenment—a movement that based political, social, and cultural thought on the practical, non-emotional, and ordered precepts of realism and rationality. Romantics, in contrast, embraced emotion with the belief that passion represented the essential human experience. They celebrated imagination, which unshackled their minds from the practical or achievable and permitted them to stoke their ambitions with a visionary fire. Romantics also longed for the elsewhere of both time and place. They sought to escape into the past or race into the future, envisioning exotic lands, better fields to sow, better markets to exploit, and better lives to live.[10] The emergence of U.S. romanticism, furthermore, coincided with the most intense period of U.S. expansionism, and the connection between the two was inextricable. The crucial elements of romanticism—emotion, imagination, and the elsewhere—were present at the core of the expansionist movement.[11]

With Lane's life as a lens, therefore, an examination of adventurism in the nineteenth-century United States provides a new perspective on the forces behind expansion, looking beyond the more traditional approaches that emphasize politics, economics, and diplomacy. Adventurism reveals that romantically charged ideas about gender and ethnicity fueled the continental ambitions of the United States, and although recent scholars have acknowledged the racial dimensions, they have largely interpreted expansion as a pessimistic phenomenon—driven by anxieties over slavery, industrialization, Anglophobia, and other fears.[12] A study of Lane's life experiences offers a more optimistic interpretation, suggesting that expansionists dreamed of an empire with confident, arrogant, and aggressive images that revealed as much about their nation as it did about themselves.

Although Lane led an extraordinary life, fraught with the incidents of adventure, he has not been the subject of a biography.[13] Perhaps the dearth of personal papers has hindered the study of Lane's experiences. His home burned in 1905, destroying any records that might have better illuminated his life and thoughts.[14] Although other collections contain his letters, few of his writings before 1860 survive. Fortunately, his memoirs provide important information about the course of his life, but in it, Lane revealed little of himself, and the book is as much an expression of his attitudes in 1887, when he wrote it, as it is a reflection of his experiences from 1835 to 1865. A careful reading and thorough research draws out the more private person and places him within the social and cultural context of his times.

Lives lived, however, are seductively linear, and biographies tend to follow a strict narrative structure. This treatment of Walter Lane, however, deviates slightly from this convention. The first part of chapter 1 treats Lane's childhood and family history thematically, exploring how and why the forces of adventurism, romanticism, and U.S. expansion called him away. Then, a narrative follows Lane as the romantic adventurer during the Texas Revolution, the U.S.-Mexican War, and the Gold Rush. In the late 1850s, he settled in Marshall, Texas and attempted to connect with family and community by compromising with domesticity. Here, the narrative pauses to reflect on Lane's life to that point—further illuminating his ideas about gender and hostility toward marriage. The narrative resumes with Lane's Civil War career, revealing his ambition for higher rank and his transformation into a paternal adventurer. The final two chapters thematically explore Lane's last years as a retired adventurer. During Reconstruction, he attempted to establish business and political careers, with disappointing results. His elusive attitudes toward race emerged during his role in the so-called redemption of Harrison County from the Republicans and black voters. His leadership in Texas reunion organizations illustrated the important function of these organizations as arenas for retired adventurers to romanticize the past. Furthermore, his recollections helped shape the lore and myth of the heroic interpretation of Texas history. The epilogue draws the biography to a conclusion, identifying the legacies of Lane's experiences, regarding the individual, society, and the culture in which he lived.

• 1 •

THE ROAD TO SAN JACINTO, 1817-36

On *August 10, 1821,* the merchant vessel *Medford* arrived at the busy port of Baltimore. In-bound from Cork, Ireland, the ship crossed the Atlantic in fifty days of uneventful sailing. Once the crew secured the moorings, its handful of passengers disembarked. Among their number, William and Olivia Lane and their seven children looked forward to their new lives in the New World. At four years of age, Walter Paye Lane, the youngest son of William and Olivia, probably could not have comprehended the significance of the new experiences arrayed before him.[1]

That same day, some seventeen hundred miles away, on the prairie along the Guadalupe River, Stephen F. Austin approached the villa of San Antonio de Béxar. He traveled there to request that the Spanish government confirm the colonization contract of his ailing father, Moses Austin. On August 12, he arrived at the provincial capital, negotiated for ten days and received confirmation as successor to his father's contract to settle three hundred families in Texas. Austin had initiated events that would dominate the remainder of his life and, in time, capture the imagination of the youngster standing on the wharves with his family in Baltimore.[2]

Walter Paye Lane, or "Nonny," as his family knew him, was a native of County Cork, Ireland, born to parents William and Olivia on February 18, 1817. His father, according to one description, "was of literary tastes and poor," while another noted that he "had the reputation of being a scholarly man with fine conversational powers." Olivia was "the wise, discreet and heroic mother." Beyond his parents, Walter's Irish ancestry remains unknown. Walter's niece noted that the Lane family had descended from English aristocracy, but William apparently claimed little of that inheritance.[3]

William Lane left few clues that would reveal his reasons for leaving

Ireland, but the depression of 1818 likely played a key role. During the Napoleonic Wars, Cork thrived as a major supply port for the British military, and prosperity created a population boom. After the British defeated the French in 1815, agricultural and mercantile prices fell, and returning soldiers exacerbated Cork's problems with overpopulation. In the hinterland, the Irish middleman system of subletting and subdividing finite land resources contributed to the depression. Prospects of land ownership in the United States, and a chance to start anew, beckoned to many Irish families. One such immigrant of the era explained that "unless a young man has capital . . . he may toil all his life, and never find an independent feeling occupy his breast," but in the United States, if he worked hard, "he will eventually succeed." Under these circumstances, William Lane gathered his family, boarded the *Medford,* and sailed to a new life.[4]

When he landed in Baltimore, William declared to customs that he intended to reside in Kentucky. He may well have scouted lands or even attempted farming there, but by 1828, he had settled in Guernsey County, Ohio. He obtained about 125 acres in Oxford Township, northwest of Fairview, a small community on the old Zane Trace, near the Belmont County line.[5] The land was rugged hill country, deep in the trans-Ohio outcropping of the Allegheny Plateau, covered with a dense forest of mixed hardwoods. One local observer described the terrain as having a "romantic appearance . . . [T]here are no valleys but those shut in and surrounded by other hills, and this makes the whole scene one of beauty and charm to the passer-by." This broken topography confined any farming or grazing to the narrow valleys and hillsides. A contemporary booster blamed the lack of agricultural production on non-resident land speculators, who owned all the good land and would not sell at reasonable prices. This section, however, was not conducive to large-scale and profitable agriculture.[6]

If these less-than-productive fields did not draw him there, then perhaps the promise of work on the National Road lured William Lane to the Fairview area. On March 3, 1825, the U.S. Congress appropriated $150,000 for the extension of the road from Wheeling to Zanesville, Ohio. Farmers worked on the road as laborers or contractors, and most were crews of Irishmen, who graded the route, paved the roadbed with crushed stones, and built those peculiar S-shaped bridges unique to the Wheeling-Zanesville section. By June 1826, the National Road employed 826 men. The U.S. government often paid crews in acreage along the route rather than in dollars, and this might have been the means by which the Lanes received their plot.[7]

Of his childhood near Fairview, Walter Lane left no recollection with which to identify any enduring influences, but as his actions would soon demonstrate, movements on a national scale would draw him away from his family's home. An expansionist surge compelled Americans west across the Mississippi and often brought them into conflict with Native and Latin Americans. Expansionists of the 1820s and 1830s invigorated their rhetoric with powerfully romantic images designed to incite emotional responses, stoke eager imaginations, and arouse longings for the elsewhere. In 1821, scarcely a month before the family's arrival, a Fourth of July orator at Baltimore expressed these romantic notions; he envisioned that within a century, the United States would possess two hundred million people, fifty states, and "cover the expansive arch of heaven from the Atlantic to the Pacific, tinging the tops of the Rocky mountains, and glaring upon the broad surface [of] the Gulf of California."[8]

The coupling of expansionism and romanticism created a powerful, adventuristic impulse. Thousands in Lane's generation sought the emotional stimulation of risk-taking and renown, and in the face of peril and violence, they imagined new meanings of Americanness and manliness. They sated their yearning for the elsewhere in sublime landscapes and with promises of prosperity, and many believed that their adventurous experiences would transform them into memorably vital men.[9]

In the humble setting of Fairview, Ohio, these forces reached Walter Lane. The National Road itself was a conspicuous symbol, if not a tangible example, of the westwardly expanding nation, bringing through the middle of the community travelers from the East, who expressed their dreams of new lives elsewhere, and travelers from the West, bringing tales of such exotic places like Missouri, Arkansas, and Texas. At Fairview, drivers often changed their teams and stayed overnight. The Bradshaw Tavern was renowned as the best inn between Wheeling and Zanesville, and as one long-time resident noted, "Many tales were told by the travelers as they sat about the big fireplace." The National Road, with its dusty course disappearing behind some wooded hillside, leading to someplace else, would have been a powerful lure to a young man bored with the doldrums of the rural Ohio landscape.[10]

Lane's affinity for fiction, however, provided him with an immediate opportunity to escape into worlds not his own and feed his appetite for excitement. He read the works of William Shakespeare, Daniel Defoe, and, above them all, Walter Scott and his heroic tales of medieval Scotland and England. Scott's novels sold over a million copies in the United States and inspired many American romantics. Although more often associated with the cultural phenomenon of Southern honor, Scott was no less popular in the North, and he was certainly known of in Guernsey County.[11]

The martial spirit of Scott's lore was one feature that Lane would try to exemplify. In the novel *Ivanhoe* (1819), Scott explained the lure of combat through the words of his title character. During the siege of Torquilstone, Wilfred Ivanhoe defended his code of chivalry against Lady Rebecca's questions. "The love of battle is the food upon which we live," the knight stated, "the dust of the *melée* is the breath of our nostrils! We live not—we wish not to live—longer than while we are victorious and renowned. Such, maiden, are the laws of chivalry to which we are sworn, and to which we offer all that we hold dear."[12] This romanticization of warfare and heroic celebrity appealed powerfully to Walter Lane, and it resonated throughout his life.

Living in Guernsey County during the 1830s, however, Lane did not need to travel to England or transport himself through time to find the adventure he sought. The frontiers of North America offered ample opportunity for those romantics of a martial inclination, and stories of strife with Native Americans preoccupied Lane's imagination. Living in Ohio, he had never encountered an Indian, but sensational accounts of warfare filled the local newspapers. Under headlines such as "Indian Battle" and "An Indian Horse," the *Guernsey Times* often featured the fictional struggle in the West, presented in a prose calculated to incite the emotions of its readers. On occasion, editors devoted their entire front pages to tales such as "The Dark and Bloody Ground" and "The Ghost Riders: A Legend of the Great American Desert" that recounted the perceived heroics of the Anglo-pioneers of the trans-Appalachia area and beyond.[13]

The appearance of these accounts in local papers suggests that the imagined peril of Native America was an important topic to the community in which Lane lived, and he personally exhibited these anxieties. In the spring of 1836, during his steamboat voyage between Louisville and New Orleans, he shared a stateroom with an Episcopal minister. Sleeping in the upper bunk, Lane dreamed. "I raised a fearful cry of '*Murder!*' 'Indians, kill them, ——them.'" Lane recalled that the minister woke up and tried to leave, but "I fell down on top of him. He tried to shake me off, but I thought he was the 'Big Brave.'" After the minister sounded a cry of alarm, a party of gamblers intervened and awoke the sleepwalker. Lane's nightmare was indicative of an obsession with ideas about Native Americans that he acquired from sources other than personal experience.[14]

Similarly, Texas preoccupied the imagination of U.S. editors and their readers, and the newspapers along the National Road between Wheeling and Zanesville were no different. As early as the 1820s, these publications reported Anglo-American colonization projects in Texas as well as any conflict between these settlers and their Mexican hosts. In November 1834, the *Guernsey Times* printed a prophetic article that stated, "[I]t is so obviously the interest both of Mexico and the United States to make the Rio Grande the dividing line, that we do not doubt but sooner or later that river will be fixed upon by the two governments."[15]

In the fall of 1835, when Anglo-American colonists and Tejano settlers resisted the centralist policies of Mexican President Antonio López de Santa Anna, many U.S. editors rallied to support them. As early as August 1835, the *St. Clairsville Gazette* reprinted New Orleans notices that war in Texas was likely. As the conflict gained momentum, so too did the reports from Texas, which by November dominated the local papers. "The situation of Texas is the most interesting topic that now engages the minds of the people," declared the November 6 issue of the *Wheeling Tri-Weekly Gazette.* On the 18th, the paper reported, "*The war is begun,* and the Texians so far are the victors," noting the clash at Gonzales, traditionally regarded as the first battle of the Texas Revolution.[16]

Although other states of the Mexican union had rebelled against Santa Anna and failed, Texas possessed one advantage that they did not—assistance from the United States. To sustain their cause, Texans relied on financial aid, material contribution, and most importantly, volunteers from the United States. The editor of the Wheeling *Gazette* called for official non-interference but suggested, "Aid can be furnished [to] our countrymen in Texas, by men going 'by pairs and singly,' for which our government cannot be made responsible." Many U.S. citizens embraced this idea, such as the fifty men from Wheeling who organized a company for Texas in New Orleans in late September, defying U.S. neutrality laws.[17]

Influenced by these sympathies and by his own yearning for adventure, an eighteen-year-old Walter Lane decided to enter the conflict on the side of the rebels. In November 1835, he embarked for Texas, taking passage aboard a riverboat at Wheeling and steaming down the Ohio to Louisville. He was not interested in the complex causes of the war.[18] Instead, he responded to the rhetoric present in news reports that appealed to his pride in his fellow Anglo-Americans, who ostensibly fought for the uncomplicated principles of liberty, justice, and self-rule. Reports of battles fought in the chaparral and on the gulf also promised excitement to any who might cast his lot with the Texans. When he left his parents' home, Lane set out alone, and he followed no ideology other than a romantic notion of adventure.[19]

Lane was not alone in his desire to seek excitement in that clamorous province. Nineteen-year-old John C. Duval of Bardstown, Kentucky, enlisted in a company after hearing stories about Texas. Evoking the romantic elsewhere, Duval admitted, "[I]nsensibly, an ardent longing sprang up in my bosom to see for myself the 'broad prairies,' the beautiful streams and vast herds of buffalo and wild horses." Even forty-year-old Micajah Autry, a veteran of the War of 1812, admitted to his wife, "I feel more energy than I ever did in anything I have undertaken," as he boarded a steamboat at Memphis, plying for Texas. He would die at the Alamo. The same romanticized notions of warfare that inspired Lane compelled Virginia native John Sowers Brooks to seek his destiny in Texas. "I am acting, my dear sister, in that sphere which nature designed me to fill. *I am a soldier of fortune;* and all the premonitions of my child hood early told me that I should be one. . . . My prayer has been, since my earliest recollection, to die on the field of battle, with the shout of victory in my ears." Brooks did not find the glorious death he envisioned. Mexican guards beat him to death at Goliad.[20]

Samuel H. Walker, with whom Lane would later serve during the U.S.-Mexican War, epitomized this romantic adventurer. With echoes of Ivanhoe's creed, he wrote from Florida, "[T]hat unextinguishable love of chivalric immortal fame still clings to my heart." Writing in 1842, Walker illustrated how romantics allowed their emotions to influence their decisions. "[T]hough the passionate fondness of my friends & relatives often effect [*sic*] my feelings[, t]he love of Fame still urges me on[.] I was thus admist [*sic*] all these contending passions." Adventure provided Walker, Lane, and men like them with an avenue to attain prestige and emotional gratification, as well as claims to a meaningful manliness. "Heaven forbids that I should ever mistake the path of true glory," Walker wrote, "forgetting the true and proper elements of a great man in his pursuit of that honourable [*sic*] distinction." Just as Lane had, Walker looked to that fabled place across the Sabine to sate his need for adventure. "My Brother still advises me to return home[,] but to return without wealth or Fame[,] it is too bad, therefore be not surprised if my next communication to you should be written in Texas." When he left Ohio for Texas, Lane embraced the same ideas that Duval, Autry, Brooks, Walker, and a generation of American men expressed.[21]

When he steamed into Louisville, Kentucky, Lane stopped to visit his older brother. Wade F. Lane had recently moved to that river port and established a wholesale grocery firm. The elder sought to douse his younger brother's ardor. "He partly put the notion of Texas out of my head," Walter admitted. Wade employed him as a clerk, providing him with crucial training that he would use throughout the remainder of his life. The brothers boarded at the home of the distinguished John J. Marshall, lawyer, state legislator and soon to become judge of the Louisville Circuit Court.[22]

Louisville, however, was not the place to reside in order to abandon notions of Texas. The town was an active center for Texas aid and recruitment. Many citizens participated in mass meetings, passed resolutions of support, collected subscriptions, and organized military companies. The Lanes' host family energetically supported the cause, especially Marshall's son, Humphrey. Despite the enticements, Wade kept Walter busy learning the trade of a merchant and managed to delay his journey to Texas for several months.[23]

During this time, the winter of 1835 and 1836, a lull settled over events in Texas. In early December, when the rebels ousted Mexican forces from San Antonio, they removed the immediate cause for conflict. The provisional Texas government, meanwhile, set out to defend against Santa Anna's counterstrike. They called for a convention to determine whether Texas should continue to support the Mexican Constitution of 1824 or declare its independence. By the spring, independence was the nearly unanimous choice. The government also sent a delegation of three commissioners to the United States on a mission to rally support, execute loans, and spread the gospel of Texas independence. On March 3, 1836, two of the agents arrived in Louisville. They were Branch T. Archer and Stephen F. Austin, the empresario himself.[24]

After his first night in Louisville, the welcome that Austin received encouraged him. He expressed his optimism in a letter home: "Every thing is cheering in this part of the world for Texas. The hearts of this people are with us—Nothing is now needed but union at home and an *absolute* and *immediate* declaration of *independence*."[25] Indeed, two days before on the 2nd, the convention that met at Washington-on-the-Brazos had declared independence, but Santa Anna had already invested the Alamo, an old Spanish mission just outside San Antonio. There, on the 6th, the Texas garrison, under William B. Travis, fell with all its defenders slain. But news of these weighty events would not reach Louisville before Austin left and not before Walter Lane could reaffirm his Texas ambitions.

On March 7, 1836, some twelve hundred Louisville citizens gathered for a pro-Texas meeting at the Second Presbyterian Church; John J. Marshall presided. After calling for order, he stated the purpose of the meeting and introduced Austin, who "rose amidst the cheering of the multitude," as a local newspaper reported. When the audience quieted, Austin spoke. He began by reviewing the history that resulted in the conflict, citing Santa Anna's dictatorial policy as the root of Texan grief. He gave a review of the resources of Texas, after which he concluded, "I have shown that our cause is just and righteous, that it is the great cause of mankind, and as such merits the approbation and moral support of this magnanimous and free people." Archer spoke next, and Humphrey Marshall followed, passing a resolution, welcoming the Texans as brothers and as being "worthy . . . to establish upon the broken fetters of military despotism and misrule, the fair fabric of a virtuous Republic." Lane did not mention if he attended this mass meeting, but sometime during their stay in Louisville, Austin and Archer met with the young man. Knowing of Lane's interest in Texas, John J. Marshall arranged for an introduction, and Lane visited the commissioners in their hotel room, where they described their country and their cause and provided him with letters of introduction to Gen. Sam Houston and Gov. Henry Smith.[26]

With his enthusiasm for Texas renewed, Lane booked passage aboard a steamer bound for New Orleans, taking quarters in the stateroom. His nightmare of Indians and his assault on the minister occurred during this voyage, and when he arrived in New Orleans, Lane took a few days to tour the sights. From New Orleans, Lane opted for the overland route to Texas, boarding another riverboat and plying back up the Mississippi into the Red River. He landed at Natchitoches and set out on foot, following a road that wound through the dense pine forest of western Louisiana. He passed Fort Jessup and crossed the Sabine River at Gaines's Ferry.[27]

Lane's first glimpse of Texas presented a rich forest of tall pines that cloaked a hill country, less rugged than the Allegheny landscape to which he was accustomed. Beneath the blanket of pine needles, the earth revealed a ruddy complexion, which gave this section of Texas its name, the Red Lands. Lane reached San Augustine sometime in late March. A recent visitor described the town as "a new place, not two years since the first house was built. Has now about a dozen finished and going up. Laid out in the woods, on *red land*." Lane complained that he arrived "with about *six bits* in my pocket," but found a party organizing a company for Houston's army. The provisional government allowed men of means to avoid service by hiring substitutes, and Lane encountered one such individual, who provided him with "a fine horse, double-barreled gun, and a brace of pistols to take his place." Handsomely supplied with the accoutrements of war, he declared, "I was all right then."[28]

The cause of Texas independence, however, was in peril. The force of individualism that Anglo-Texans sought to preserve threatened their undoing. Troubled by factious in-fighting, the convention that declared independence struggled to organize an effective government. To meet the impeding arrival of Santa Anna and his soldiers, they appointed former Tennessee governor Samuel Houston as commander of a non-extant army. He failed to bring under his control the forces commanded by Travis and James W. Fannin. Their headstrong personalities led them toward their defeats at the Alamo and Goliad. This individualism further hindered Houston's efforts to cobble together an army at Groce's Retreat.[29]

In this environment, where "every man was his own captain," the individualist mantra of the period, military organization was mercurial. Lane, for example, would serve in two different companies in as many weeks. On the 15th, he joined Capt. William Kimbro's company, and the next day, his comrades elected him sergeant. He later joined James Chessher's Jasper Volunteers. He likely made this switch based on Chessher's promise of joining General Houston, but events in East Texas prevented that.[30]

If the Texas Revolution was a clash of cultures, then the Red Lands was its most volatile region. There, Anglo-Texans lived in close proximity with Tejanos, native Hasinais, and a community of dislocated peoples across the Angelina River that consisted primarily of Kickapoos, Delawares, and Shawnees, under the nominal leadership of Cherokees. Although Houston had obtained assurances of non-interference from the Cherokee association, rumors of Indian attacks, Tejano duplicity, and collusion with the advancing Mexicans alarmed the Anglo inhabitants. Although ready to march for Houston's army, Captain Chessher deemed that the situation in East Texas required his presence at Nacogdoches, about thirty miles west of San Augustine on the Camino Real. He assured the leaders there, "We are convinced that the Indians intend attacking your place; we shall march immediately." With Chessher's company, Lane arrived at the old Spanish settlement, where officials managed to gather about 250 men.[31]

After several days, Chessher selected Lane to deliver messages to General Houston and provided him with an order to impress a horse if his failed. Refugees from the war zone filled the roads over which Lane traveled. Hundreds of Anglo-Texans, mostly women and children, fled the advance of Santa Anna's army, tossing broken equipment or encumbering luxuries. The Runaway Scrape, with its abandoned hopes and discarded dreams, represented one of those inconvenient realities of war that romantics like Lane often overlooked.[32]

Indeed, in his memoirs, Lane omitted the Runaway Scrape, but his journey from Nacogdoches to Groce's Retreat included two moments impressed upon his recollections. The first occurred when his horse became fatigued, and he attempted to execute the requisition that Chessher provided for a fresh mount. "I never tried that game but once," Lane assured his readers. He showed the owner his orders, but the reluctant Texan replied, "Hold on a minute and I will show you an order *against* my horse being *pressed*." He entered his house, Lane recalled, and reemerged "with his *big* son and two double-barreled shot guns, and told me to git." When Lane relented, the old man invited him to stay the night. At supper, the owner advised, "Sonny, never try that dodge *agin* in Texas."[33]

The second episode occurred on the road the next day. Lane chanced upon a group of six Native Americans, probably Hasinais. They were the first Native Americans he personally encountered. "I came near falling off my horse." They compelled him to stop, curious about his shotgun. When one reached for it, Lane "waved him back, and cocked one barrel, and told him: 'No see' . . . when they all burst into a laugh and said: 'White man skeeered.'" Lane admitted, "God knows I was." They left him frightened but unharmed, and he continued his mission.[34]

These two moments reveal multiple meanings about Lane's adventurous career. In both, he exhibited a straightforward sense of humor, with himself as the object of jest. This ability to laugh at oneself was an important quality among adventurers. It reinforced the egalitarian ethic of the expedition because it signified that one did not perceive himself as superior to his comrades. The incident with the horse owner marked the tension between duty and individualism. Lane valued both his own determination to follow orders as well as the old man's pragmatism and magnanimity. His conversation with the Indians showed his willingness to admit fear—at least to his readers—a theme throughout his memoirs. By transcending moments of trepidation, Lane exhibited his capacity for courage. The meeting further demonstrated how extra-cultural encounters bristled with violent potential. Lane reacted by presenting his firearm, ready to shed blood. Lane's inclusion of both of these anecdotes, and others like them, further suggested that these minor incidents shared equal space with renown, wealth, and transformation as the impetus behind adventurous careers. Both stories also illustrated the value of storytelling in conveying these ideas, and Walter Lane would become a practiced storyteller by the time he committed his recollections to paper.

After these episodes, Lane arrived at Groce's Retreat and delivered to General Houston Chesser's dispatches and the letters of introduction that Austin and Archer provided to him in Louisville. During his meeting, a group of volunteers called on the general and requested a furlough, so that they might assist their families in the Runaway Scrape. Understanding that these men would probably leave with or without permission, he granted their request and immediately employed Lane as a clerk to facilitate the paper work.[35]

As this moment demonstrated, the twelve hundred men that Houston assembled were a contentious group. To many of the soldiers, the general's withdrawal to Jared E. Groce's plantation on the Brazos was a headlong retreat, but Houston argued that he needed time to drill his ill-disciplined troops. The Texas government also felt that he was moving too slowly, and newly appointed ad interim president, David G. Burnet, dispatched his Secretary of War, Thomas J. Rusk, to urge the general into action, or take command himself. When Rusk arrived, Houston convinced him of the wisdom of the delay, and the secretary joined the army as second in command. On April 12, the general ordered his force to strike camp, and after two days crossing the swollen Brazos, he marched eastward down sodden roads.

With the destruction of Texas forces at the Alamo and Goliad, Santa Anna recognized that the only remaining rebel force of consequence was Houston's army, and in late March, he departed San Antonio in search of his quarry. He crossed the lower Brazos on April 9 and soon after learned that the Texas government had moved to Harrisburg. Santa Anna opted to abandon momentarily his pursuit of Houston and capture the rebel government, but Burnet and his cabinet escaped by mere hours. On the 18th, the Mexicans torched the town.[36]

During this time, Lane "got tired of acting aid," as he described his clerkship, and requested a transfer to the scouts under Henry W. Karnes. Houston consented, and on April 16, Lane joined the unit as a private. Karnes had organized his company on March 20 at Beeson's Crossing of the Colorado River. Karnes, Erastus "Deaf" Smith, and Hendrick Arnold—all veterans of the campaigns about Béxar during the fall of 1835—formed its nucleus, and in this group, Lane met three men who would become lifelong friends: Robert K. Goodloe, Young P. Alsbury, and William Crittenden.[37]

On the 18th, Houston's army arrived at the smoldering ruins of Harrisburg on Buffalo Bayou. The general dispatched Karnes's company across the bayou to act as pickets and to scout the advance. Deaf Smith intercepted a Mexican courier, and from this intelligence, Houston learned for the first time that Santa Anna himself commanded the force before them. Armed with this intelligence, Houston broke camp and moved his army to the southern bank of Buffalo Bayou, near its junction with the San Jacinto River. To his south, across an open field, Santa Anna camped just inside a stand of timber. The New Washington road lay on Santa Anna's left, while the San Jacinto flowed at his right. In his rear, a marsh opened into a small lake.[38]

Early the next morning, April 20, the Texans discovered a party of Mexicans transporting supplies across the bayou. Rusk took two hundred men, including Karnes's company, and captured the Mexican boats, laden with the plunder from Harrisburg. The Mexican soldiers escaped across the bayou and took shelter in a nearby house. Rusk called for volunteers to swim across and retrieve a small boat so that the Texans might cross over and capture the detachment. Lane and Crittenden accepted the charge. "We neared the shore below the house," Lane said of the crossing. "I was getting tired, but suddenly a *big alligator* put his head up, some ten feet from me, to see what was the matter. The surprise was mutual. The alligator dived in front of me, as I thought to get one of my *hind* legs, and I fairly flew ashore." Lane and Crittenden succeeded in gaining the boat, and, harassed by Mexican gunfire, they rowed back to Rusk. The Secretary of War sent twenty men back across the bayou. They accepted the surrender of the Mexicans. When artillery boomed across the prairie, Rusk ordered his force back to camp and found the two sides engaged in a artillery duel, which accomplished little more than announcing each other's presence.[39]

Anxious to receive accurate information of the Mexican troop strength, General Houston called on his reliable scout, Deaf Smith. The spy noted Lane's fine horse and chose the inexperienced trooper to accompany him. They rode to the rear of the Mexican position, and Lane held their horses while Smith counted Mexican tents with his field glass. "The enemy ran out a company of soldiers and commenced firing on us," Lane recalled. "The balls whistled over our heads—greatly to my demoralization—but Smith did not notice them." A squad of Mexican cavalry rode out to chastise the spies, and Smith casually remarked, "Lane I think *them* fellows are shooting at us; let us *git*." Lane wasted little time. "I never obeyed an order more cheerfully in my life . . . while under fire I expected to be murdered at each round." Lane openly revealed his fear to the readers of his memoirs, but in that moment, he could not admit it to Smith. "I knew [they were shooting at us] 20 minutes before but was ashamed to tell him."[40]

When Lane and Smith returned, they found the camp abustle with activity. After the exchange of artillery, Sidney Sherman, commander of the rebel cavalry, argued heatedly with Houston to allow him to attack the Mexican piece and capture it. Sherman had the sympathy of the soldiers. With a larger force arrayed before him, Houston was once again confronted by his unruly subordinates. He had little choice but to compromise with Sherman and permit him to reconnoiter the enemy position with the futile directive not to engage them.

Lane arrived in time to join the sixty mounted Texans who trotted out to probe the enemy. The Mexican cavalry formed a line of battle, and their officers antagonized the Texans with jeers and challenges. Sherman would not let the opportunity pass and ordered Lane and his comrades to charge the Mexican position. "[W]e went through them like a stroke of lightning," Lane described, and "chased them back to their infantry." After several charges and counter-charges, the Mexican cavalry withstood the Texan strike. Defying orders, Jesse Billingsley marched his infantry past an infuriated Houston to support Sherman, bringing with him Edward Burleson's entire regiment. Sherman ordered his cavalry to withdraw and support the infantry. Unfortunately for Lane, his horse—perhaps imbued with the spirit of Texan individuality—considered other alternatives. "My horse—a powerful animal—had got excited, and having more *zeal* than *discretion,* took the bit in his teeth and ran me headlong into the midst of the enemy, much to my disgust." Sherman called for his men to withdraw. "I was unanimously in favor of it, but my horse wanted to go through. A Mexican lancer settled the difficulty by cutting at my head with his sabre." Lane grappled with the lancer, when another rushed up and knocked him off his horse. "I fell on my head, stunned and senseless."[41]

An ambitious volunteer from Georgia, Mirabeau B. Lamar, noticed the altercation between Lane and the lancer and rushed to Lane's aid. He shot the Mexican but judged the prostrate Lane as killed and rejoined the withdrawing Texans. When he awoke, Lane found himself alone on the field. "I regained consciousness and my feet at the same time. Twenty Mexicans were round me when I rose, but it so surprised them to see a *dead* boy rise to his feet and run like a *buck,* that I got ten steps before they fired at me." Captain Karnes spotted his downed trooper and ordered his company to wheel about and race to his assistance. Lane "did some of the prettiest running to catch up," and reached an old timer—with an equally old horse—and rode to safety. When he arrived in camp, fellow trooper Robert Goodloe dressed Lane's wound.[42]

The dissension in Houston's army continued into the morning and early afternoon of April 21, 1836. "The men wanted to fight," Lane explained, "Gen. Filasola [*sic*], with the main Mexican army, was some eighty miles off, and if he joined Santa Anna we would be 'rubbed out.' Gen. Houston wanted to wait a few days for reinforcements . . . but the men sent up their officers, demanding *fight.* So *fight* it was." Another volunteer recalled that when the officers confronted Houston, an animated discussion ensued. The general finally jumped up, exasperated, and reportedly said, "Then fight and be damned." At about three in the afternoon, the general arrayed his 900 soldiers in a thin line across the prairie and ordered them forward against Santa Anna, reinforced to 1,250 with the arrival of Gen. Martín Perfecto de Cós. Without a horse, Lane joined an infantry unit. He probably served under Sergeant Goodloe in a company of other soldiers who lost their horses during the previous day's skirmish. Lane marched somewhere in the middle of the advancing line.[43]

The Texans initially maintained order as they crossed the bayou grass. Once they discovered the advance, the Mexicans fired a barrage of artillery, "but, as we were going up a slight ascent, they overshot us," Lane explained.

After a Mexican lancer unhorsed him during Sidney Sherman's skirmish, Lane ran to a volunteer who carried him to safety. The image of the old horse endured in his memory. Lane recalled, "She was a sorrel mare and thin in flesh; I would know her hide if it was dried on a fence even now." Charles Shaw, *Texan Cavalry Retreats.* Oil on canvas, 1986. Courtesy of The San Jacinto Museum of History, Houston, Tex.

"We never fired a gun till we got within forty yards." Employing traditional military tactics, Houston ordered his troops to halt, aim, and fire; but his unruly men eschewed proper formation. After their first volley, the Texans charged the Mexican breastworks of crates, feed sacks, barrels, and various other supplies. Lane rushed into the fray. "In a second we were into them with guns, pistols, and bowie knives, and there rose a cry of: 'Remember the Alamo!' In a short time they were running like turkeys, whipped and discomfitted." Any semblance of unit cohesion disappeared, as Houston's army melted into the fleeing Mexicans. Lane's friend, Young Alsbury, remembered that the charge "was by no means marked for its modesty . . . in a few minutes, evry [*sic*] officer became a private, and evry [*sic*] private became his own officer."[44]

Lane's squad reached the Mexican artillery commanded by Gen. Manuel F. Castrillón. The officer faced the rush of Texans and, according to Lane, declared in his own language, "I have been in forty battles and never showed my back; I am too old to do it now." Secretary Rusk rode forward and called on his men to spare the general, but they ignored the order and shot him down. As he continued through Santa Anna's camp, Lane encountered one of his comrades threatening several wounded Mexican soldiers in a hospital tent. The gruff Texan demanded, "Bring out the *chist,* or be J——I'll blow ye brains out," but Lane realized that the chest held only medicine—not gold. Lane assured, "I told him of his mistake and got him out."[45]

In less than a half hour, the Texans swept through the Mexican camp. The battle was over, but the real butchery had just begun. Those Mexicans who tried to surrender found their opponents were in little mood to give quarter. "The greatest slaughter in the battle occurred between the breastworks and the lake," one Texan surmised, and most participants and later scholars agreed. The Texas officers attempted to rein in their men, but like Rusk trying to spare Castrillón's life, they met with little success. Adj. Gen. John A. Wharton "tried to get us to cease," one soldier reported, "and grabbed a Mexican and pulled him up behind him on his horse, saying that was his Mexican," but the rebels ignored Wharton and killed the soldier.[46]

Similar incidents continued as the Texans pursued the Mexicans to the lake behind Santa Anna's camp. "[T]hey took to water, like ducks, to swim across," Lane wrote, "our men firing at their heads." A fellow rebel soldier saw that the Mexicans "would dive to get away from our shots, but the minute they would raise their heads they were picked off by our men." Another veteran described the affair as the "first sport and best target practice of the day." According to Lane, somebody called for a cease-fire, and miraculously, the Texans complied. This individual called out to the Mexicans, offering not to harm them should they return. Many accepted, but when they neared the shore, the soldier urged his comrades, "Now, boys, give it to them." Lane estimated some two hundred Mexicans perished there.[47]

And the carnage continued elsewhere on the battlefield. Thomas F. Corry, a volunteer from Ohio, left the target shooting at the marsh—"this work did not suit my feelings," he recalled—and met John Forbes, commissary general of the army. While they conversed, a pair of Texas soldiers approached, escorting two Mexican prisoners—a man and a woman. A Texas officer rode up and ordered, "Kill them, God damn them. Remember the Alamo." The two soldiers fell on the male prisoner with their bayonets and while Corry rushed to intervene, Forbes "thrust his sword through the woman's breast, the blade entering in front, and coming out at her back." Corry lamented, "This dreadful deed paralysed me," and he admonished Forbes, "Damn you, you have killed a woman." Walter Lane encountered Forbes later in the afternoon. After rounding up Mexican soldiers, Lane and several comrades returned to camp with a group of prisoners, and the commissary general attempted to repeat the act of running his sword through one of the wounded prisoners. Fortunately, one of Lane's comrades warned Forbes away with the threat of his firearm. A military inquiry later cleared Forbes of wrongdoing, believing that he mistook the woman for a man. This ruling, however, seemed to have excused the killing of prisoners of war.[48]

The brutality that Lane witnessed contrasted starkly with the excitement of the previous day and with the romantic images he read in Walter Scott's novels. One commentator felt that the cavalry skirmish of the 20th "comes nearer the feats of the Nights of old than any thing recorded in modern times." The conduct of the rebels on the 21st, however, hardly fit the chivalric creed that *Ivanhoe* and "the Nights of old" represented, and it offended Lane's sensibilities. Referring to the treachery at the lake, he indignantly declared, "I never fired a shot." However the Texans might rationalize the carnage—justice or revenge for the Alamo and Goliad—they nonetheless exhibited their own capacity for the same barbarity that they claimed was unique to the Mexican character.[49]

Although the rout of Santa Anna was complete, the rebel officers knew that it was not a decisive victory. Somewhere to the southwest, beyond the swollen rivers of the gulf prairies, Gen. Vicente Filisola commanded a force twice the size of the one that the Texans had defeated along the San Jacinto. Rusk resumed the negotiations with Santa Anna, captured on the 22nd. The Mexican President asked the Texan Secretary of War if he should order Filisola out of Texas. Rusk agreed. When Santa Anna's lieutenant, Juan Almonte, wrote the order, he asked Houston how he should date it. Houston answered, "Lynchburg, I believe, is the name of this place." Perhaps mindful of how important the name would be to public memory, Wharton interceded, "San Jacinto, Genl.—let it be San Jacinto."[50]

Although the cruel realities of war might have surprised Lane, his experience did not diminish his enthusiasm to remain in the army. Two days after the battle, Karnes's company underwent a reorganization, and Lane's comrades elected him second lieutenant, a fact that he proudly claimed was "quite an honor . . . for a 19-year old boy." This acknowledgment gratified him. Indeed, in a company that included a number of veteran scouts, Lane could not have received a more manifest sanction of his new-found manhood.[51]

After the battle, Lane took a turn on guard duty and shared a cigar with Santa Anna. He rode with the cavalry under Edward Burleson to deliver Santa Anna's orders of withdrawal to Filisola and escorted the sodden army to the Colorado River. Meanwhile, Houston transferred command to Rusk, so that he could travel to New Orleans and seek treatment for his wound. On May 10, Rusk issued a proclamation, warning Texans that the war was not over. He implored them to continue in the service and called for more volunteers. He challenged his men to "drive the enemy from your soil, secure your rights and avenge the death of your brethren whose bleaching bones yet lie on the prairies at La Bahia." Meanwhile, on the 14th at Velasco, Burnet and Santa Anna signed a series of agreements to end hostilities and provide the means by which the Mexican government would recognize the independence of Texas.[52]

After Rusk moved the army to Victoria, little else broke the monotony of camp life. Volunteers from the United States continued to arrive, anxious for a fight but with few prospects. While waiting to serve out his term, Lane became ill. Karnes's company planned to disband, and the Mexicans gave no sign that they intended to renew hostilities—despite Rusk's concern. Lane, therefore, decided to request his leave. On July 16, 1836, Rusk issued a discharge and, according to Lane, signed it with this compliment: "Although unusual in a discharge, I cannot help testify to the gallantry of Lieut. Lane at the Battle of San Jacinto."[53]

Afterward, Lane returned to Nacogdoches and lingered for several weeks before he retraced his travels back to Fairveiw, Ohio. He noted, "I remained with my parents . . . and ventilated my laurels." He had quite a story to tell. Despite Lane's painful encounter with a Mexican lancer and his witnessing Anglo-Texan brutality, Texas had met his expectations for adventure. He confronted his fears of Native America and experienced the rush of battle. He received the approbation of his fellow men, and he could now call them fellows, because his election to lieutenant confirmed the sanction of his manly peers. Despite the havoc created by an army of captains, the Texans defeated Santa Anna at San Jacinto and on that tenuous foundation, they constructed an equally tenuous republic.

• 2 •

LOS PIRATAS DE TEJAS, 1836–37

Neither the battle of San Jacinto nor the treaties of Velasco settled the conflict between Mexico and Texas, and both sides understood this at the time. Texas authorities clamored for more volunteers to finish the war, while Mexican officials promised counterstrikes, and armed clashes did occur. During the 1840s, Mexico mounted two campaigns into Texas as far as San Antonio, and the Texans responded with disastrous expeditions to Santa Fe and Mier. More immediately, during the summer of 1836, the war continued on the Gulf of Mexico. Texas naval vessels and privateers cruised the gulf waters from the mouth of the Mississippi to the Campeche Banks, clashing with Mexican warships and merchantmen.[1]

When he returned to Texas, Walter Lane embraced this conflict. In early September 1836, he arrived at Velasco. Despite being the Republic's busiest port and its temporary capital, Velasco was a crude village. One observer described it as having "about one dozen poor houses, looks old and decaying," while another condemned the place as "a miserable little village consisting of two stores and a hotel, so called, and five or six grog shops." Lane remained in this setting for several days when the schooner *DeKalb* arrived from New Orleans with about forty volunteers. Although it sailed as a common merchant, the vessel came to Texas prepared for a new mission as a privateer. Commanded by Capt. Nathaniel Hoyt, on leave from the Texas Navy, the schooner bristled with guns but needed sailors to man a cruise off the Mexican coast.[2]

With the Texas Army languishing in camp at Victoria with little expectations for battle, privateering offered Lane the opportunity for the adventure he sought. A cruise was very much an expedition at sea. It offered the comradery of an exclusively male environment, striving for a common purpose.

It could alleviate the yearning for the elsewhere by sailing to far-off, exotic shores, and it could deliver excitement, with contests against nature and Mexican merchantmen.

As its owners worked out the bureaucratic details with the Texas government, Lane joined the crew of the *DeKalb*. Built in 1829 in Dorcester County, Maryland, the 112-ton, two-masted, square-stern schooner measured seventy-four by twenty-three by eight feet. A Texas official described it as "sailing fast and of light draft," and another predicted that it would significantly contribute to the naval service. The owners of the *DeKalb*, James Reed & Company, were merchants in New Orleans and active supporters of the Texan cause. They outfitted the vessel with a battery of eight side guns and an eight-pound "long tom" mounted on a pivot. They sold the schooner to Grayson and Shreve of Velasco, who renamed it the *Thomas Toby*, in honor of the Republic's new agent in New Orleans.[3]

Texas colonists had early recognized the strategic necessity of defending the coast during their struggle with the Mexican centralists. Despite the long border with its neighbor, Texas trade with the United States consisted largely of maritime commerce, especially with New Orleans. The rebels needed supplies and volunteers, to fight the superior Mexican forces. "As to the state of the seaboard," Gen. Samuel Houston suggested in March 1836, "keep the navy busy. To it we must look for *essential* aid." Similarly, Mexican generals recognized the need for establishing supremacy of the gulf coast to defeat the rebelling province. The first strike against Texas came via an amphibious assault, led by Martín Perfecto de Cós. Although Antonio López de Santa Anna attacked overland—against the counsel of his lieutenants—he nonetheless dispatched José Urrea to sweep the coastal plains from Matamoros to Goliad, in order to reopen supply lines. Although Urrea succeeded, supplies remained difficult to obtain, because a small Texas flotilla managed to thwart Mexican transports.[4]

On November 25, 1835, the provisional government of Texas issued a decree for the purchase of a navy. Severely strapped for cash, however, the government could only purchase four vessels. To supplement the little fleet, Gov. Henry Smith advocated the use of privateers, a tactic favored by the United States during its War for Independence and the War of 1812. Strictly defined, a privateer was a vessel—owned, equipped, and manned with private capital—that received the sanction of a belligerent, to raid the ocean-borne commerce of its enemies. Theoretically, this license—usually called a letter of marque and reprisals—provided the privateer with a measure of protection should an enemy capture its crew. If the enemy respected the license, the crew would remain regular prisoners of war, rather than suffer the fate of pirates. Governor Smith argued that the use of privateers provided the best means for Texas to achieve this naval presence. "My own mind is satisfied that the whole of our maritime operations can be carried out by foreign capital and foreign enterprise." In this context, "foreign" invariably meant the United States. On the 27th, Smith signed "An Ordinance and Decree for granting Letters of Marque and Reprisal," empowering the government to issue privateer commissions. The ordinance restricted operations to the Gulf of Mexico, stipulated that privateers should condemn all prizes—captured ships—in Texas ports, and claimed for the government ten percent of the proceeds.[5]

The Texas privateer system represented a significant element in the conflict between Texas and Mexico.[6] These independent war vessels fired the first salvo of the Texas Revolution, when the *San Felipe* and *Laura* captured the *Correo de Mejico* on September 2, 1835. As many as twelve privateers plied the Gulf, as transports and fighters, from the beginning of hostilities, until a storm destroyed the remaining vessels in October 1837.[7] As the regular navy only employed four national vessels, twelve was not an insignificant number and required no small effort on the part of numerous Texas patriots and profiteers. Strategically, the policy never achieved the expectations of its authors and ultimately failed, but these Texas vessels succeeded in maintaining supply lines and projecting an illusion of force.

By the time Walter Lane joined the crew of the *Thomas Toby,* the enthusiasm for privateers in Texas had waned. After the battle of San Jacinto, the *Terrible* captured two prizes, but the U.S. Navy seized the little schooner after New Orleans merchants expressed their concern about the threat to their commerce with Mexico. In September 1836, when the *Toby* sailed into Velasco, only two other privateers operated in the Texas service, but the schooner *Flash* and the steamboat *Ocean* served primarily as transports.[8]

Despite Lane's inexperience in maritime service, Capt. Nathaniel Hoyt signed him as a lieutenant, perhaps out of respect for his former commission in the Texas Army. A twenty-seven year old native of New Hampshire, Hoyt was an experienced sea captain. Before the Texas Revolution, he plied the Gulf trade between the United States and Mexico, and during the war, he transported volunteers and goods to the rebels. Hoyt joined the Texas Navy as an officer and took a leave of absence to command the *Toby.* One observer described Captain Hoyt as "a vulgar, rude, coarse-looking man," and after he arrived in Velasco, the writer reported that his disposition offended some of the local ladies.[9]

Sometime in late September 1836, Hoyt received orders to cruise near Tampico and Vera Cruz, in an effort to intercept two new Mexican brigs that had left Baltimore. These warships represented a threat to Texan naval supremacy, considering that the *Toby* was the only active vessel in the Texas fleet. In a letter to ad interim president David G. Burnet, a Texas agent in New Orleans expressed his fear that the Mexican vessels had already reached Vera Cruz. "This is almost a death blow to our trade," he lamented: "[the Mexicans] will be enabled to Blockade all the ports of Texas." With Lieutenant Lane and the rest of the crew, the *Toby* set out from Velasco and cruised "so long as water and provisions lasted," as Hoyt reported. They never found their quarry.[10]

Despite failing in their mission, Hoyt and his crew managed to draw the consternation of Mexican officials. They cruised along the coast, between Tampico and Sisal. Without authority, Hoyt declared Vera Cruz and Tampico under blockade. On October 4, the *Toby* entered the port of Tampico. A Mexican newspaper reported, "[I]t was seen at a distance at the bar[,] a schooner with the flag adopted by the seditious ones of Texas with superior running ability, armed and with people correspondent with its office of piracy." Hoyt found the schooner *Segunda Juana* unloading, just beyond the range of Tampico's guns. The Texans seized the vessel and sent it to Galveston for condemnation. The Mexican press complained, "This boldness[,] with which they have the shamelessness of insulting the national honor, gives us new rights to revenge such outrage." The audacious privateer returned to Tampico and began bombarding the fort with the long tom of the schooner. The Mexicans responded in kind, and for twenty minutes, the *Tom Toby* dueled the fortress with "a lively cannonading," as Lane described it.[11]

After Tampico, the *Toby* sailed down the coast toward Sisal. On October 12, under the guise of a British flag, the privateer stole into port. "There were several vessels at anchor under the guns of the fort," Lieutenant Lane wrote, "Passing an American vessel our own captain hailed her, and asked which vessel was Mexican. Her captain laughed, and pointed to a brig close to the fort. He knew us." The brig was actually the large schooner *Mexicano,* formerly the *Mentor,* which Hoyt had commanded in 1834. The *Toby* eased next to the merchant vessel. "[We] threw twenty armed men on board," Lane recalled, "who slipped the cable, [and we] made sail . . . under a heavy fire from the fort."[12]

Hoyt sailed for Velasco, but before reaching home port, they spoke to the *Louisiana,* a U.S. ship, and after inspecting the vessel, found an opportunity to "ventilate his laurels," as Lane would have described Hoyt's braggadocio. The captain gloated over his recent success and issued a challenge to all Mexican ships. By October 29, the *Toby* and its prize arrived at Velasco. The *Mexicano* was a valuable prize, carrying a large cargo of coffee and sugar.

At 180 tons and mounting three guns, the schooner would have been a welcome addition to the Texas fleet. Secretary of the Navy, S. Rhodes Fisher, considered both the *Mexicano* and the *Segunda Juana,* but a lack of funds prevented their purchase.[13]

Although the 1836 cruise of the *Toby* inflicted little physical destruction, the damage to the collective Mexican psyche was effective. During the bombardment of Tampico, one newspaper noted that the Texas raider "frighten[ed] the good people of the town nearly out of their witts [*sic*], who supposing her to be the vanguard of the Texian Navy, turned out *en masse.*" Recording the same event, another correspondent noted, "The mere appearance of the Schooner Tom Toby . . . spread general alarm over the whole coast." The Mexican military sent officers to place Tampico in a defensive position because of the actions of the *Toby.* The material losses were mere nuisances, but the privateer system permitted Texans to exploit the illusion that they possessed more naval might than they truly had.[14]

Mexicans were not alone in their objections to the Texas privateers. New Orleans citizens were also vocal against the system. In May 1836, a group of merchants and insurance companies petitioned the U.S. Navy to protect their commerce with Mexico, and Commodore A. J. Dallas dispatched the U.S.S. *Grampus* in response. Many New Orleans merchants, however, were ardent supporters of the Texas cause and actively outfitted privateers. One editorial tried to explain this ambiguity. "We are sincere in advocating their [the Texans] struggles for independence . . . but we must deprecate any spoilation on American trade . . . Merchants care little for the cause of belligerency." To pass in and out of the port, Texas privateers carried cargoes and manifests, disguising themselves as transports. This was made possible by the sympathies of the custom collector, James W. Breedlove.[15]

Lane and his shipmates saw no more action as 1836 drew to a close. In November, the *Toby* sailed for New Orleans to refit. It crossed through a violent norther but on the 16th managed to reach its destination. After the New Year, with repairs complete, the privateer returned to sea but opted to remain near the mouth of the Mississippi, prowling for Mexican vessels embarking from the Crescent City. On February 1, however, a severe storm swept the Louisiana coast. A wave tossed the privateer and when it came down, Lane "thought the jar would drive the mast through her bottom." Captain Hoyt placed crews, armed with axes, to cut down the mast should a similar wave approach. After the storm, the schooner finally came to rest in the mud near the mouth of Bayou La Fourche. The crew tried to float the *Toby* by unloading its cargo but did not succeed.[16]

For ten days, the privateer remained stranded at the mouth of the

Lafourche, and the idle time allowed the disaffected among Hoyt's crew to plot a mutiny. The trouble began when a local man floated down to the schooner on a skiff, and the doctor and the purser of the *Tom Toby* convinced Captain Hoyt to allow them to return with him. A Lieutenant Richards and a Midshipman Johnston followed the three and killed them to prevent them from alerting anybody of the *Toby*'s plight, because they planned to wrest the schooner from Hoyt's control. A newspaper later reported that the "surgeon was afterward found with his feet tied to a stake, and the top of his head shot off. The [purser] was shot and sunk in the bayou." The two sailors returned and hid a bundle of bloody clothes. Lane discovered the evidence and reported it to the captain, but Hoyt already knew, having overheard Johnston and Richard talking, with Captain Paul of the marines, about their plan to overpower the ship. Hoyt deployed his loyal crew members to arrest the mutineers at a given signal—three coughs. He placed Lane and a squad over Paul. Lane recalled that at the signal, "I threw my arms around Capt. Paul, with a cocked pistol to his breast, telling him: 'Make a move and I'll kill you.' The seamen seized him on each side, threw him down and tied him." The other crewmen apprehended Richards and Johnston and prevented the mutiny.[17]

With the mutineers in chains, Captain Hoyt managed to float the schooner and opted to sail up the Lafourche rather than attempt to recross the bar. At some point below Thibodaux, he left the schooner, went to New Orleans, and reported to Algernon Thurston, a Texas agent. On February 10, Hoyt left the city with the local marshal and a steamer and returned on the 28th with the *Tom Toby* in tow, during which time Lt. Walter Lane celebrated his twentieth birthday. Lane and others signed a bond for their appearance at the mutineers' trial and, as Lane recalled, "dined and feted" in New Orleans. The court found all three men guilty and sentenced them to hang. Only Richards, "a hardened villain" according to Lane, suffered this penalty. Johnston's family managed to have his sentence reduced to imprisonment, and the court pardoned Captain Paul per the jury's request.[18]

The *Tom Toby* underwent repairs in New Orleans. During this time, Grayson and Shreve attempted to sell it to the Republic of Texas for $15,000 in land scrip, but after several weeks of negotiations, Grayson and Thurston could not come to terms with each other. "The enormous price asked for the Tom Toby," Secretary Fisher informed Thurston, "I presume will entirely close the door to your treating for her."[19]

The Texas government, nevertheless, urgently needed the services of the privateer on the Texas coast. After a year of inactivity, the Mexican government declared Texas in a state of blockade and sent a squadron of three brigs and two schooners off to the newly established port of Galveston. The flotilla began making prizes of the New Orleans and Texas trade. Although the U.S. Navy deployed the *Natchez* to the area and managed to rescue several U.S. ships taken by the Mexicans, the Texans were utterly unprepared. The three remaining national vessels and the *Tom Toby* were refitting in U.S. ports. The *Terrible* lay on the banks of the Mississippi with a rotting hull, and the steamers *Laura* and *Ocean* continued along the Texas riverways as transports. Only the lightly armed transports *Flash* and *Sam Houston* patrolled the coast, while the Mexican squadron captured at least five U.S. vessels. The Mexican warship *General Terán* exemplified Texan futility, when on April 12, 1837, it seized the *Julius Caesar* near the mouth of the Sabine. The *Flash* and the recently commissioned *Sam Houston* sailed forth to assist the distressed schooner, but the *Flash* managed only one shot before retiring. The Mexican brig escorted its prize back to Matamoros.[20]

On April 17, two Mexican brigs, the *Vencedor del Alamo* and the *Libertador,* intercepted the Texas warship *Independence,* returning from a refit. After a six-hour running battle, which could be heard in Galveston, the *Independence* surrendered within sight of the Texas coast. According to a sailor on the captured vessel, the presence of the *Tom Toby* could have averted defeat. "I feel convinced that had the *Tom Toby* or *Brutus* . . . been with us, we should have proved too many for them. But had three of our schooners been together, both brigs would have been inevitably captured." Indeed, the *Toby* and *Independence* were scheduled to sail in convoy, but the privateer was delayed for eight hours, arriving at Galveston the next day.[21]

Within a few weeks, Captain Hoyt, Lieutenant Lane, and the crew piloted the *Tom Toby* down to their old haunts of the previous year, stalking along the coast between Tampico and the Campeche Banks. On May 24, the schooner revisited Sisal harbor, under the auspices of the U.S. banner. Hoyt sent Lane and a squad of eleven sailors, to slip alongside a merchant brig. "As we drew near her she showed Spanish colors, so we could not touch her," Lane explained. The brig proved to be the *Emilio.* As the Texans prepared to return to the *Toby,* a small lighter, the *Sabina,* filled with women from the town, eased up to the brig. Lane and his comrades seized it. "The ladies screamed when they saw we were white men, but we told them we would not harm them—merely wanted their boat." Lane and his crew helped the ladies into the *Emilio* and quickly raised sail for the *Toby.* Although Mexican reports claimed the action took place beyond the range of Sisal's guns, Lane recalled that "the fort opened fire on us, putting two balls through our sail." As the privateer escaped with its little prize, Hoyt replaced the U.S. flag with the Lone Star of Texas, to make certain the enemy recognized the perpetrators.[22]

As the *Tom Toby* cruised toward Campeche, the crew sighted a sail on the horizon and gave pursuit. Near Sabinas, the Texans overtook the Mexican brig *Fenix,* inbound from the Turks Islands, hauling salt and a cache of brandy. "After two hours of stirring chase," Lane recalled, "we overhauled and captured her." Hoyt permitted the thirty passengers and crew of the prize to row ashore and dispatched the brig to Galveston under a prize master. Lane remained aboard the privateer.[23]

The Mexican press railed against *los piratas de tejas.* "It is truly very sensitive that such an insignificant pirate as the Tomas Toby is found being conspicuous with such liberty on our coasts, and it will probably terminate our languid commerce." Identifying the privateer by name, the newspaper testified to the *Toby*'s growing reputation since the summer before, but the author of this editorial directed most complaints toward Mexican authorities. "It would be very expedient that our squadron leave as soon as possible to look for this pirate, in order to punish and to impede his daring." Because of a lack of funds, however, the Mexican flotilla lay inactive at Vera Cruz, which allowed the privateer to cruise the Yucatán coast with impunity.[24]

Indeed, Captain Hoyt returned to Sisal to cut out the schooner *Correo de Campeche* but mistook the *Emilio* for a warship and retreated. On May 31, the Texas raider seized a fishing boat, and a few days later, sighted the schooner *Eulalia* sailing to Campeche from Havana. The *Toby* fired on it and chased it ashore. The *Eulalia*'s crew saved it from capture, and they salvaged its cargo by tossing it to shore.[25]

On June 2, Hoyt returned to Galveston and condemned his prizes, but the crew reserved the *aguardiente* off the *Fenix* for themselves. "A few days afterwards," Lane wrote, "the prize money was distributed among the crew, and we were having a gay time." The celebrating did not last long, for Hoyt learned that a vessel laden with $80,000 in specie had left Mexico for Spain. The privateer sailed in pursuit but never encountered its target. Hoyt, Lane, and mates cruised fruitlessly that summer, before returning to Galveston sometime in August.[26]

The Republic, meanwhile, reopened the question of acquiring the *Thomas Toby,* as well as the *Fenix,* from Grayson and Shreve. Both vessels impressed naval inspectors. The Republic, however, purchased neither because of the timely arrival of a French squadron into the gulf. The French government blockaded Mexican ports to enforce the repayment of a loan and effectually immobilized Mexico's navy.[27]

When Captain Hoyt—who had ambitions to command the more impressive *Fenix*—learned of the decision not to purchase these vessels, he took command of a U.S. merchant ship. Though he reported to his superiors seven times, he did not return to Texas until 1841. Lane and the crew of the *Tom Toby,* however, remained on board in Galveston while the vessel was idle and awaited new orders or a new captain. They received neither before October.[28]

On the night of October 5, 1837, a hurricane inundated Galveston. It had tracked across the Yucatán peninsula and on the 2nd, struck the mainland at the mouth of the Rio Grande. In a long, merciless arc, the massive storm followed the coastline from Matamoros to New Orleans, eventually passing through the Carolinas and wasting itself in the cooler waters of the North Atlantic. The hurricane devastated the young port of Galveston, destroying most of the vessels anchored in its harbor. The *Tom Toby,* with its crew aboard, did not fare well. "[T]he 'sly coon,' in the shape of a terrible tornado, sprang up," Lane remembered, "It blew fearfully until about 12 o'clock, at which time a *tidal wave,* about fifteen feet high, struck us, tore us loose from our moorings, and sent us flying over the city of Galveston (that now is), and struck us, prow foremost, into a sandy bank, some two miles beyond." Fortunately, no one aboard perished. As for the schooner, it settled at the bottom of West Bay, somewhere off Virginia Point.[29]

During its career, the *Thomas Toby* out-performed its fellow privateers and rivaled the vessels in the national service. Forgotten in the histories of the Republic and scarcely mentioned in the histories of the navy, the *Toby* succeeded in its mission to complement the financially strapped Texas Navy, with private capital and private enterprise. Like the other Texas privateers, it did not fare well in coastal defense, but Hoyt, Lane, and their crewmates effectively employed the schooner as an offensive weapon that projected an illusion of might that often preoccupied Mexican officials.

• 3 •

RED LANDER, 1837-44

After Walter Lane survived the storm of October 1837, he returned to San Augustine, but after swimming in the Trinity River, he contracted an illness. Fortunately, when he arrived in the Red Lands community, he found his old cavalry mate, Dr. Robert K. Goodloe, who secured room and board and nursed Lane through his sickness. After Lane's recovery, Goodloe arranged for him to teach at a subscription school. They signed up a class of forty children and a few adults. "Two or three of the latter gave me much trouble," Lane admitted, "for they knew more of arithmetic than I did." He had to work through the night before class in order to solve math problems for the next day, but he managed. He took quarters in the home of Obediah Hendrick, a resident of East Texas since 1826. When the school term ended in early 1838, Lane received some money from his brother Wade, which enabled him to leave his school, "thanking my stars that I had gotten out with credit from a position I felt totally incompetent to fill."[1]

Meanwhile, the years 1838 and 1839 proved to be an era of continuing violence for the young republic. The unresolved issues between Anglo-Texans, Tejanos, and Indians resurfaced in the Red Lands. After the revolution, the community of six hundred Tejanos found themselves as a people under siege, suffering from Anglo-American intrusion on their land, threats of disenfranchisement, legal and personal harassment, and suspicions as an enemy. "It would be difficult to assume that these people [Tejanos] always received fair and honorable treatment at the hands of the Texians without an infraction of the truth," John S. Ford, a resident of San Augustine, later admitted.[2] In the spring of 1838, Vicente Córdova and other Tejano leaders wrote to Samuel Houston, recently elected president of the Republic, seeking support for the maintenance of peace. But Thomas J. Rusk, commander of the local Texas forces, would not forward the letter until late August.

Weary of the lack of redress, Córdova decided to assert Tejano rights by force of arms. On July 20, he met with Indian leaders at the Cherokee village and received a message from Gen. Vicente Filisola at Matamoros. Filisola promised Mexican aid to the Tejanos and Indians, should they revolt. The Texas government learned of the communication, and Houston alerted Rusk, imploring him to keep the information from the public.

On August 4, however, the Anglo-Texan community became aware of trouble, when a group of Tejanos fired on and killed one of a party of white men who were searching for stolen horses near Nacogdoches. When the Anglo-Texans followed the trail, they determined that the Tejano party had grown to an alarming size. Rusk received information that Córdova commanded the loyalty of about one hundred Tejanos and that he sought assistance from the Indians. The old bugbear of Tejano and Native American collusion appeared once again in the Red Lands. Rusk dispatched a company from Douglas to the Angelina River to prevent this collaboration and issued a call for volunteers.[3]

Citizens at San Augustine quickly mobilized. On August 8, Walter Lane and other men rallied at the court house and formed a company of mounted volunteers. The Texans adhered to the tenets of the American militia tradition by electing their officers. Ford, who joined the unit as a private, recalled, "Elections were primitive affairs, when two candidates were in the field for captain, they were placed some distance apart. At the word 'march' the friends of the respective candidates fell into line by the side of their favorites." Thus, the volunteers elected former Texas senator Henry W. Augustine captain. Despite his former rank of lieutenant in the Texas Army, Lane rode with the company as a private.[4]

On August 10, Córdova and other Tejano leaders issued a declaration of grievances, describing their actions as necessary to defend themselves and their families. "The citizens of Nacogdoches," the document announced, "tired of suffering injustices and the usurpation of their rights, cannot but state that having gathered together with their weapons in hand, they are determined to shed their last drop of blood in order to protect their individual rights." The Tejanos stated that they had never accepted the authority of the Republic of Texas and promised to fight for the Mexican Constitution of 1824.[5]

The same day of the declaration, Augustine's company of 120 troopers reached Rusk's camp, and with the arrival of other volunteers, the Anglo-Texans mustered a force of about 600 soldiers. President Houston traveled to Nacogdoches and ordered Rusk not to cross the Angelina, hoping to find a diplomatic means to end the crisis. An exasperated Rusk later wrote, "[H]ad I been governed by [Houston's] peremtory order I have not the least doubt that an Indian war would have been now raging here." Rusk found justification to ignore Houston's orders when he received a report that Córdova was moving in the direction of the trans-Angelina Indians. The general crossed into Cherokee territory and dispatched Captain Augustine's company to pursue the Tejano trail.[6]

At the village, Rusk interviewed Bowls, leader of the Cherokees. Bowls professed friendship and claimed to have convinced the other groups in his association not to join the revolt. Rusk continued his pursuit of Córdova, arriving at the Neches Saline saltworks, where "there was scarcely anything visible to follow," as trooper Ford recalled. The general called off the pursuit and returned to Nacogdoches, where he ordered the volunteers disbanded. This show of force, according to Texas authorities, prevented a war with the Tejanos and the Indians. Rusk claimed that it "excited strongly that which can only be depended upon in Indians[,] their fear."[7]

Augustine's troopers experienced no action, but they reveled in their adventure. Ford remembered the masculine comradery that Lane often enjoyed while on an expedition: "More good feeling and hilarity never prevailed among the citizen soldiers of any country." Perhaps referring to the pranks and teasing associated with these groups, Ford commented, "Everything was given and taken in good humor." The company returned to San Augustine, where on August 22, Lane and the rest of the men received their discharges and $12.09 for their trouble.[8]

Córdova eluded Rusk's attempts to capture him, and he maintained a small force of Tejanos that occasionally harassed Anglo settlements, but in March 1839, he received word that the promised assistance from Mexico would not arrive. Córdova left for Matamoros. Texas authorities arrested the Tejanos who remained and put them on trial. Walter's brother, George Lane, served as a prosecutor. He had graduated in 1837 from Transylvania University in Kentucky and located his law practice in Milam—between San Augustine and the Sabine River. The Texas authorities eventually dismissed all of the cases, but they achieved their larger goal. After the removal of Córdova and his followers, the surviving Tejano community never again presented a risk to Anglo control in East Texas.[9]

The Republic and its citizens in the Red Lands took the Tejano uprising seriously, but they were more concerned about the trans-Angelina Indians. In 1838, the Cherokees and their affiliated groups numbered about 2,500 people. The Anglo-Texans possessed long memories of Indian support of

Mexican authorities, dating to the battle of Nacogdoches in 1832. Certainly, Walter Lane and other Red Landers recalled the crisis of March 1836, and reports of imagined and real emissaries from Matamoros stoked their anxieties of a Tejano alliance. Although Bowls declared his friendship when Rusk marched through his village, Ford believed otherwise and expressed the concerns of many East Texas Anglos when he noted that "the evidences of their [Cherokee] hostility were undoubted by us. This caused many a prudent man to consider the danger of having a people about half civilized, possessing property, arms, and munitions of war and harboring a hereditary enmity to us, living as our near neighbors, really in our midst." Ford wrote this in hindsight, informed of the events to come, but the logic of his words was the same that the policymakers used at the time. Indeed, George W. Bonnell, the Indian affairs commissioner of the Republic, remarked in 1838, "[M]ost of them [the Indians] have the sagacity enough to know that the White Man and the Indian cannot flourish in the same vicinity."[10]

The Anglo-Texans justified the concerns of the Native Americans. The Texas Congress had not ratified the treaty that Houston negotiated with the Cherokee association in February 1836. The agreement recognized the affiliated groups as a single community, guaranteed them title to their lands, and specified a boundary. By 1838, President Houston, an adopted member of the Cherokee before he came to Texas, was still debating with the Congress to establish a "line between the whites and the Indians." This policy, Houston warned, "alone can save Eastern Texas from ruin, and the country generally from imminent danger."[11]

A more immediate cause for Indian concern occurred when the Republic opened the General Land Office in January 1838. As early as 1835, the provisional government of Texas issued a decree that promised to pay its soldiers with land, so that by the time the land office opened, the Republic teemed with veterans, locators, and speculators with scrip in hand, anxious to make their claims. As a result, during the spring and summer of 1838, numerous surveying parties surged onto the Anglo-Indian frontier. The Native Americans were not ignorant of what the surveyor's transit represented, and they made a deliberate effort to hinder these expeditions.[12]

Lane joined the rush. On June 29, he applied for and received a donation certificate—a grant of 640 acres for his service at San Jacinto. In late August, shortly after Lane received his discharge from Augustine's company, a land locator by the name of William M. Love arrived from Franklin—a town at the extreme edge of the Anglo-Texan settlement, about 150 miles west. He was an agent for William F. Henderson, deputy surveyor of the Robertson Land District, and he came to San Augustine looking for men interested in surveying their claims. Fresh from the campaign against Córdova, Lane agreed to accompany Love—joining yet another expedition, perhaps looking forward to the same levity. At least two fellow troopers from Augustine's company—Richard Davis and William M. Jackson—also decided to take part. They might have been adventurers, enjoying the all-male environment of the expedition as much as Lane. Others, like former Texas congressman Samuel T. Allen, cooperated because such endeavors were costly to land locators like himself.[13]

The problem of expense arose when it became evident that the Indians did not welcome these expeditions. To defray this cost, surveyors like Henderson and Love organized companies of Texas Army veterans and land locators. These men, providing their own horses and weapons, worked at their own expense. Veterans possessed a personal interest in surveying their own lands, while the locators received pay through contracts with scrip holders, either by shares of land or by cash wages.[14]

At Franklin, Love's crew from East Texas met the others who heeded Henderson's call. The company elected a Mr. Neill captain, and in early September—probably on the 1st, as was custom—the expedition of about twenty-five mounted men left Franklin and traveled due north. After four days and about one hundred miles, the company reached Richland Creek in present-day Navarro County. As they neared their destination, the band encountered numerous groups of Indians, who greeted the surveyors cordially while slaughtering buffalo for their winter stores. The company located their base camp and settled down amidst several hundred Indians. The groups varied but most appeared to be Kickapoos.[15]

The surveyors worked two days without incident. They labored from morning until evening, returning to the same camp. On the second day, Henderson concluded that the compass was faulty and sent Love and Jackson back to Franklin to replace the magnet. This reduced the company to about twenty-three.

Early on the third day, the party picked up their line along a creek branch, and at about 9:00 A.M., they stopped for breakfast. A Kickapoo leader and a group of his men entered the camp, to warn them that Hainais were planning to attack the Texans. Lane was confident. "We thanked them for the information, but said we were not afraid of the [Hainais], and said if they attacked us we would *clean them out.*" The leader was unimpressed and urged the men to leave, fearing that if the Hainais killed them, the Kickapoos would get the blame. "They begged us feelingly to go," Lane remembered, "but as we would not, they planned a little surprise for us."

The company returned to their work while several Indians followed, distracting the surveyors with questions they deemed annoying. As the company came upon a dry creek, the Indian who vexed Lane shook hands and dashed away. As Lane and his comrades passed, a band of Kickapoo rose from the creek and opened fire. Captain Neill quickly rallied his company and ordered a charge. The mounted Texans routed the Kickapoos from the ravine and pursued them into a stand of timber, about a mile distant. From the woods, a larger force appeared and countered the Texans' charge, and a third group of mounted men swept down from the prairie. The company retreated. As the Kickapoos encircled them, the surveyors leapt into a dry wash and hugged the sides for protection.

The gully was scarcely five feet deep. A few bushes scattered about its edge. A cottonwood tree, standing at its head, provided the defenders their only breastwork. The Kickapoos placed a group just beyond gunshot to keep the company in place. Another group, positioned below the gully, managed to kill most of the surveyors' horses. Surrounded by some 200 Indians, with no water and only a few surviving horses, the surveyors recognized their desperate situation. They decided to employ the customary strategy in frontier defense: holing up and praying that the Indians would lose interest. If the Kickapoos insisted on a fight, however, the company resolved to wait until nightfall and try to escape under cover of twilight.

The battle continued throughout the day. "Whenever one of our men would put up his head to shoot, twenty-five Indians would pull down on him," Lane recalled. "The Indians had climbed up in these cottonwood trees in order to shoot over into the creek."[16] Into the afternoon, the combatants exchanged fire. Captain Neill fell wounded and requested that Euclid M. Cox take over as commander. The company agreed. Cox was a former Austin colonist and a veteran of the early battles of the Texas Revolution. Acting on his new responsibility, he climbed the bank and took position behind the lone cottonwood. He shot at the Kickapoos in the trees below the creek and maintained his post for several hours, before taking a bullet through the spine. Under heavy fire, Lane rushed up to Captain Cox and dragged him back into the gully. The company did not elect a replacement. Heartened by Cox's fall, the Indians mounted an assault on the ravine, but the surveyors drove them back. The Kickapoos continued to test the surveyors' defenses but never could move them from their position.

As night enveloped the combatants, as many as twelve surveyors managed to survive—although most had sustained injuries. They had hoped that if they could make it until dark, they might be able to steal away, but to their dismay, a bright September moon illuminated the prairie. They waited until midnight, hoping that the sky would cloud over, but it never did. The surveyors concluded that they should attempt an escape, reasoning that despite the odds, some of their number might succeed.

The able men placed the wounded upon the remaining horses and led them into the open moonlight, determined to reach the timbered bottoms a quarter mile away. The Kickapoos immediately attacked. "All rushed around us in a half circle pouring hot shot into us," Lane remembered. "We retreated in a walk, wheeling and firing as we went, and keeping them at bay." The mounted men made easy targets, despite being placed atop the horses to facilitate their escape. As one spot emptied, those on the ground lifted another man into his place. Lane and a companion helped the wounded Neill onto one such horse, but they scarcely made ten steps before the Kickapoos shot down the rider and his mount. Riding his fleet horse, a surveyor, Mr. Violet, managed to outrun his pursuers, but in the unreliable light of the moon, he and his horse tumbled headlong into a gully, snapping his thigh.

Having escaped the day's fight unharmed, Lane took a bullet in the same volley that killed Captain Neill. "I was shot through the calf of the leg, splintering the bone and severing the 'leaders' that connected with my toes." He managed to reach the next gully, and with Henderson, Violet, and a Mr. Button, he hid in the brush. These men were fortunate, for their prediction proved accurate. Most of the casualties that the surveyors sustained occurred during this escape attempt. Only three others survived, seeking their own means of flight.

Henderson hastened to Lane's side and quickly bandaged his wound. As he worked, some fifty Indians entered the ravine and finished off one of the wounded. Lane believed that the Kickapoos intended to track down all the survivors, to ensure that no one could charge their people with the deaths. The Indians searched down the dry creek toward Lane and Henderson. The two men crawled out and lay quietly, according to Lane, "with our guns cocked ready to give them one parting salute if they discovered us. They passed us by, so closely that I could have put my hands on any of their heads." From somewhere on the prairie, a conch shell blew, a signal for the Indians to regroup.

Lane and Henderson reached Richland Creek, where they found a puddle of water. Lane "pitched headforemost," as he described it, into the muddy pool and drank greedily. They found Button and Violet and decided to rest a moment, but realizing that they had only few hours left of darkness, they elected to get as far as they could before sunrise. Violet, suffering a broken thigh, could only crawl and pleaded with Lane to stay with him, but Lane refused. After tending to Violet's injury and promising to return with help, Henderson and Button, with Lane in tow, began the trek back to Franklin.

The trio hid in the brush during the day. That evening, the three arose from their hideout, but as Lane stood, his wounds overcame him, and he passed out. Button wanted to leave him, but Henderson adamantly refused. Lane overheard the conversation as he regained his senses and blasted Button. "I rose to my feet, and cursed [him], both loud and deep, telling him he was a white-livered plebian, and, in spite of his 180-pounds, I would *lead* him to the settlement." Lane apparently refused to endure Mr. Violet's fate. With the debate resolved, the men continued the trek through the night and into the next day. They followed a series of buffalo trails, hoping to find water but only became lost. They suffered terribly from thirst. Lane complained that "the country was so dry that the earth was cracked open."

On the third day after the battle, the three men sighted the Tehuacana Hills, atop which flowed the Tehuacana Springs. The hills were still six miles in the distance, and a disheartened Button refused to continue. Lane and Henderson "abused and sneered at him for having no *grit,*" and managed to get him moving again. As the trio neared the spring, a party of Kickapoos rode up to them. The battered men realized that these men were not aware of the recent battle, and they prudently explained that they had been in a fight with the Hasinais. Convinced, the Kickapoos helped the men to the water and from there took them to their camp. They dressed the surveyors' injuries, fed them, and gave them quarters for the night.

The next morning, Lane, Henderson, and Button left the Kickapoo camp, anxious to get as far away as possible, lest the Kickapoos discovered the truth of the battle. The trio scarcely traveled three miles before another party of Indians confronted them. Lane realized that they merely wished to trade, "showing an old, dilapidated rifle, to trade for our good one. We soon found out it was *trade or fight,* so we swapped." As part of the deal, one of the Indians would guide the trio to Parker's Fort, allowing Lane to ride his horse. On the morning of the fifth day after the battle, their guide brought the three men to the abandoned outpost. Button wanted to shoot the man and take his horse, but the other two dismissed the idea. "Rather than betray confidence," declared Lane indignantly, "I would walk in on one leg."

After they parted with the Indian guide, the three men continued their journey. On the eighth day after the battle, they encountered a pair of riders who called out and ordered them to halt and to identify themselves. "I looked up, and saw two men, with their guns leveled on us." Lane waved the men off, claiming, "We are friends—white men!" As the armed men approached, the trio recognized them as Love and Jackson, the two that Henderson had sent to replace the defective magnet before the fight. They placed the exhausted

In 1885, the children of Euclid M. Cox erected this monument over the grave of their father and his comrades, near the battleground of the Surveyors' Fight. The inscription lists those who perished and those who survived, including Walter Lane. Author's photograph, Surveyors' Fight Monument, Navarro Co., Tex.

men onto their horses and led them the remaining fifteen miles to Franklin. Dismay spread through the community, and Love mustered fifty men to ride to the battlefield and aid any survivors.

Love's party found Violet, who had incredibly crawled twenty-five miles. The company then rode on to the battlefield, where they gathered the remains of sixteen men and placed them in a common grave beneath a pair of oak trees that had grown together. Love drove a nail into the tree to mark the ground. Their task complete, the company returned to Violet and carried him back to Franklin.[17]

Most accounts of the battle took great care to mention the number of Indians slain, demonstrating the toll paid for the deaths of white men, as Lane's comrades described themselves. Lane boasted that when Love reached the battlefield, his company found eighty piles of brush, under which they found "a copious quantity of blood, which proved that we had not been fooling away our time during that day." Cox reportedly made a valiant last stand, killing "eight or ten" before being overwhelmed, a tremendous feat for a man severely wounded and wielding a mere single-shot pistol.

For two months after, Lane recuperated at James Dunn's, a former Robertson colonist whose home on the Camino Real doubled as a fort. Lane mentioned that he was "kindly nursed and attended by sympathetic ladies," a welcome respite from the perils of the manly expedition. Instead of a "good feeling of hilarity," as Ford described the jaunt against Córdova, the Surveyors' Fight resulted in the deaths of sixteen of Lane's comrades and an unknown number of Kickapoos. He was one of only seven surveyors who survived.

After Lane recovered at Dunn's Fort, his brother George escorted him back to San Augustine. He rented a space in town, while Lane took a clerk's position at Matthew Cartwright's store, relying on the experience gained at his brother Wade's establishment in Louisville. His employer was one of the wealthiest men in Texas, a dealer in vast tracts of Texas land, a cotton broker, and a merchant. Thus situated, Lane resumed his place in the Red Lands community.[18]

The Kickapoos, in the meantime, gained no advantage after their victory over the surveyors. They retired to their village in present-day Anderson County. Responding to rumors that Córdova had joined them, General Rusk attacked on October 15th, routing the Kickapoos and Tejanos from their village. Many of them retreated north of the Red River. The rest sought refuge with the Cherokee.[19]

Any consideration that the trans-Angelina Indians might have received from a sympathetic Sam Houston, however, vanished with the inauguration of Mirabeau B. Lamar as president in December. In a message to Congress, Lamar denounced his predecessor's "moderation" and "mercy" toward "the wild cannibals of the woods," and recommended a policy "of an exterminating war upon [the Indian] warriors, which will admit of no compromise and have no termination except in their total extinction or total expulsion." A congress that had been reluctant to sanction Houston's strategy of accommodation eagerly rallied around Lamar's policy, but he needed no justification to implement his anti-Indian agenda. The trans-Angelina Indians had few friends in the Republic with any political clout.[20]

Meanwhile, on May 17, 1839, a ranging unit defeated a small band of Mexicans and Indians on the San Gabriel River. They proved to be an escort to Manuel Flores, a Mexican emissary who carried belated promises of military aid for Córdova and the Cherokee association. When the government received the papers, Lamar snatched the opportunity. The president sent a letter, dated May 26, to Bowls, leader of the Cherokee, informing him that the Texas government intended to remove his people. Executing the order, General Rusk informed the Cherokee that they should leave immediately. Bowls replied that he needed to consult with his people, and Rusk gave him until morning. The next day, when a Texas officer arrived at the Cherokee village to receive Bowls's answer, he found it empty. Rusk dispatched Gen. Kelsey H. Douglass in pursuit, who clashed with the withdrawing Indians.[21]

The intervening ten months since the disaster on Richland Creek gave Lane ample time to recuperate his appetite for adventure. As rumors of war circulated in the Red Lands, he took leave from his employer. On July 15, Lane enlisted in a company organized by his old captain, William Kimbro. That night, after news of Douglass's skirmish arrived at San Augustine, Lane and his comrades, "being hilarious over the victory," as he remembered, wanted to celebrate but had to improvise without a cannon to fire. The men filled a bottle with gunpowder, buried it on the public square, and laid a "train" of powder to ignite it. "It fell to my lot to touch it off," Lane wrote. "The artist who laid the train being poca baucho [*sic*]—that is, a little drunk—spilt about a pound of powder at the end of the train." Lane did not see the pile in the dark—being perhaps *un poco borracho* himself—and lit the charge. The "powder flashed into my face, knocking my hat fifteen feet high, throwing me on my back."[22]

The hilarity of that evening prevented Lane from accompanying his comrades to the front, and he missed the decisive battle with the Cherokee at the Neches River, where on July 16, Anglo-Texans killed the eighty-year-old Bowls and about one hundred of his comrades. Instead, Lane lay in bed with turpentine-soaked cotton on his face, administered by the good doctor John S. Ford. On the 22nd, after regaining his health, Lane joined J. E. Hamilton's mounted company, pursuing scattered Indian groups, razing their abandoned villages, and burning their fields. Finding no resistance, the volunteers returned home and disbanded on August 10.[23]

With the expulsion of the trans-Angelina Indians from East Texas and the destruction of the Tejano community, Anglo-Texan residents of San Augustine could devote their efforts to cultivating their frontier village into a rural community. The citizens included such prominent Republic officials as former President Sam Houston, Vice-President Kenneth L. Anderson, and Texas minister to Great Britain James P. Henderson, and such wealthy families as the Cartwrights and Garretts. These people completed the transformation with remarkable speed. By 1840, many fine homes replaced the crude buildings that Lane had encountered when he first arrived there in 1836. Two newspapers vied for public interest, and as many as three academies educated the community children and young adults. The town boasted an acting troupe and often heard academic lectures on a variety of subjects. Lying on the principal overland route from the United States, San Augustine claimed the only inland customhouse of the Republic.[24]

After his tour in the so-called Cherokee War, Lane teamed up with fellow trooper Samuel Jordan and established their own mercantile firm. They opened a store in Hamilton, which Sam Houston and other San Augustine speculators had recently platted. The promoters situated the town on a bluff overlooking the Sabine River in northern Sabine County and hoped that its location would attract steamboat traffic, but the river would not permit it. Between 1838 and 1840, only five steamers attempted the journey, and three sank. The Hamilton project was one of many that boosters and speculators established along Texas rivers, hoping to repeat the success that the promoters of Houston and Galveston had experienced. On the Sabine, Hamilton vied with Belgrade, Sabine Town, Salem Town, New Columbia, Pendleton, and others for the scarce river boat traffic. Hamilton—like its peers on the Sabine—never realized the ambitions of its creators.[25]

The partnership with Jordan was the first of several that Lane would enter into during the idle moments of his life, and the early 1840s was one such time. Lane left little record of his activities during this period, but he apparently continued to reside in San Augustine and attempted to establish stronger ties to the Red Lands community. He associated with such local elites like Cartwright and Obediah Hendrick, joined the local Masonic lodge, and served on a committee to celebrate the anniversary of the battle of San Jacinto. Lane later commented that in San Augustine, he "made a good many friends in as kind a community as it has ever been my fortune in which to live."[26]

But in 1843 or 1844, Lane decided to escape this sedentary life. He described this seemingly sudden decision as "getting tired." He dissolved his partnership with Jordan and set out for San Antonio. Lane explained, "I had no particular business there, but was in search of adventure." True to the image he formed of himself, Lane apparently lost interest in the Red Lands as the region had rapidly transformed from a frontier to a rural landscape. The romantic longing for the elsewhere was an ever-potent pull in his life.[27]

Lane, however, may have left San Augustine for a different reason. At age twenty-seven, the next logical step in establishing community ties would have been marriage. His brother George married in 1841, but Lane never recorded any relationships he might have had with women. A revealing remark in his memoirs, however, suggested that he had suffered from a romance that had soured. He stated, "I had been atrociously lied to by *white* women." Written in the context of the U.S.-Mexican War only three years after he left the Red Lands, he might have targeted the comment at a specific, unnamed belle of San Augustine. A sudden and dramatic gesture of escape certainly fit Lane's character. Much later in life, when he lost an election for county office, he indignantly declared that he was moving West. Writing in 1886, Lane was nearing his seventieth birthday and had been a resident of Marshall, Texas, for thirty years. He did not act on his threat. In 1844, however, no such hindrances as age and decades-old community ties could sway Lane from leaving. Whatever his motivation—whether a fit of petulance or a longing for adventure—his experiment with the settled life had failed, and he left for San Antonio.[28]

• 4 •

STORMING MONTERREY, 1844-46

I*n 1844, when he arrived* in San Antonio, Walter Lane found the place in a state of uneasiness. Its inhabitants, Tejanos and Anglo-Texans, had endured Mexican border sorties and Comanche incursions. This disquiet created an environment that attracted men who embraced violence. In San Antonio, Lane met one such group, led by John C. Hays.

Hays was the same age as Lane—twenty-seven—and in 1838, he had served with Lane's former comrades, Henry Karnes and Erastus Smith. Hays had already attained renown as a soldier, fighting against Mexicans and Comanches in the San Antonio region. He had participated in Alexander Somervell's 1842 campaign to the Rio Grande but did not accompany those whom the Mexican Army had captured at Mier. Presently, he was a captain of a ranging company that a January 1844 act of the Texas Congress had authorized. Charged with patrolling the Hill Country to the north and west and the semi-arid chaparral to the south, Hays established camp on the Medina River south of San Antonio and invited Lane to visit. There, Lane met a group of veteran fighters. Among them, Walter Lane made fast friends, including Michael H. Chevallié, Gouvenier H. Nelson, William S. Oury, and Samuel H. Walker. Perhaps these men would provide better company than the planters and merchants back in the Red Lands.

Lane did not officially enlist in Hays's company. Instead, he accompanied them on a few scouting expeditions, describing himself as an "amateur." He divided his time between the ranger camp and San Antonio over the next two years, but he did not mention how he earned a living. Perhaps his venture with Samuel Jordan had been profitable enough that he managed to keep a savings. Meanwhile, Hays's company was very active, expecting another attack from Mexico and engaging Comanches at Nueces Canyon, Walker's Creek, Agua Dulce, and Paint Rock. Lane probably did not participate in these fights, celebrated in the lore of frontier warfare, but perhaps he assisted in the escort of Henri Castro's colonists, protecting the Convention of 1845 in Austin, or participated in the numerous scouts toward Corpus Christi and the Rio Grande. He nevertheless acclimated himself to the life of a ranger and soon gained the respect of the veterans of the company.[1]

During this period, on December 29, 1845, Texas joined the United States as the twenty-eighth state. Mexico had never recognized the independence of Texas and protested its annexation. U.S. President James K. Polk, who, in 1844, had campaigned on an expansionist platform, sent an emissary to confirm the border at the Rio Grande and to negotiate the repayment of several million dollars in claims that U.S. citizens had against Mexico. The emissary also had secret instructions to make an offer to purchase California. The newly installed government in Mexico, headed by José Joaquín de Herrera, refused to receive the diplomat, and in response to this rebuff, Polk ordered Gen. Zachary Taylor from his post at Corpus Christi to the Rio Grande. Polk counted on Mexican troops crossing the river and clashing with Taylor to spark a little border war, but they did not immediately take the bait. Frustrated, Polk resolved to go to war anyway. He decided to use U.S. claims on Mexico and their refusal to accept a minister, as the justification for hostilities. Although not expressed publicly, Polk and his advisers already planned to seek California and New Mexico as indemnity for war costs, suggesting that Polk based his war aims more on territorial expansion than on protecting the Texas border. Fortunately for Polk, on April 25, 1846, a small detachment of Mexican lancers crossed the Rio Grande and fought with U.S. dragoons, killing sixteen. Now that "American blood" had been "spilled on American soil," as Polk claimed, he found his occasion for war and on May 11 presented his war message to the U.S. Congress, which passed the measure by a decisive 214 to 16 vote.[2]

At the front, Zachary Taylor had already issued a call for volunteers. Some of Hays's rangers, such as Samuel Walker and Benjamin McCulloch, were already operating at the scene performing scout duty, and Hays had received permission from Texas governor James P. Henderson to raise a regiment. Sometime in May 1846 in San Antonio, the rangers organized a company and elected veteran Christopher "Kit" Acklin captain. Although they had witnessed Walter Lane only as an amateur, the company elected him first lieutenant, which he accepted as a position of "high honor." Hays declared Point Isabel—Taylor's supply station on the south Texas coast—as the rendezvous for his regiment, and on June 6, Acklin's company arrived there and entered the U.S. Army. With the arrival of other companies, the rangers formed a regiment and selected Hays colonel, Walker lieutenant colonel, and Chevallié major. The U.S. officially accepted the unit as the First Texas Mounted Riflemen, but the public recognized them as Hays's Texas Rangers.[3]

McCulloch's and Robert Gillespie's rangers would arrive later, but even without those veteran companies, the group that assembled at Point Isabel represented an impressive array of martial talent. As many as twenty men had served at San Jacinto with Lane, including captains Thomas Green and James Gillaspie. Green and Capt. Eli Chandler were both experienced rangers. This collection of soldiers also included West Point graduate Henderson Yoakum, a number of recruits from recently disbanded Louisiana regiments, and Lane's former captain during the Texas Revolution, James Chessher. In addition, the regiment enlisted as many as twenty-five veterans of the Mier expedition, including Sam Walker, second in command. Having suffered through the infamous "black bean" episode and performing forced labor while inmates at Castle Perote, many of these embittered men believed their grievances entitled them to seek vengeance upon Mexico and its people.[4]

While Hays organized his command, General Taylor defeated Mexican forces in the opening battles of the U.S.-Mexican War at Palo Alto and Resaca de la Palma and occupied Matamoros. As more volunteers arrived in the lower Rio Grande Valley, General Taylor prepared for his anticipated campaign on Monterrey—the capital of Nuevo León and the largest city in northern Mexico. First, he secured the town of Camargo, some 140 miles upriver, from whence he planned to launch his invasion into the Mexican interior. Before he could advance, however, he needed to ascertain that partisans did not threaten his left flank. Taylor heard rumors that such a group had gathered in the vicinity of San Fernando. He called on Hays and his rangers to investigate.[5]

In late July, Captain Acklin had become ill, and on August 1, he relinquished command of his company to Lieutenant Lane. On August 8, at the head of the company, Lane left Matamoros with the remainder of Hays's rangers. Although they had not yet fired a shot, war correspondents already began creating the mystique that would soon surround them. A New Orleans reporter grandly predicted, "[D]o not be surprised . . . if you hear of them having possession of Tampico." Yet another offered a more colorful description of their departure, reporting that they left for San Fernando "to the tune of Yankee Doodle—a negro mounted on a jackass playing the tune most admirably on a violin."[6]

Before he dispatched the rangers, Taylor ordered Hays to respect the neutrality of civilians and pay for any supplies he might press as part of a policy to appease noncombatants. If he could mollify the civilians, Taylor could concentrate on the Mexican military, rather than commit scarce resources to police duty. On the morning of August 13, as the Texas Rangers neared San Fernando, the *alcalde*—a town official—informed Hays that the townspeople did not intend to contest his entrance and requested that the riflemen spare their lives and property. Hays gave his assurance. Mexican civil officials and U.S. troops would repeat this ceremony throughout northern Mexico over the next two years. The alcaldes of Matamoros dispatched the same message to Taylor before he entered that town, as did the governor of Coahuila before U.S. forces occupied Saltillo. In all cases, Taylor and his lieutenants promised to respect civilian property and lives, but with so many ill-disciplined volunteers stationed in close proximity to a less than grateful populace, keeping these promises proved difficult.

Hays located his camp outside of town, although he did permit some of his men to take quarters in the local homes. They partook the hospitality of the townspeople. One trooper reported, "At night we are treated to sweet music, struck from the trembling chords of the guitar and harp by the delicate and tapering fingers of a fair *señorita,* while we sit quietly and puff our *cigaritos* in the cool breeze." The citizens entertained the rangers by holding several fandangos. Another trooper recalled that the sojourn at San Fernando "was one continued *fete,* and on leaving, the heart of many a dark eyed brunette went with them. Either in fighting or in love, these Texans are hard to beat." These accounts, however, were written by New Orleans reporters, who had enlisted in Hays's rangers. They no doubt embellished the romance of San Fernando in order to appeal to their readership, but fandangos, feasts, and other forms of entertainment occurred throughout the U.S. occupation of northeastern Mexico. Most U.S. soldiers accepted the sincerity of Mexican hospitality, but a few recognized it as a means to placate them until they rode from town.

The occupation of San Fernando, however, did not pass without bloodshed. On the night of August 12, while the rangers camped outside of town, a mounted Mexican brazenly rushed through Hays's pickets. When he refused to heed the order to halt, the guards fired on him and killed both the horse and rider. Later, a Mexican civilian in the employ of Walker's mess stole twelve horses. The rangers apprehended him and sentenced him to flogging, but upon his release, one of the aggrieved rangers shot and killed him. Perhaps the Texans felt that rushing an enemy picket and horse theft justified the use of deadly force, but these incidents and many to follow demonstrated the volatile nature of the occupation of northeastern Mexico. Unfortunately and perhaps correctly, the Texas Rangers earned the reputation of being culprits of these unpleasant encounters.[7]

On August 16, Walter Lane and his fellow riflemen departed San Fernando, striking west across the countryside and on the 21st, reached the villa of China. As in San Fernando, the inhabitants offered little resistance, but the unpleasantness continued.[8] The rangers caught a man accused of stealing a horse, bypassed the formalities of a trial, and immediately shot him. But the Mexicans were not utterly helpless. On or about September 15, Mexicans killed three men near town.

Colonel Hays, having departed for Taylor's headquarters at Camargo, left the command to Sam Walker, who admonished his ill-behaved troopers. On August 27, he declared that any soldier "found sleeping on his post, or guilty of any pilfering or plundering or any disgraceful transaction . . . shall forthwith be dishonorably discharged." In addition, Walker promised to publish the soldier's name in the New Orleans *Picayune,* with his residence and place of birth. If the soldier tried to return to the regiment, he would order him shot.[9] Although the Texans threatened lethal justice to police themselves, they apparently never acted upon it as they had against Mexicans.

Lieutenant Lane, who remained in command of Company B during the scout and most of the occupation of China, understood this harsh justice. As events soon to follow and throughout his life, would demonstrate, he was uncompromising. He had little tolerance toward anyone who might violate a value system that was starkly clear in his own mind. His self-righteousness more often resulted in harsh words, but under extraordinary conditions, Lane would enforce his code of justice with the penalty of violence and death.

Hays's rangers remained in China for several weeks. On September 11, Taylor issued his marching orders to Governor Henderson, who personally led Texas forces. On September 12, Captain Acklin returned to Lane's company and reassumed command. Henderson and his Texans departed China the next day and caught up with Taylor's army on the evening of the 19th, just a few miles north of Monterrey.[10]

The final march covered only twenty miles. Crossing over a rise in the road, the entire valley of the Río Santa Catarina opened before Lane and his comrades, shrouded in a morning mist. Only the tall spires of the cathedral marked the location of the city of some twelve thousand people beneath the fog. As the veil lifted, the Texans could see Monterrey's white, sun-bleached buildings huddled beneath the looming heights of the green, piñon-covered Sierra Madre. A grid of streets and plazas spread across the north bank of the

Santa Catarina, which flowed from a deep canyon in the west and into the countryside to the east. The road from Saltillo wound from that canyon. Two sentry peaks, Loma de Federación on the south and Loma de Independencia on the north, protected the western approach. Even from their vantage point, the Texans could see the heavily fortified Bishop's Palace and its contingent of white army tents atop Independencia. In the foreground, the valley lay under heavy cultivation, with an occasional herd of cattle and peasant huts. At the junction of the Marín road from the northeast and the Monclova road from the northwest, the Black Fort contested any hostile entry. Gen. Pedro de Ampudia and some seven thousand Mexican regulars, had spent the last two months constructing fortifications and artillery emplacements. They waited for the approach of the U.S. Army.[11]

Through the remainder of the day, Taylor dispatched his engineers to examine the Mexican works. In the afternoon, he ordered Maj. Joseph F. K. Mansfield to reconnoiter the formidable Black Fort. The task of accompanying the engineer, with an escort of twenty rangers, fell to Lane. The defenders of the fort opened on them with musket fire, frightening Mansfield's horse. Lane remembered, "I told him to get down and I would hold his horse, so that he could get a better view." The lieutenant then ordered his men to scatter, so as not to give the Mexicans an easy target. Mansfield protested, fearing that the enemy would target their fire on him as the only dismounted man. "I told him, emphatically, no!" Lane assured the West Point graduate that he would remain at his side "and share his danger." He continued, "[W]e were officers, receiving big pay, and that it was nothing more than right that we should take more risks than privates."[12] Risk-taking was a crucial component of the masculine performance on the expedition, and Mansfield's demur likely cost him manly prestige among the rangers. Upbraiding Mansfield, however, might have elevated Lane in their estimation. It certainly did in his own mind.

That evening, as the scouts delivered their findings, Taylor formed his battle strategy. He decided to send Gen. William J. Worth and his division around to the western approaches of the city and take the positions on both Federación and Independencia hills, while Taylor led a diversionary force against the eastern works. Worth's movement would block reinforcements from Saltillo and divide the attention of the Mexican defenders.[13]

To support Worth, Taylor attached the First Texas Mounted Rifles to his division. In the afternoon of September 20, Hays's rangers took the lead of Worth's division of regulars that consisted of brigades under Thomas Staniford and Persifor Smith. They cut through the cornfields, sugar cane, and chaparral across the northern suburbs of the city. Worth's column made little progress before the sun set, having just reached the Monclova road, and the Texans halted in a farmyard, where pigs, goats, and chickens wandered. The rangers set about with swords and rocks, climbing and chasing, to avail themselves of a meal. Such casual disregard of Mexican property characterized the conduct of many soldiers in the U.S. Army and contributed to the distrust that many locals would harbor against them. Distracted by this merriment, the men did not see the Mexican cavalry deploying on a nearby ridge. They fired into the melée, which resulted in "such a getting down out of trees and scampering generally," a ranger described. Hays quickly rallied his men and placed Acklin and Samuel Ballowe's companies, dismounted, on the road. They managed a volley before the Mexican cavalry withdrew. As a storm broke over them, the Texans rested at the farmyard, before Worth recalled them to the main camp for the night. The force had to sleep in the open and without fires, but the night passed without incident.[14]

Worth's men arose early the next morning, the 21st, and pushed forward with the First Texas Mounted Rifles on point. As the column rounded a hill, they passed through a hacienda called San Geronimo, where they encountered about 200 soldiers of the Jalisco and Guanajauto cavalry regiments under Lt. Col. Juan Nájera. Hays dismounted five companies, including Acklin's, behind a hedge while Worth placed regulars in support. The Mexicans charged into them. "On they came," described a trooper of McCulloch's company, "at a full gallop, led by their brave Lieut. Col . . . in dashing style, with pennons of green and red fluttering in the wind." Worth's men responded with rifle and artillery, "emptying many a saddle," Lane recalled. This was the first engagement of the war for Lane and most of Hays's men, whom Worth praised as having "received the heavy charge of cavalry with their unerring rifles, and usual gallantry." The Texans lost one man killed and reportedly buried thirty-three lancers and their commander Nájera. The day was still early, and Worth pressed his men forward to seize the Saltillo road.[15]

When he reached the western approaches, Worth decided to attack, first Loma de Federación on the south side of the river. Defended by a small redoubt on its western end and the fort El Soldado on its east, Federación was less formidable than Independencia, atop which sat the menacing Bishop's Place, the key to Monterrey's western defenses.

The attack on Loma de Federación commenced at noon, September 21. Lane and his detachment did not participate in the initial assault, but after regulars under Capt. Charles F. Smith and rangers under Major Chevallié stormed the works on the western summit, Gen. Persifor Smith ordered the balance of Hays's Texans into the battle. Lieutenant Lane and his squad crossed the Santa Catarina and climbed the hill under an intense barrage of artillery and muskets. Once they gained the summit, the rangers and U.S. regulars overran El Soldado.[16]

After the battle, the bulk of the assaulting force returned to camp. During his ascent, Lane encountered a horribly wounded John Waters of McCulloch's company. "He was shot through the upper lip," Lane described, "knocking out his teeth, by a spent grape shot, which lodged on the side of his neck, under the skin." The poor ranger could not speak and motioned for Lane to cut out the shrapnel, but he did not have the proper instruments. Although badly disfigured, Waters survived.[17]

U.S. soldiers celebrated their triumph on Federación, but they only completed half the work. Independencia and the Bishop's Palace still loomed over them. As he conferred with his lieutenants, scouts, and engineers, Worth permitted his soldiers to rest. Few had eaten since they had left General Taylor thirty-six hours before. They left the stolen chickens and pigs uncooked, because Worth forbade campfires. The rangers, therefore, shared corn with their horses. Despite their hunger and the sudden storm that pounded Monterrey, all looked forward to some recuperation.

Lane, unfortunately, would not benefit from the lull in the action. As evening fell, Lieutenant Colonel Walker ordered him to select twenty men and ride toward Monterrey and Loma de Independencia, as close to the enemy's position as he could without being discovered. His relief, Walker informed, would be the attacking force. "Although highly flattered by the compliment," Lane admitted, "as the night was dark and rainy, and I did not know a foot of the road, I would have cheerfully given the only three dollars I had in the world if he had dropped the mantle on some other officer's shoulders." Lane nevertheless accepted his orders and made his way through the storm and down the Saltillo road, to about a half mile short of the Bishop's Palace. He placed two sentries another two hundred yards in advance. "I relieved the sentinels every hour, in person, and could plainly hear the Mexicans relieving theirs." At three in the morning of September 22, the attacking force under Lt. Col. Thomas Childs arrived, with Hays in advance. Lane reported to the ranger colonel "that everything was quiet in front, and that, evidently, they had no suspicion we were going to attack the palace." Lane was probably overly optimistic, but Hays transmitted the intelligence and relieved Lane by ordering him to the rear.[18]

The attack commenced at dawn. Childs, an old veteran of the regular army, divided his force in two, with himself, Hays, and half of the rangers on the right, and Capt. J. R. Vinton of the artillery, Walker, and the other half on the left. Up the muddy ascent, the Texans and regulars gained the height above the Bishop's Palace and began firing down on the defenders

Lane participated in the storming of the Bishop's Palace with Samuel H. Walker and the Texas Rangers. In this watercolor, Samuel Chamberlain contrasts the disciplined tactics of the Mexican troops with the haphazard action of the rangers, who display their unshaven faces and buckskin jackets and wield their long rifles and Bowie knives. Samuel Chamberlain, *Texas Rangers in Combat in the Courtyard of the Bishop's Palace.* Watercolor and gouache on thin, light-gray paper, [n.d.]. Courtesy of The San Jacinto Museum of History, Houston, Tex.

but had little effect. They held the position until Lt. John F. Rowland blasted a hole through the wall with a twelve-pound howitzer. Lane, in company with Walker and a few of his comrades, rushed through the breach, as the Mexicans retreated into the city below. The U.S. soldiers turned the guns of Bishop's Palace on the retreating Mexicans. Throughout the remainder of the day, Worth waited vainly for orders from Taylor. The commanding general remained inexplicably idle while Worth's men ascended Loma de Independencia and made no effort to communicate with them. While he waited, Worth rearranged his artillery and formed a plan for the assault on the city itself.[19]

On the morning of the 23rd, Worth heard the first signs of battle in the eastern neighborhoods of Monterrey. Actually, the action was no more than a skirmish, but the general construed it to be Taylor's main assault, and he ordered an attack from the west. Worth devised another two-pronged advance, with the rangers divided to assist both forces. Hays accompanied Capt. Theophilus Holmes, Eighth U.S. Infantry, on the right or the south, advancing down Calle de Monterey, while on the left, Walker's force, including Lane, fought with Capt. Richard B. Screven, also of the Eighth, down Calle de Itúrbide. Ampudia's men barricaded the streets and manned the roof tops, firing on the *norteamericanos.* "The street-fight became appalling," one of McCulloch's rangers remembered, "the artillery of both sides raked the streets, the balls striking the houses with a terrible crash."[20] Their position became worse when Taylor withdrew his force, allowing Ampudia to concentrate on Worth.

The intense fire forced the U.S. soldiers to take refuge in the buildings. The soft adobe and stone construction of the walls, however, could not check their advance. They took Bowie knives, spades, and the butt of their rifles and bore their way through the walls of Monterrey, slowly outflanking the Mexican soldiers on the rooftops and behind barricades. One ranger claimed that they taught this "mode of warfare . . . to the regular troops, who knew nothing of street fighting as the modus operanda of the Texans."[21]

As they dug their way into each house, the rangers opened the doors, admitting the wounded from the streets. They also came into contact with the female citizens of Monterrey. Most often, the Texans remembered them with fondness. *Mexicanas* tended to all of the injured, one of Lane's comrades remembered, "regardless of peril, . . . and they showed the same tenderness towards our own men as they displayed towards their fathers, husbands and brothers."[22] From other women, the rangers purchased tortillas as the battle stormed outside, but the encounters were not always welcomed. One unfortunate soldier found a group of women praying. They rose and began hugging him, asking for his protection. The Texan shook free, posthaste, and ran back into the street, warning his comrades, "[D]on't go in there, them women will smother you to death if you do; they tried to come it on me, but zounds, didn't I make a break for it!"[23] As later events illustrated, Lane probably would have sympathized.

The fighting continued on the streets and in the homes of Monterrey. In one room, the Texans found a large table laden with food and silverware. "A fine-looking old gentleman bowed politely and invited us to help ourselves," explained a trooper, and he frankly admitted, "I fear we would have done so anyhow."[24] Through the walls and over the rooftops, the U.S. soldiers fought their way toward El Plaza Mayor. Both units occasionally cheered to one another as they advanced down different avenues, until they finally reached to within a block of the main plaza.[25]

As night fell, Worth withdrew Hays's men back to Loma de Independencia and left Walker encamped in advance near the post office and the governor's home. Lane remained with Walker. The two rangers appropriated General Ampudia's quarters and availed themselves of his bed. As he wanted to be prepared for action, Lane "laid down by the side of the [lieutenant] colonel, *sans ceremonies,* with *boots* and *spurs* on." Sleeping together was a common occurrence for nineteenth-century men and meant little more than convenience, but for Lane, sharing sleeping arrangements with fellow members of the expedition appeared to carry special meaning as an important indication of friendship.[26]

Battle resumed at daylight, September 24. This time, Lane and his comrades had command of the housetops, and Maj. John Munroe of the artillery placed a twelve-pound mortar on a two-story building. Overlooking the plaza, Lane watched as Munroe shelled the Mexican positions, but after a few moments, a Mexican officer emerged on the street below the Texans with a white flag and a bugler. "My men on the house-tops, not knowing or caring what it meant," the lieutenant admitted, "promptly fired on them, killing the trumpeter and wounding the officer." Walker admonished his men to respect the flag of truce and when another appeared, he chose Lane to receive the message. The lieutenant climbed down from atop the building and walked out to the officer, who was justifiably concerned for his safety. Lane took him to Walker, and he informed the Texans that he carried Ampudia's request for surrender terms. Walker charged Lane with guiding the messenger to General Worth, whose headquarters lay toward the rear.[27]

Ampudia, however, had already contacted Taylor during the night, asking for terms, but the U.S. general did not inform the troops on the square. In any event, Lane and his men soon learned of a cease-fire, until the generals could agree on terms of surrender. Lane claimed, "After two hours' negotiation, in which they beat our officers 'all hollow' as diplomatists, the enemy got permission . . . to march out with their arms, baggage and artillery, with bands playing and all the honors of war."[28] Indeed, Taylor granted Ampudia those terms and in return, he received the immediate surrender of the Black Fort and evacuation of Monterrey within one week. They also designated a line south and west of Monterrey, across which neither army could cross for eight weeks.

Many of his subordinates and his superiors in Washington, D.C., censured Taylor for his armistice. By means of the agreement—so Taylor's critics claimed—Ampudia preserved his army to fight again and received eight weeks by which to pass through the Sierra Madre and fortify Saltillo. When he made the agreement, however, Taylor still faced hard fighting. Although the Mexicans defending El Plaza Mayor were essentially defeated, the forces in the Black Fort still presented a formidable obstacle. Low on supplies, the armistice allowed Taylor to secure the crucial city of Monterrey without expending further resources. Consequently, between September 26 and 28, General Ampudia evacuated the city.[29]

Taylor's armistice angered most of the Texans, including Lane. Many felt that Taylor cheated them from the prize that they had worked so hard to attain—crushing the Mexican forces. While Lane and his men waited for hostilities to resume, Pvt. James Chessher—who had been Lane's captain during the Texas Revolution—expressed their eagerness for bloodshed by pointing out two "Mexes," as he termed them. "Well don't none of you shoot at them, they are my game—there's plenty all around for you." When word of the armistice reached them, a war correspondent reported: "a burst of indignation and angry discontent was manifested on every side. No loud huzza rent the air at our triumph over the enemy." A member of McCulloch's company agreed, "The Texians were maddened with disappointment. . . . It was a terrible moment." Lieutenant Lane mirrored this bitterness, admitting, "I never felt meaner in my life."[30]

Regardless of their disappointment, their role in the taking of Monterrey garnered the Texas Rangers much attention in the national press. Reporting the battle, the *New York Herald* claimed, "The Texan volunteer troops have gained imperishable renown. . . . [T]he deadliness of Texan retribution found no obstruction to its revenge in the walls of stone which had been reared to oppose its advance," and claimed that General Worth called the Texas rangers the "best light troops in the world." In a November 6 issue, the paper published an article entitled "The Texas Rangers—Who Are They?" Newspapers across the nation published similar articles, and within a year, Samuel C. Reid published a popular book about his experience with the riflemen from Texas.[31]

The anger and meanness that Lane and others expressed in response to Taylor's armistice, however, suggested that the battle had not sated their thirst for bloodshed. Indeed, their conduct in the days following the surrender tarnished any laurels the rangers received. Luther Giddings, an Ohio volunteer, described their behavior as a "lawless and vindictive spirit," while a Texan recorded in his diary that "rumor say's several Mexicans killed—Texians done it of course." In another case, an obscure report noted that a Mexican killed a ranger, and in response, the Texans sought revenge by killing eleven Mexicans—presumably citizens. The degree of retribution was hardly proportionate, but the report remains unsubstantiated.[32]

Walter Lane did not mention if he had participated in this "lawless and vindictive" behavior; although he had admitted that after watching Ampudia march from Monterey, he "never felt meaner." Certainly, murder ran contrary to his sense of honor, or at least, to the notion that he presented of himself. In his memoirs, he censured those who shot at the Mexicans swimming in the marsh at San Jacinto and had indignantly protected the life of the Kickapoo scout, whom Mr. Button wanted to kill after their escape from the Surveyors' Fight. But Lane kept silent on his conduct and that of his fellow rangers after Monterrey.[33]

The armistice, meanwhile, guaranteed that the Texans would see little fighting in the near future, so many clamored for their discharges. General Taylor gratefully obliged, adding that "with their departure we may look for a restoration of quiet and order in Monterrey," but when he addressed them directly, Taylor complimented the rangers for their "efficient service" during the campaign. On October 2, Lane and his fellow Texans disbanded. Giddings witnessed their departure. "[W]e saw them turn their faces toward the blood-bought State they represented, with many good wishes and the hope that all honest Mexicans were at a safe distance from their path."[34]

Although he actively participated in the storming of Federación and Independencia, the fighting down Calle de Itúrbide, and hazardous picket duty on the night of September 22, rarely did observers single out Lieutenant Lane in official or personal accounts, like many of his comrades.[35] But according to Hays, each ranger performed so conspicuously that "to undertake to designate the conduct of individuals might have the appearance of calling the roll of my command." Many years later, however, one trooper who "burned powder with Lane at Monterrey," remembered that "[I]n those days there was no hold back in Lane. He was as gay and gallant a fellow as I ever saw."[36]

• 5 •

THE FAULT OF ALL TEXANS, 1846-48

After *his discharge in Monterrey* in October 1846, Walter Lane returned to San Antonio. Despite his disappointment with Zachary Taylor's armistice, he decided to raise his own company of Texas Rangers and rejoin the war. Advertising Lane's call to arms, the *Texas Democrat* in Austin described the former lieutenant as an "old Texian," and recounted his service at San Jacinto and with John Hays in Mexico. The writer vouched for Lane's reputation. "Persons wishing to engage in military pursuits cannot find a more competent, brave and meritorious young gentleman than Mr. Lane, to command them." Lane's friend and fellow ranger, Gouvenier Nelson, assisted him and traveled to Fayette County to recruit. Finding volunteers, however, proved difficult, because Lane and Nelson wanted a company to serve for the duration of the war. No one knew when peace would come, and few were willing to make such an indefinite commitment. A man of no less reputation than Benjamin McCulloch could barely muster thirty men under these circumstances. Hays and Michael Chevallié cancelled their plans to raise a regiment for the same reasons.[1]

The inactivity at General Taylor's front also dissuaded many from enlisting. Gen. Pedro de Ampudia abandoned Saltillo shortly after his exit from Monterrey, and Taylor consequently occupied that forward position. Any further movement toward the interior of Mexico would prove difficult. A vast desert lay between Saltillo and San Luis Potosí to the southeast and Zacatecas to the southwest. If the war should continue, Pres. James K. Polk and his advisers agreed that an assault on Vera Cruz, on the gulf coast, would present the best route to Mexico City.

In the meantime, Lane and Nelson managed to raise a company of about one hundred rangers. It included as many as twelve troopers from Hays's

First Texas Mounted Riflemen, four former Mier prisoners, and fifteen volunteers from Mississippi. Young P. Alsbury, who had served with Lane under Henry Karnes at San Jacinto, joined as a private. They organized the unit on February 13, electing Lane captain and Nelson first lieutenant. Taylor's inspector general, George Croghan, arrived in San Antonio to enroll Lane's company into the U.S. Army. The old soldier impressed Lane. A veteran of the War of 1812, Croghan had distinguished himself at the battle of Fort Stephenson, near Sandusky, Ohio. The people of Ohio, among whom Lane spent his adolescence, revered him as a hero. Croghan officially mustered the company into federal service on February 19, a day after Walter Lane's thirtieth birthday.[2]

On February 24, Robert H. Taylor's company from Bonham, which included future Texas governor James W. Throckmorton, also entered into federal service in San Antonio. On March 6, George W. Adams enrolled a company from Red River and Limestone counties, which included William Crittenden, another one of Lane's old friends from Karnes's spies. The three captains decided to form a battalion. They acknowledged that Lane had enlisted first and held seniority, but he waived his claim to the rank of major in favor of Mike Chevallié, recently arrived in San Antonio. The others agreed.[3]

While the command organized in San Antonio, the situation on Taylor's front changed. In an impressive demonstration of initiative, determination, and coercion, the once-exiled president, Antonio López de Santa Anna, gathered a force of about 20,000 soldiers and left San Luis Potosí. By the time he crossed the harsh landscape and reached the pass of La Angostura, south of Saltillo, the Mexican general could field only 15,000 men. Taylor and his lieutenant, Gen. John E. Wool, deployed their 4,500 troops in the pass and within the ravines to their left. For two days, on February 22 and 23, 1847, the two armies clashed. Santa Anna beat Taylor back toward the small hacienda of Buena Vista. Although U.S. forces reeled from their assaults, the Mexican forces suffered heavy casualties, and then Santa Anna received dispatches that informed him of a rebellion in Mexico City. On the brink of victory, he ordered a withdrawal, leaving Taylor in possession of the field. Unfortunately for Walter Lane and his fellow rangers in San Antonio, the battle of La Angostura, or Buena Vista, as the U.S. veterans called it, ended large-scale action in northeastern Mexico. On March 9, Gen. Winfield Scott landed near Vera Cruz and launched his campaign against Mexico City.

The operations in northeastern Mexico, however, had always been more a matter of occupation than one of warfare. The battles of Monterrey and Buena Vista only briefly interrupted the two years in which U.S. forces occupied the Mexican states of Tamaulipas, Nuevo León, Coahuila, and portions of Chihuahua and Zacatecas. Taylor established military governments but implemented a policy of appeasement, which included respect of private property, payment for supplies obtained from Mexican farmers and merchants, guarantees of religious freedom, Indian protection, amnesty for past service against U.S. forces, and other measures. Furthermore, Taylor often left Mexicans officials alone, to attend to exclusively Mexican affairs. This program, however, was not an example of U.S. humanitarianism. Instead, this was a pragmatic measure designed to obtain the neutrality of the Mexican people, which would permit the deployment of troops in offensive operations, rather than requiring them to serve as a police force.

Taylor and Wool found that volunteers presented the greatest hindrance to maintaining a passive Mexican population. As early as August 1846, Taylor wrote to President Polk, "The only obstacle I encounter in carrying out this desirable policy [appeasement], is the employment of volunteer troops." Later, in June 1847, he explained, "Were it possible to rouse the Mexican people to resistence [*sic*], no more effectual plan could be devised than the very one pursued by some of our volunteer regiments." Unfortunately for Lane and other Texas soldiers, they were the most visible of the volunteers and received most of the blame for crimes against the Mexican people.[4]

General Taylor discovered the Texans' penchant for violence against Mexicans early in his campaign on the Rio Grande. After the battle of Resaca de la Palma, he learned about a Texas trooper in Samuel Walker's company who had scalped a Mexican. Incensed, he had John Bate Berry brought before him and demanded an explanation. The scout offered a tearful account of his past experiences with Mexicans. According to his comrade, Creed Taylor, Berry tearfully stated, "General, I served under Sam Houston, I was at Mier where my brother was butchered like a dog by the Mexicans; I was at Salado and drew for the black bean, I was in Perote driven to work like an ox, and I have sworn by the eternal to kill Mexicans as long as I live." These Texans, the general learned, carried a special malice toward their southern neighbors.[5]

Many, like Berry, entered the war for the express purpose of killing Mexicans. "Few . . . can realize the hatred and contempt the pioneers of Texas . . . bore towards the Mexicans," Creed Taylor explained. "The blood of our countrymen called to us from the Alamo, Goliad, Refugio, San Patricio, Santa Fe, Mier, Salado, and Perote, and we rejoiced in the prospect of wreaking vengeance on the nation which had clothed our houses in the garb of mourning." Texas volunteers often used the idea of vengeance as justification for their crimes in Mexico. When U.S. authorities established a court in Monterrey to settle disputes between Mexicans and U.S. soldiers, citizens filled the docket with grievances against Texans. Luther Giddings, a volunteer from Ohio observed, "[The Texans'] answers to the complaints . . . almost invariable [*sic*] began, continued and ended with the Alamo, or Goliad or Mier." The Texans who enlisted under Captain Lane in San Antonio carried with them this vengeful spirit. Although they were not involved with the more notorious atrocities in northern Mexico, Lane's men would contribute to the tarnished image of the Texas Rangers in the war.[6]

However loath General Taylor was in calling on Chevallié's battalion, he desperately needed their services. In advance of Santa Anna's movement from San Luis Potosí, Gen. José Urrea, an old nemesis of Texas from the 1836 campaign, rode at the head of a mounted column that struck at Taylor's supply line between Monterrey and Matamoros. On February 22, he attacked a large supply train, killing as many as fifty teamsters and capturing the escort of thirty soldiers. The Texans, under Chevallié and Lane, were well suited for the type of operations required to reopen Taylor's supply lines. Fast moving, ready to ride at a moment's notice, the rangers could scout vast distances and engage the equally fleet cavalry under Urrea or the squads of partisans under Antonio Canales. Taylor seemed willing to endure a measure of the rangers' peculiar capacity for violence in order to benefit from their service.[7]

On March 8, 1847, the rangers left San Antonio and rode toward the Rio Grande via San Patricio. Chevallié sent Lane ahead to Camargo, in order to request supplies.[8] When Lane arrived, he located the quartermaster's office but found the major in charge too busy feting with his fellow officers to give the Texan immediate attention. After Lane protested, the assistant reluctantly notified the quartermaster, who agreed to receive the irritated ranger. When he walked into the back room, Lane recalled, "I found about a dozen officers, all in fine uniform, enjoying a dinner which, from the number of turkeys, chickens and the quantity of champagne on the table, must have been very appetizing." The captain recognized one of the officers as the son of John J. Marshall, with whom he and his brother, Wade Lane, quartered in Louisville during the winter of 1835–36. Humphrey Marshall, according to Lane, refused to acknowledge him. The dismissive quartermaster and the haughty Marshall emasculated Lane in the presence of his fellow officers. This denial of peer sanction threatened his manly status.

When he invalidated Lane's requisition because Chevallié had not yet been confirmed as the battalion commanding officer, the quartermaster decided that as the senior officer of the regiment, only Captain Lane had the authority to sign it. No doubt feeling a measure of self-satisfaction, the Texan declared that he would sign it "as I happen to be Capt. Lane, the senior officer," and suggested that Marshall could identify him, "if he was not ashamed to do so." The volunteer colonel rushed up to shake Lane's hand and professed that he did not recognize him at first, but Lane did not believe his old friend. Marshall, who led the Kentuckians at Buena Vista, introduced the Texan to the other officers, and the quartermaster offered him a place at the table. "I proceeded with great relish to *line* the inner man," Lane recalled.

While Marshall confirmed his identity and the quartermaster officially recognized his rank, the other officers might have reserved judgment in regard for Lane's masculine credentials. To obtain their approval, Lane evoked the custom of storytelling. Over dinner, he entertained his fellow officers with "some exploits I had gone through, by flood and field, all of which Col. Marshall solemnly asseverated, he being nearly drunk by that time." Storytelling was an important part of the adventurous expedition, permitting veterans to present their credentials for review. The acknowledgment of his rank, an invitation to associate with brother officers, and Marshall's "asseverations" of his tales confirmed Lane's status as a man among men.[9]

On March 23, the battalion reached Camargo with about three hundred rangers. Two days later, the three companies officially organized as a battalion and elected Chevallié major. General Taylor immediately employed them in pursuing Urrea and escorting supply trains. The Mexican cavalry had already withdrawn to Tula, on the opposite side of the Sierra Madre. The rangers, however, demonstrated their effectiveness as scouts, by providing Taylor with accurate intelligence. Chevallié selected Cadereyta, east of Monterrey, as his headquarters and for the next several weeks, dispatched his scouts and escorts from there. Giddings, who was personally acquainted with the difficulties of escorting supply trains, credited the rangers with restoring order to the region. "Even the robbers, awed by the rapid and searching patrols of the few companies of Texas Rangers, again in the field, were perfectly quiescent; and our trains were permitted to pass unmolested."[10]

Captain Lane played a conspicuous role in these operations. Sometime in the middle of May, Chevallié dispatched Lane to hunt down a partisan company, near Cerralvo, under José Nicolás García. On May 27, the captain dispersed a camp of thirty Mexicans but failed to capture them. During the night, however, a pair of citizens, professing to be wealthy rancheros, entered the ranger camp and requested an audience with the captain. They concealed their identities by blackening their faces with gunpowder and covering their heads with scarves. According to Lane, they were as eager as the rangers to see García captured.

The rancheros led Lane and his rangers to a small village and pointed out a house. "We immediately entered," Lane recalled, "when a beautiful woman sprang out of bed." She was Antonia García, wife of the partisan captain. Lane asked for her husband, but she claimed that he was not there. He did not believe her. "[A]s I had been atrociously lied to by *white* women, I did not give much credence to the assertions of the Mexican sister." Lane found a man hiding under the covers, and his guide confirmed that they had found Nicolás García. The captain ordered the suspected guerrilla to dress and consider himself under arrest. Antonia implored Lane for mercy, but he explained that they were taking García to Cerralvo, where he would receive a "fair trial, as he was accused of a great many atrocities perpetrated on Americans." In the same breath he mentioned "fair trial," Lane emphasized the "great many atrocities." The captain's assurances probably comforted Antonia very little.

On May 28, García received his trial at Cerralvo, and his jury—likely formed of Texans—found him guilty and sentenced him to die. Lane set the execution at noon the next day. At the appointed time, Lane placed a firing squad on the plaza, and as the Texans arranged the execution, Col. Alexander Doniphan's Missouri regiment entered town. They were marching home, having received their discharge. "No inducement of the officers could make the men leave until they saw the Mexican shot," Lane claimed. "Several came up to the executing party and offered to give them ten dollars for their places." The captain did not mention if any succeeded.[11]

Several of the Missourians, however, remembered the episode differently. Although many felt that the execution was justified, a few expressed indignation. Frank S. Edwards claimed that the Texans fabricated the charges "as a cloak to their insatiable desire to destroy those they so bitterly hate." Writing sixty years later, Odon Guitar described the episode as "one of the most outrageous events of the Mexican War." Far from wanting to join the firing squad, Guitar claimed that the outrage was so strong in the Missouri regiment that it nearly caused a general mutiny, until Colonel Doniphan and his officers interceded and maintained order.[12]

Lane, meanwhile, offered García amnesty if he would name his confederates, but the Mexican proudly refused. He claimed, according to Lane, that he had killed many *norteamericanos* and would kill more if allowed. The alleged partisan chief calmly rolled a cigarette while a priest offered the last rites. Lane asked Garcia if he would turn away or wear a blindfold. "He said neither, he wanted to look them in the face," Lane recorded. When the captain gave the order to fire, García "drew himself up and threw out his breast. . . . Three balls went through his head and three through his breast. He sprang three feet in the air and fell dead." Everyone remarked on how defiantly Nicolás García met his fate. Although satisfied that justice had been served, Missourian Jacob Robinson summed up the feelings of many who were present: "[W]e turned our horses and resumed our march in silence, sincerely regretting that so brave a man should die in such a manner."[13]

A few days later, Captain Lane found himself involved in another controversy. General Taylor ordered him to scout the vicinity of Linares, where rumors had placed General Urrea. In the company of Lt. George T. Shackleford of the Sixth Infantry, Lane and his rangers reached Linares after riding for three days. They arrived after nightfall, and the captain dispatched three squads to search up the streets toward the main plaza, where he thought the enemy might have camped. He instructed his men that "if they came across any armed Mexicans, to order their surrender, and fire upon them if they refused."

The squad under Henry Earll, second lieutenant in Lane's company, encountered José María Arsipe, reportedly armed and riding towards them in the moonlight. The Texans ordered him to halt, but he replied, "Damn the Americans," and rushed away. Pvt. John J. Glanton gave chase and, according to Lane, implored him in Spanish to halt. When Arsipe refused, Glanton shot him down. After the squads reached the plaza and discovered no sign of the enemy, they returned and reported to a relieved Lane. He sent a message to the alcalde, Guillermo Morales, and demanded that he send forage and rations to a hacienda that lay outside of town. The next morning, the alcalde called on the captain, protested the shooting of Arsipe, and requested that the rangers return his horse to his family, to which Lane agreed.[14]

The battalion remained in Linares several days before returning to Monterrey. When he reported to Taylor, Lane found the general in one of his infamous fits of anger. "[H]e commenced abusing my command as a set of robbers and cut-throats." Apparently, Morales had sent word of Arsipe's killing, accusing the rangers of murder and of refusing to pay for their provisions. Lane defended his men, explaining that they killed the Mexican for refusing to halt and that his quartermaster had the receipts proving he had paid for the supplies. Lane suggested sending for Shackelford, who would support the Texans' account. Taylor refused and ordered Glanton's arrest.[15]

Lane defied Taylor. In his autobiography, he relished the memory. "This, I flatly refused to do." He claimed that because he gave the order, he deserved the punishment. When Taylor asked him if he was disobeying a direct order, Lane replied, "I most emphatically do. And, furthermore, you are a general and I am a little [captain]; but I won't stand here any longer and hear my men and myself abused." Taylor ordered his arrest, but the captain rode out of Monterrey to his camp, then advised Glanton to flee.[16]

Taylor's adjutant general, William W. S. Bliss, followed Lane, placed him under arrest, and instructed Captain Adams to deliver Glanton. Lane recorded smugly, "[I] pulled out my watch, looked at it, and told Bliss that I thought by that time John was about eleven miles on the road to San Antonio; I didn't think there were any dragoons in Gen. Taylor's command who could overtake him on 'Old Charlie.'" The captain explained the circumstances of the scout to Bliss and once again requested Shackelford's statement. Bliss obtained the information, which later satisfied Taylor.[17]

If Lane's account was accurate—if Arsipe had charged on Lieutenant Earll's detachment and did not heed repeated warnings to stop—then contemporary observers might have deemed the shooting justified. Lane, however, did not personally observe the affair, and Glanton had a long history of inappropriate violence. During the 1840s in East Texas, he reportedly killed men on both sides of the Regulator-Moderator conflict. He fled before residents could hang him. After the U.S.-Mexican War, Glanton killed a fellow ranger in Texas, and he later led a group of scalp hunters in Chihuahua, receiving bounties for killing Apaches. Chihuahua authorities banished Glanton when they received reports that he often turned in Mexican scalps, as well.[18] Captain Lane might not have known of his murderous disposition, but Glanton's conduct before and after the episode at Linares casts a dubious light on actions that Lane believed were justified.

The Glanton affair, however, upset Taylor more than Captain Lane remembered, or was willing to admit. The general decided to transfer the unruly Texans to John Wool's command in Saltillo. "You will find Chevallie [*sic*] a good partisan officer," Bliss informed, "but his people have the fault of all Texans i.e. an indifference to human life. On almost every detachment they have managed to kill a Mexican and it is in consequence of a recent occurrence of that kind near Linares that the Genl [*sic*] has hastened their departure from Monterey [*sic*]." Bliss added that Wool should keep the rangers in camp, to prevent any further mischief.[19]

In June 1847, Chevallié reported to Wool, who placed the rangers at a forward position called La Encantada, some fifteen miles south of Saltillo, at the southern end of the narrow valley where U.S. and Mexican forces had fought the battle of Buena Vista. Sometime in July, Chevallié became ill, and Lane assumed command of the battalion.[20]

Even at their remote post, a few rangers continued to rob and pilfer. On July 21, five Texans attacked a Mexican traveling between La Encantada and Buena Vista, in an attempt to take his money. Wool also received reports of Texans interfering with the herding of cattle for U.S. troops, and he railed on Chevallié, "If you cannot control your men . . . we will be compelled to send you back to the Rio Grande. I will not have men under my command who will not obey orders." On August 16, when he learned that the rangers had killed cattle and sheep at Vaqueria, Wool issued Orders Number 405, warning that he would discharge the perpetrators, but if he could not identify them, he would discharge their entire company. "[I]nstead of claiming credit for having fought the battles of their country," Wool further explained, "they will be able to boast of depredations in Mexico."[21]

On August 31, amidst this controversy, Major Chevallié resigned his commission. Lane recalled, and a contemporary newspaper agreed, that he resigned after an altercation with Wool, when the general refused to discharge several rangers who the major deemed unfit for duty. Perhaps Chevallié simply tired of the general's continual criticism of his unit, but the official returns cite ill health as the reason. Whatever the circumstance, Chevallié left the service and relinquished command of the battalion to Walter Lane. On September 27, the battalion confirmed Lane's rank when they elected him major.[22]

At La Encantada, Lane and his rangers settled into the routine of camp life and scouting. When he dispatched them, Wool always included reminders of good behavior with his instructions. On one such mission in August 1847, the general instructed Lane to ride toward San Miguel, a large hacienda west of Saltillo, and arrest a bandit by the name of Gonzales, who reportedly attacked a supply train carrying corn to Saltillo. Wool reminded Lane, "You will take care that your men do not commit any depredations in the course of your tour." On October 1, to Captain Taylor, the general ordered, "In your intercourse with the people . . . [you] will see that your men commit not the slightest depredations, and before starting, you will admonish them particularly on this point." On the 16th, when he sent Captain Adams southeast to Hedionda to protect Mexican herders, Wool's subordinate relayed, "The General trusts they will not by their conduct add to the list of depredations already too long."[23]

The rangers under Lane's command, however, continued to justify Wool's concern. In October, Captain Taylor sent Lt. Simeon Nunelee to arrest the alcalde of Yerba Buena for abetting bandits. "In so doing it unfortunately became necessary to take Human Life," Taylor casually reported. Those lives were, of course, Mexican, and the rangers killed four during the incident. Another episode testified to the harsh justice that the Texans enforced. While away pursuing Indians, a Mexican stole their blankets at San Miguel, and he received one hundred lashes for his offense. In Parras on November 25, an Irishman not connected to the U.S. forces shot and killed Otto Peltz, a private in Lane's old company. In retaliation, "one of the Rangers blew the assassin's brains out," according to George H. Tobin, part-time ranger and correspondent of the New Orleans *Delta.* Then the Texans "got on a spree and killed a few jackasses and bulldogs, and two Mexicans who had managed to get mixed up in the business." Between April and September 1847, as many as thirteen rangers received dishonorable discharges for a variety of offenses—stealing from Mexicans, attempted murder, or worthlessness. That same period also witnessed thirty desertions, including thirteen who left La Encantada on September 13. Little wonder Wool felt compelled to constantly admonish Lane's command about their conduct.[24]

Although not directly implicated in these incidents, Lane—as commanding officer—was responsible for the behavior of his men. The captain, apparently, did not take this responsibility very seriously. In December, José Ignacio Arsave of Parras wrote to John F. Hamtramck, commanding volunteers in Saltillo, and listed a number of complaints against the rangers under Lane, including assault, robbery, the discharge of firearms, and other rowdiness. Arsave had complained to Lane, who offered no answer. "I do not know why I do not deserve from Major Lane the honor of a reply to the note that I directed to him the last time they began the disorders." To assuage the inhabitants, Wool barred Lane's rangers from Parras. In another case, three Texans robbed a rancher of $600. U.S. authorities arrested the sergeant involved, but the others managed to escape, "so Capt. Lane reports," Wool informed, perhaps insinuating that Lane might have facilitated their escape, as he had Glanton's.[25]

Whatever the captain's culpability in these cases might have been, he certainly did not have Wool's confidence. The general recognized Lane as a hindrance to maintaining good behavior when Chevallié left the service. As an indictment of Lane's inability to discipline his men, Wool lamented, "The circumstances [of Chevallié's absence] has given me much trouble, for no one of the command besides the Major, appears to have any control over his men." He further implicated Lane when he added, "I would except Capt. Adams."[26]

On October 20, General Wool provided Lane with instructions for another scout toward Parras. The general had received intelligence that the governor of Chihuahua, José María Aguirre, was organizing partisans in Pastora, San Miguel, and Castanuella. He instructed Lane, "Should you meet any of the Guerrillas you will show them no quarter. In doing this be careful not to confound the innocent with the guilty." Wool added that Lane should supply the command with corn from the hacienda Arriva and not pay, as he suspected that its inhabitants abetted partisans. He reiterated that Lane should "impress upon them [Lane's men] the distinction which should be made between men in arms and men peaceably following their usual avocation." Major Lane completed his mission with little incident.[27]

In addition to scouting, escorting supply trains, and combating guerrillas and bandits, Lane's rangers also fought against Indians. The states in northeastern Mexico had a long history of violence with Native Americans, usually Comanches or Apaches. Traditionally, the Mexicans of Tamaulipas, Nuevo León, Coahuila, and Chihuahua felt neglected by the central government in Mexico City, that rarely possessed the means to provide adequate protection. They also blamed the U.S. government. With Indian protection, however, the U.S. military discovered another opportunity to further their appeasement program, by providing the Mexicans in the northeastern states with a measure of security that some had not felt since 1835. Although no amount of killing Comanches could undo the wrongs committed against Mexicans, fighting Indians provided the Texans with an opportunity for action that might benefit the Mexican populace.[28]

That moment arrived on the morning of November 21. Lane's pickets raced into La Encantada, interrupting breakfast. They reported that a body of Comanches had attacked a nearby village where they were stationed, and they had narrowly escaped with their lives. Lane immediately assembled his rangers, calling on those who had good horses. "I knew it would be a long chase, and I was determined to see the color of some of those Comanches' hair before I returned to camp." After six miles, Lane sighted the dust created by the Comanche *caballado,* or horse herd, and gave pursuit. Riding hard for three hours, the rangers finally caught up with the "Red devils," as Lane termed them, at a place called Los Muchachos, and formed for battle. According to one account, Lane attempted to talk with them, but they answered with a volley of arrows. While the Comanche leader encouraged his men, Lane "rode down the line and asked: 'Are you all ready for a charge?'" When they replied to the affirmative, Lane gave the command, "Charge! and go through them!" The Texans, the major claimed, "literally obeyed, our men going through them like they had been greased, and the Indians scattered in all directions."[29]

The rangers chased the Comanches to the foothills of the Sierra Madre. Lane found one of his men engaged with a Comanche and rode at "full speed . . . shot the Indian through the breast, and, running my horse against him, knocked him a distance of ten feet upon a pile of rocks." Tobin probably exaggerated when he reported that "Maj. Lane killed several in single fight." At the end of the battle, Lane counted one of his own killed and fourteen wounded and estimated forty Indians killed and wounded. He captured a considerable amount of horses and mules and rescued several Mexican children.[30]

Lane regarded the battle as a singular moment of his adventurous career. In addition to capturing the caballado and freeing children, the rangers collected bows, spears, shields, and other accoutrements of Comanche warfare. For several days, officers of the U.S. Army visited the Texan camp to view the booty. "The sight was novel to them," Lane explained, "as most of them had never seen an Indian." For Lane, the relics represented material evidence of his manly exploits—evidence of his exceptional experiences. Until his last days, he would display them for any who might listen to the stories that they confirmed. He imbued those stories with the romantic's enthusiasm—even in the very moments of experiencing them. The day after he arrived at La Encantada, for example, the major prepared to intercept the remaining Comanches but took the time to write to Captain Nelson, who had resigned and yet remained in Saltillo. "I start for Parras to-morrow with my whole command, again in pursuit of the Indians. . . . They have been devestating [*sic*] settlements, killing the Mexican hombres, and carrying off the women." With a flair reminiscent of Walter Scott, Lane added, "This you know is unchristianlike, and we go to show our gallantry in defense of the fair. Mount and come with us, for we are certain to have a brush."[31]

The letter generated a measure of notice for Major Lane. Nelson forwarded copies to the Monterrey *Gazette* and the Matamoros *American Flag*. According to one editor, the latter was "at this moment one of the most frequently quoted papers we know of on this continent," as it served as a clearinghouse of information regarding the war in northeastern Mexico. Lane's account of the fight at Los Muchachos appeared in such locales as New Orleans, Cincinnati, Clarksville, Texas, and the *Daily American Star*—a U.S.-operated newspaper in Mexico City.[32]

The battle with the Comanches, however, brought Lane into another conflict with Mexican citizens. From the Indians, he captured horses and mules, presumably taken from Mexican haciendas. Several citizens convinced Wool that they owned some of the animals, but Lane determined that they were running a scheme. "I found out the Mexicans would come to my camp, and view the horses and mules, take on a piece of paper their brands, and then go to Gen. Wool and prove by two witnesses it was their property." When one Mexican claimed a horse belonging to one of the rangers, Lane decided to put a stop to the practice. He ordered several of his men to take the Mexicans out "and settle the horse question with them; which they did, giving them about *one hundred apiece,* the Mexicans barely escaping with their lives." Lane did not specify whether the claimants were flogged or beaten, but the result was the same. "These were the last that ever visited my camp for horses or mules." The major was satisfied with this brutal form of deterrence, and he took the caballado to Saltillo, sold it, and divided the money with his men.[33]

Nothing in Lane's language suggests that this assault was racially motivated, but only in Mexico did he preside over an execution, or assault people whom he thought deserving. During the Civil War to come, Lane exhibited a harsh and arbitrary attitude toward shirkers under his command, but he never punished them with physical violence. Tobin summarized Lane's attitude toward Mexicans perhaps as well as anyone. In January 1848, when Wool appointed a court to try several Mexicans suspected of killing three Mississippi volunteers, Tobin wrote, "May the Lord have mercy on their souls, as Major Lane, of the Rangers, is President of the Court."[34] At the very least, the assault on the horse claimants, together with García's execution and the Glanton affair, confirms Walter Lane's contribution to the brutality of the U.S. occupation of northeastern Mexico.

Gen. Winfield Scott, meanwhile, brought active hostilities between the United States and Mexico to a close. On April 8, 1847, he launched his invasion of the Mexican interior from Vera Cruz and clashed with Santa Anna at Cerro Gordo on the 18th. Scott fought four major battles in the suburbs of Mexico City before occupying the capital on September 14. Although regular hostilities had ceased, several months passed before Mexico could organize a government willing to negotiate a peace settlement.

In the northeast, a few changes occurred. General Taylor, tired of commanding an occupation force, found it difficult to cultivate his presidential aspirations from Monterrey. In October, he left Mexico and on November 25, General Wool assumed command. Clashes with native groups continued, as did banditry and murder of both Mexican civilians and U.S. soldiers. Despite his reputation as a martinet, Wool experienced the same problems regarding volunteers and civilians that had vexed Taylor. He nonetheless expanded his area of occupation west to Parras in Chihuahua and south to Mazapil in Zacatecas, in order to collect a new tax that the U.S. Army had levied on Mexican citizens. On February 28, 1848, he ordered the Second Mississippi Regiment and Lane's battalion, under the command of Col. Charles Clark, to Mazapil. Arriving on March 7, Clark and Lane established their headquarters at Cedras, just west of Mazapil on the Zacatecas-Saltillo road.[35]

During this period, Major Lane became disgruntled with his status. On February 4, he wrote Wool on behalf of himself and Captain Adams, requesting the general recommend them for commissions in regiments that he heard were organizing for California and New Mexico. Two weeks later on the 20th, Lane again wrote Wool, believing that his rank entitled him to a larger command, and on April 7, after returning from a scout, he requested a leave to visit central Mexico. The familiar adventuristic longing for diversion and renown tugged again at Lane.[36]

Wool assuaged his restlessness by sending him on an audacious scout. In early March, the general summoned the ranger to Monterrey and gave him orders to take four hundred men and Capt. John Pope of the engineers on a reconnaissance toward Matehuala, a city in the northern section of the state of San Luis Potosí—180 miles southeast of Saltillo. Lane suggested that he could better execute the scout with a smaller command. "[W]e would penetrate into the country . . . and get out with whole bones," Lane explained, "for, any small party of Mexicans we could *whip,* and any large force we could [out] *run.*" After Pope supported the idea, Wool reluctantly consented.[37]

On March 12, 1848, Lane, Pope, and fourteen rangers departed from Mazapil. They rode west through desert, mountains, and valleys, dotted with haciendas, herds of cattle, and flocks of sheep. They paused to rest their horses in Salado, the location of the infamous execution of seventeen Texans. At dawn on the 14th, they entered Cedral, a small town about five miles north of Matehuala. "It is beautifully situated on an eminence and commands an extensive view of the surrounding Country," Pope described. Lane called on the alcalde to provide supplies and quarters for his men and horses. When the inhabitants realized that the rangers were not the vanguard of Wool's army, they gathered around the intruders, yelling, "Kill the Americans!" Lane and Pope agreed that they had over-stayed their welcome and quickly departed.[38]

On the morning of March 16, after 225 miles and four days, Lane's scout returned to Mazapil. Captain Pope believed they had achieved their objective. "I deem the reconnaissance to Matehuala entirely effected as we approached within eight miles and attained a point from which the position of the town was plainly to be seen."[39] The scout was perhaps the most impressive of Lane's career in Mexico. His previous missions to Linares and Parras occurred over routes that had been scouted before and covered considerably less distance. Few, if any, U.S. troops had ever reached as far as Cedral.

Soon after Lane returned to Mazapil, several of his men approached him about riding back to Salado. There, in 1843, Mexican soldiers had executed seventeen Texans—one in ten of the prisoners that the Mexicans captured at Mier. Stationed at Concepción, about five miles west of Mazapil, Lt. William H. Francis and the battalion's interpreter, John E. Dusenberry—a former Mier prisoner—wanted to exhume the remains. They asked the major for permission, and he reportedly replied "that he highly appreciated their motives, but could not formally give them the permission . . . though he privately winked at the plan."[40]

On May 2, 1848, Francis and Dusenberry, with nine other rangers, left Concepción and arrived at Salado the next morning. They secured the alcalde, warned the inhabitants not to send messengers, and forced the exhumation of the Mier prisoners. Then, the detachment returned to Concepción. The men chose Fayette County as the place in Texas to deliver the remains, and Lane's battalion raised several hundred dollars to defray expenses. They declined to receive donations offered by the Mississippi volunteers wishing to bare the burden alone, but called on Louis P. Cooke, a Texas congressman who served on Wool's staff, to request assistance from the general for transportation. Wool permitted Dusenberry to escort the remains to Texas. He took the bodies to La Grange, and the citizens buried them on a bluff overlooking the Colorado River. Much later in life, Walter Lane claimed that he led the mission to Salado and personally demanded the return of those cherished remains.[41]

In the meantime, movements toward peace had taken place in central Mexico. On February 2, 1848, U.S. and Mexican representatives agreed to a treaty that they signed in a suburb of Mexico City called Guadalupe Hidalgo. On March 5, the U.S. military agreed to an armistice that brought an end to hostilities throughout Mexico. The Treaty of Guadalupe Hidalgo fixed the Texas boundary at the Rio Grande and transferred New Mexico and Alta California to the United States. Mexico ceded over 500,000 square miles, half of its national territory. In return, the United States agreed to pay $15 million in addition to assuming U.S. claims on Mexico. The treaty consummated Manifest Destiny, transforming the United States into the continental nation that its people had long imagined.

On June 12, 1848, General Wool announced the peace to his troops occupying northeastern Mexico, and he began preparations for withdrawal, placing the rangers in the rear to prevent straggling. "The soldiers on the march would naturally want to 'skip out' of ranks, to buy chickens and eggs and court the senoritas," Lane explained. "At nightfall we generally had about two wagon loads of stragglers. I would, according to orders, send them to Wool's camp, under guard. But, as I had been once *young myself,* and still had a taste for the *fine arts,* I ordered the officer to dump them out close to their camp, and no doubt all got in." Lane did not explain what he meant by "the *fine arts,*" but it might have been a rare admission for a fondness of women.[42]

During the withdrawal, Lane participated in at least two banquets, cele-

By the 1870s, Lane falsely claimed credit for exhuming the Mier prisoners. In 1936, the State of Texas seemed to perpetuate that honor when it erected this shaft over their tomb. On the right face, a plaque commemorates, "In memory of Walter Paye Lane (1817–1892) through whose personal initiative . . . the remains of 16 members of the Mier Expedition . . . were returned to this place for burial." Author's photograph, Tomb on Monument Hill, La Grange, Tex.

brating the American success in Mexico. He found both personally gratifying. He first attended Wool's grand feast, aboard a steamboat laying in the Rio Grande at Camargo. With some forty fellow officers present, Wool toasted the major of the Texas cavalry. According to Lane, the general thanked him for his service and complimented him on his ability to promptly field a scout at a moment's notice. At a time of celebration, Wool chose not to dwell on the unruly conduct of the rangers. Major Lane basked in the general's acknowledgment and recognition in the presence of his "brother officers."[43]

On June 30, the same day that Lane disbanded his battalion, the citizens of the recently established town of Rio Grande City—directly across the river from Camargo—invited Wool and his staff, as well as Lane and his battalion, to a public dinner to celebrate the Fourth of July and the end of the war. "I can hardly find words . . . to express to you the feelings of gratification which your kindness has excised in my bosom," Lane gushed, "for nothing can give more pleasure to the soldier . . . than to find that his conduct while in the field has met with the approbation of his fellow citizens." Many civilians of northeastern Mexico would have recognized the irony of his words. Nevertheless, on the morning of the fourth, Major Lane and many of his discharged rangers joined the townspeople at the Rio Grande Hotel for a round of toasts and feting.[44]

Despite the platitudes and laudatory nature of the toasts, Major Lane and his battalion of Texas Rangers left a mixed record during their service in Mexico. The command performed valuable service under Taylor and Wool as scouts, obtaining important intelligence. They were less effective in countering partisan activities, policing against bandits, and as protectors from the Indians, but neither Taylor nor Wool could completely solve those puzzles. Although the men in Lane's command were not responsible for the more heinous crimes committed in Mexico, their conduct was less than exemplary. Contact between them and the Mexican populace often resulted in violence and perpetuated an atmosphere of anxiety and ill-feeling between the occupiers and the occupied.

Although he commanded a battalion, Lane did not receive the renown that many of his companions had. John Hays, Ben McCulloch, and Samuel Walker achieved lasting fame for their role in Mexico, while Richard Gillespie and Michael Chevallié received wide-ranging press at the time. Despite the reprinting of his letter about the fight at Los Muchachos and an occasional mention in the popular correspondence of George Tobin, Walter Lane remained anonymous to most in the United States.

The major, nonetheless, felt proud of his career as a soldier in Monterrey and Los Muchachos and as commander of a ranging force. He certainly felt justified in his conduct during the execution of García, the Glanton affair, and the assault on the horse claimants—although those who suffered as a result might have felt otherwise. General Wool, furthermore, placed little confidence in Lane's ability to curb the depredations of his men. Lane's experience in Mexico, however, provided him with the excitement for which he always yearned. Battling Mexicans and Comanches in the exotic landscape of northeastern Mexico's Sierra Madre provided him with the incidents that romantic adventurers craved. Furthermore, Lane kept almost exclusively masculine company, and his comrades gratified his notions of manhood with his election to major and expressions of respect by his "brother officers." In the end, as he celebrated with the citizens of Rio Grande City, Lane was satisfied with his small, but symbolically significant role in furthering the territorial expansion of the United States.

• 6 •

BY FLOOD AND FIELD, 1848-58

After his tour in Mexico, Walter Lane entered the most restless period of his life. The gold mania swept him away to California, where his fortunes waxed and waned. He traveled to Peru and Panama, and after a half-hearted attempt at the settled life, he organized an expedition to the Gadsden Purchase. During this time, Lane indulged his adventurous disposition but with a decided emphasis on attaining wealth. At moments, however, his ardor for adventure seemed diminished. He was no longer an adolescent and his fortunes continued to elude him, but the expedition, placer camps, and military outposts continued to provide the masculine spaces where Lane felt the most comfortable.

Before he set out on his travels, Lane returned to southeastern Ohio, perhaps for the last time. His mother, Olivia, apparently had passed away, and his father, William, sold their Fairview town lot in August 1847. He resided in neighboring Belmont County, probably with one of his daughters.[1] While visiting his family, Walter Lane first heard of California gold.

By December 1848, the gold news reached the communities along the National Road. On the 20th, under the title of "The Gold Business," the *Wheeling Times and Advertiser* reprinted a letter written on the American River, above Sacramento. "Yesterday I dug and washed out a pound of gold myself," the correspondent reported. "The rush of people here is immense. The amount of Gold taken out of the earth here is prodigious." Such reports of quick riches dominated the *Guernsey Times* from January to March 1849, reporting the latest from California, offering tips to potential immigrants, and noting the departures of organized companies. As early as January 5, the *Times* printed "Hints for Emigrants to California," and on the 19th, began carrying an advertisement for "Signor D'Alvear's Goldometer." Writing in

March from Middlebourne, the next village on the National Road from Fairview, a resident described the sentiment of southeastern Ohio when she wrote, "The 'California fever' is raging to an alarming extent."[2]

In early 1849, Lane took leave from his family and probably traveled by steamboat from Wheeling to Missouri. One of his older brothers, William H. Lane, lived in Liberty, less than fifteen miles across the Missouri River from Independence—one of two major staging towns for the overland trek to California. Major Lane arrived at his brother's home sometime in April and sought men interested in accompanying him across the continent. Seven Liberty residents agreed to join—perhaps attracted by his reputation as a Texas Ranger, which he no doubt encouraged with his tales of "exploits . . . by flood and field," as he described his penchant for storytelling. Jasper M. Hixson, a Liberty merchant, joined and recorded the journey in his diary. He characterized Lane as a "professional Indian fighter," buying into Lane's reputation. The other members of the party included Hixson's brother, Henry; his uncle, Jasper the elder; Paley Carpenter, Thomas Conington, John York, and Daniel Mosby. The company totaled eight men. They purchased three wagons and nineteen mules. Compared to other outfits, the Liberty company was small and fast-moving.[3]

So, by late April 1849, Walter Lane once again found himself in the company of men, about to embark on yet another expedition. Whether driven by the desire to improve one's social position, or by the search for excitement in far away places, many forty-niners epitomized the romantic adventurer. As he and his companions departed Liberty in early May 1849, Hixson testified to the irrationality of his decision to leave for California. "Gold, gold, that magic word! . . . Home, family, with all the comforts that could be asked for, to render one happy, if contented, are left behind, and the rush is on to California."[4]

On May 1, 1849, the Liberty company departed at eleven in the morning. They knew that they were two weeks early if they wished to rely on the grass for forage, but they were impatient. "We wanted to be ahead and get what [gold] there was," Hixson recorded, so they pressed ahead.[5] They crossed the undulating Great Plains through cold and drizzle. They followed the Platte River to the regions where it cut into the raising grasslands, creating buttes and formations to which the overlanders attached names like Statehouse Rock, Chimney Rock, and Independence Rock. Lane and his comrades passed them all. Into the Rockies, the company trekked over mountains and into alpine valleys, through which flowed glacial-cold streams. They visited numerous mineral hot springs and mused over fantastic lava formations. They endured the heat, dust, and oppressively dark nights of the Humboldt

Desert and found respite in the idyllic meadows along the Carson River. They hauled themselves over the Sierra Nevada and descended into the American River valley, arriving at Sacramento on August 6, three months after they had left Liberty, Missouri.

Lane, however, described the journey as "tedious and uneventful." Apparently, it did not measure up to the violence and incident that he had experienced in the Republic of Texas or in Mexico. Nevertheless, the overland trek was a social experience that forged close friendships, as Hixson attested at journey's end. "I can say . . . that we came across without a hard word or feeling that I know of[.] Maj. Lane, my Uncle, Brother and Dan'l Mosby, are as noble men as ever crossed the plains."[6] Once the company reached El Dorado, however, the competitive environment of the placer camps challenged notions of friendship and manliness, compelling the miners to seek different meanings that often exaggerated and sometimes confounded, notions of adventurous manhood.

A typical day during their journey found the Liberty men awaking at dawn or earlier. They wanted to get ahead of the ox-drawn trains, which were slower and stirred up suffocating trail dust. Lane and his fellows elected Hixson as cook. On good days, breakfast might include slapjacks, bacon, and coffee, and while Hixson prepared it, his comrades readied the mule teams for the day's work. During the day, while Lane and the others drove the teams, Hixson rode ahead to locate a camp for lunch, which might consist of coffee, bread, and bacon cooked on spits. On the plains, when wood was scarce, Hixson would burn "buffalo chips." After lunch, he went ahead to find their camp for the night, and he tried to have dinner ready when they reached him. At night, the company posted guards in shifts to watch for Indians and fellow gold rushers. The conversation tended toward the trivial, according to Hixson. As was common on the expedition, storytelling pervaded. "Agriculture, Politics, or the state of the Markets are but little attended to here," Hixson complained.[7]

On the plains, well-traveled roads—augmented by ferries and toll bridges—facilitated the overland journey. The trails through the Rockies, however, were rough and narrow, and crossing the mountain streams proved precarious. The Green River ferry, for example, was a "simple wagon box, with the cracks stopped with rags," Hixson recorded. The company dismantled their wagons to fit them on the ferry, while the mules swam. As the ferryman pulled the "wagon box" through the swift currents, the gold rushers bailed water. Travel through the Humboldt desert was relatively easy on the wagons but hard on the mules, and the company often traveled for days without water or grass. Once they reached the Sierra Nevada, they encountered one last obstacle—Devil's Ladder, which ascended several thousand feet up the side of a mountain. The Liberty men hitched twelve mules to their remaining wagon, "and by cracking of whips and loud hollowing [*sic*] at the mules and energetic pushing at the wheels by all the available men, we managed to move little by little." They reached the summit near dark and the next day, began to wend their way into the American River valley.[8]

Lane and his companions also encountered a variety of wildlife. Above Fort Childs, they sighted an immense herd of buffalo stampeding through the Platte. "If one said there was 100,000 his word would not be doubted, or if the number was put at 1,000,000, or 10,000,000, no one could prove the number incorrect." Hixson estimated that the herd stretched several miles long and several hundred yards wide. The Liberty company also saw an occasional herd of antelope but found them too elusive to hunt. On the evening of June 14, near Independence Rock, Carpenter heard hooves clattering on the cliffs and awoke his comrades, reporting that their mules had escaped over the ridge. Lane and Hixson spent the remainder of the night swimming the cold waters and searching for the wayward mules, only to determine that the clatter was a herd of mountain goats passing over the ridge. Mosquitos were a great nuisance. After crossing Ham's Fork on the 23rd, the company had to contend with swarms of the insects until they left the Snake River valley on the 30th. The men covered their faces with handkerchiefs and tried to relieve their mules with smoke, bacon lard, or herbs. Nothing worked except for an occasional breeze. Along the Snake River, the company encountered numerous beavers, and once they crossed over into the Great Basin, they found trout in Goose Creek to add variety to their diet. On the Humboldt River, however, the company encountered little wildlife. "A jackrabbit would starve on ten miles square of this [desert]," Hixson commented.[9]

Despite the romanticized memory of the overlander who completed the journey in triumphant solitude, actual forty-niners defied these misconceptions. In fact, a number of institutions assisted their trek to California. From Fort Kearney, the U.S. military patrolled along the Platte River road. Private individuals maintained ferries and trading posts, such as Fort Laramie, Fort Hall, or "Peg-Leg" Smith's. Overlanders not only organized companies for the journey, they relied upon the cooperation of hundreds of others and occasionally received aid from Native Americans.[10]

Lane and his companions, furthermore, welcomed the assistance of others. On May 8, only a week into their journey, a group of seven Tennesseans joined them. The addition gave the travelers more confidence and lessened the time spent on guard duty at night. Three days later, on the 11th, they camped next to a company from Lexington, Missouri, commanded by Gabriel Brown, a veteran of Doniphan's regiment during the late war with Mexico. As long as it remained convenient, the companies arranged to camp near each other.

Dealing with other overlanders, however, was not always so congenial. Some succumbed to a vindictive spirit of competition. On May 13, while entering the valley of the Big Vermillion, the Liberty company fell in behind a slow-moving train of thirty ox-drawn wagons that would not give way. Lane and his partners decided to pass the ox teams by going off-road, but the ox drivers refused to relent. "[T]hose long whips of the bullwhackers commenced to sound," Hixson wrote, and the oxen lurched into the race. Lane's men bounded through the rough side of the road but managed to gain ground on their competitors. As they neared a rise, the road cut a file too narrow for racing wagons, but the major pressed forward. "[W]hen he saw the situation," Hixson wrote, "he raised a whoop that would have put a Comanche to blush, and his team sprang forward with renewed speed, and pushed the front cattle out of the road, and his wagon dropped in ahead."[11] The lead ox wagon broke its yoke and came to a sudden stop, creating a "telescoping" effect, Hixson noted, which permitted the remainder of the Liberty company to pass. Lane had driven his team so hard that flames shot from the hubs of his wheels, but his comrades managed to put out the fire and then reapply a fresh coat of tallow.

Lane's reputation as a Texas Ranger helped his men through a similar situation on the North Platte. On June 9, Lane drove the lead wagon into a gorge, alongside an ox train that attempted to block the Liberty company from the road. Lane and his friends brandished their firearms to negotiate their passage. "[T]he bright barrels of a number of Colt's persuaders glistened in the sunlight," Hixson proudly remembered. "[I]t was passed along their line that our crowd were Texas rangers, and it would have done you good to see them fall back and let us pass." Hixson admitted that the fifteen men of his company possessed no more or less ability in defending themselves compared to men from other sections of the country, but the major was different. "[T]here was never a man trod shoeleather braver and cooler in danger than Walter P. Lane," Hixson grandly proclaimed. Apparently, his reputation preceded the Liberty company. "[T]here were enough men on the road who had heard of him, so whenever there was a disposition to overcome our little party, if it was passed along the line that Major Lane was one of us that ended the matter."[12] Hixson may well have exaggerated, but Lane's career in Mexico did receive marginal press and veterans of Doniphan's Missouri volunteers, such as Gabriel Brown, probably remembered him as the ranger who executed Nicolás García at Cerralvo. If anyone thought twice about crossing the Liberty company, however, they probably reacted more to the reputation of the Texas Rangers than to the name of Walter Lane.

Even without the thousands who teemed from the East, the overland trail to California did not lack human habitation. The company from Liberty encountered Pottowattomies along the Kansas River and purchased trout from a native group in the Carson Valley, probably Washoes. On May 19, along the South Platte, a large body of mounted Sioux alarmed Lane's comrades, and Gabriel Brown's men recklessly fired on them. The Missourians called on Lane to take control, counting on his reputation as an Indian fighter. Perhaps Lane made the men more familiar with his victory over the Comanches at Los Muchachos, Mexico, than with the unfortunate affair with the Kickapoos on Richland Creek in Texas. His experience as an officer, however, made him a valuable asset. He reluctantly consented, and upon leaving the Liberty company, told them, "Boys, I see by your coolness you mean business. If you are captured you need expect no quarter; so reserve your fire until you can see them wink their eyes; then give them hell."[13] After a meeting, however, the Sioux agreed not to steal their mules if the overlanders would supply them with foodstuffs. The overlanders actually had more supplies than they needed and disposed of more flour and bacon the next day, in order to ration the strength of their mules.

When they reached California, the Liberty company arrived at the height of the mining season, and they wasted little time before dashing into the gold diggings. "Tell Wm. Lane the Major says he may expect to here [*sic*] from him as soon as he gets his pile," Hixson wrote of Walter Lane. Soon after his arrival near Sacramento, however, Lane withdrew from the Liberty company "in consequence of a good offer from an old Texas friend," Hixson explained. That friend was probably William S. McMurtry, who had fought with Lane in Hays's regiment and had served as surgeon in Lane's battalion in Mexico. The others had left the company earlier. No longer needing the mutual protection required on the overland journey and eager to enter the gold regions, companions often dispersed in this way once they reached California.[14]

By the end of the summer of 1849, Lane amassed enough gold dust to consider other opportunities, and the placer culture provided many. Most men in California sought their personal fortunes in the diggings. These miners, however, desperately needed the services of more traditional occupations, and they willingly paid exorbitant prices. Professionals and laborers alike commanded high wages. Enterprising men could purchase goods in Sacramento and transport them to the placer camps, where they might realize a return of 1,000 to 1,500 percent profit. A person with retail experience, such as the major, could make as much money as a merchant as he could digging in the washes of the Sierra Nevada foothills.[15]

Lane decided to forego the labor-intensive mining, take his gold dust, and purchase a load of goods to resell in the placer camps. By the end of September, he set out for Taylor City, about two hundred miles northwest of Sacramento but found too much competition and sold out, breaking even. The setback did not deter Lane. He purchased another load of goods, hoping to locate somewhere in the gold region along the American River. He hurried to beat the rainy season, transporting his goods up the river in boats, but he began too late—probably the last weeks of December. Camping along the river, a flood washed away his wares. "[A] wave striking the tent, *bang* went a hogshead of crackers, sailing through and tearing down the tent," he recalled. "Barrels of flour and lighter merchandise *waltzed* out after it, leaving me up to my middle in water." He swam through frigid and swift waters and managed to gain the shore.[16] Although no settlement lay within miles, the area teemed with prospectors. Lane found a camp of Missourians who provided him with "a pair of pantaloons, the *slack* of the seat of which reached my knees, . . . an old, swallow-tailed coat, the tails of which nearly dragged the ground, . . . a stove-pipe hat and a pair of boots four sizes too large for me." Although wearing it may have given him a comical appearance, the major gratefully accepted his new wardrobe. After taking a few welcome swigs of Pike County whiskey, he struck for Sacramento, twenty miles away.

Despite his setback, Lane found himself in good spirits. He explained, "Having the world before me, with a six-shooter and thirty dollars in gold dust, all my earthly possessions, I felt buoyant and elastic." Perhaps he felt that sense of freedom and wanderlust that had always compelled him to far off lands like Texas, Mexico, and California and placed him into predicaments like this. When he reached the outskirts of Sacramento, he found the city inundated and took passage with a man passing by on a boat. They floated into town and rowed down Main Street.

While oaring through town, Lane sighted one of his boats, under the control of "four rough-looking fellows," he remembered. He jumped aboard and laid claim to it, but the occupants drew their pistols and instead offered to kill him. Fortunately for Lane, he noticed former rangers William S. Oury and William H. Hargrove floating by, and he called for their assistance. They did not recognize the major in his "opera suit," as he described his Missouri duds. When he identified himself, Oury and Hargrove immediately jumped aboard with pistols ready, and the four "gentlemen" confronting Lane quit the boat.[17]

Finding fellow rangers floating on the streets of Sacramento might not have been as coincidental as it appeared. A great many of his comrades from John Hays's regiment and Lane's own battalion joined the rush to California. He had already met William McMurtry. Hays had settled permanently in California, where he served as sheriff of San Francisco County and surveyed the town site of Oakland. Michael Chevallié, Christopher Acklin, Ben McCulloch, Richard Roman, John Waters, and many other former rangers made the trek to California. As early as December 1849, McCulloch would write that he also met with a number of old comrades. "[M]any of our Texian friends are doing well. [O]ur state is well represented in . . . this country."[18]

Oury and Hargrove took Lane to a theater where they made their quarters in the upper rooms, as the lower section remained under water. Then they provided their former major with a better fitting wardrobe. The enterprising trio soon recognized that the disaster created an opportunity. "The city, having from four to six feet of water in each street," Lane explained, "and it running like a mill-tail through the canvass houses, floated off goods and barrels, quantities of which lodged in the timber half a mile below the city." Lane and his comrades collected sixty barrels, placed them at the theater, and advertised to the merchants, who came forth to claim their goods. They, of course, paid a salvage fee, and the Texans sold the unclaimed merchandise at regular wholesale. "I realized a nice little sum from the sale of the liquors and my boat," Lane assessed.[19]

Whatever set-backs Lane might have experienced, California—at least early—offered everyone an opportunity to remake their fortune. The major went back to mining. During the summer of 1850, he worked in the vicinity of Deer Creek, a tributary of the American River. Lane probably heard the rumors of the "pound diggings"—fields that yielded a pound of gold per day. However exaggerated, Deer Creek proved to be one of the most productive regions in California, and Lane succeeded in drawing out another large quantity of gold dust.[20]

By the fall of 1850, Lane once again decided to establish a provision store. He purchased $12,000 in goods in Sacramento. He bought a third of his merchandise on loan. This time, he managed to beat the rainy season and established a store in Nevada City. Situated along Deer Creek, Nevada City was the prototypical Gold Rush boomtown. It consisted of several hundred tents, shacks, and log cabins, hastily constructed over three deep-running brooks. In February 1851, diarist Israel Lord visited the village. The town, he described, "has one long awkward crooked street built up for quite a distance on both sides. The buildings are for the most part covered with boards split from the beautiful pines which abound here." He continued, "These 500 or 600 houses have sprung up like mushrooms or," he amended prophetically, "rather like Jonah's gourd and are probably destined to a like fate. A single spark would cause it to vanish in smoke."[21]

Culturally, Nevada City was also typical of the California Gold Rush. The population of the town was overwhelmingly male, and while it served as the center of business and trade, it also served as the center of leisure. "Gambling of course, was common," one forty-niner remembered, "and fatal affrays were frequent." Lord witnessed one of these "affrays." He wrote, "[L]ast night there was a tremendous 'row' in the street; yelling, swearing, and clashing of knives. . . . I cannot learn that any one was killed." Lane resided in this environment at least four months.[22]

As Nevada City illustrated, Gold Rush culture was as exclusively male as any Walter Lane had experienced. By 1850, men comprised ninety-three percent of the territory population. In the gold fields of Yuba County, where the major spent much of his time, the 9,500 men outnumbered the 200 women—a majority of ninety-eight percent. Many forty-niners bemoaned this disparity in the sex ratio. Not only did these miners lament the absence of female companionship, many were also homesick for the civilizing influence of women. In the early to mid-nineteenth century, men looked to women as the keepers of domesticity who bound together social and family structures and who demanded moral restraint from their male relations.[23]

Not all the miners, however, missed the presence of women. Instead, they sought adventure, masculine comradery, and flight from domesticity. Many forty-niners anticipated that their adventure in California was temporary and welcomed the respite from the social rigors of their homes in the East. Although Major Lane did not record his opinion, the attitudes that he expressed during his earlier experiences suggested that he sympathized with this latter group. Indeed, the male environment of the gold diggings was similar to the expedition—a boys' club safe from the discerning gaze of mothers and wives.[24]

Placer society also exhibited several characteristics that differed from Lane's previous experiences and that contributed to disorder and lawlessness. For one, it lacked the formal structure of the military and expeditionary companies with which Lane had served. The volunteers in the Texas Revolution and the U.S.-Mexican War were hardly examples of male restraint, but a hierarchical command structure unified disparate units and provided a code of conduct. Lane joined non-military expeditions to Richland Creek in 1838 and more recently to California. In both cases, the members organized martial command structures. In California, the forty-niners formed cooperative companies, but they often lacked the unity found in the military and lacked the hierarchy that encouraged restraint.

During the first years of the Gold Rush, furthermore, forty-niners unearthed greats sums from the earth. The equal and relatively easy access to wealth was another anomalous characteristic of placer culture. The region's prosperity created an egalitarian society, at least among Anglo-Americans. Some participants described it as anarchy.[25] The prosperity also confounded the traditional belief in the Protestant work ethic. Although labor intensive, mining the gold fields often yielded far greater riches than any yeoman farmer or diligent merchant could realize in a lifetime. Gold possessed a corrupting influence, when so many could purchase their heart's whim. Ben McCulloch warned that "*many are ruined*[,] a few become *rich,* speculation of every kind is gone into with *recklessness* that would be admirable in a *cavalry charge.*" The pious Israel Lord agreed, "What is honor worth that requires so heavy a metal as gold to hold it down on a man's conscience."[26]

Gold Rush California was a fluid and open society that challenged traditional, as well as adventurous, notions of manhood. Men not only lacked a feminine foil against which to identify themselves, the ways that they assessed each other also changed. They placed less value on feats of manliness and more on luck. In both the diggings and the saloons, men gambled on their ability to guess where the richest lode lay, or whether his cards beat his opponent's across the table. Furthermore, trust was a rare commodity in the gold fields. During the expedition, men trusted one another until one broke that trust. In California, anonymity was a danger, and a man had to earn trust. In such a context, miners placed a premium on the value of relatives and friends. This crisis in trust might have compelled Lane to join fellow rangers like Oury, Hargrove, and McMurtry, rather than continue with his comrades from Liberty.[27]

As many opportunities California might offer Lane, the region seemed to conspire against him, teasing him with riches only to snatch them away. At his store in Nevada City, Lane recalled that "a little *fire* broke out one night." The buildings of the mining town were of the temporary variety—poorly constructed of wood and canvas. Nevada City was not much more than a tinder box. On March 11, 1851, arsonists struck at two in the morning, believing that rich gold deposits lay under the town. The "little *fire*" quickly erupted into a conflagration. "I had barely time to grab my boots and clothes and break out of the back door." The tall pine trees that grew between the buildings caught fire. Their blazing tops scattered embers over Nevada City, assisting the exploding powder kegs in spreading the flames. The fire burned half of the town, including all of its business section.[28]

Although Nevada City soon recovered, the fire of 1851 devastated Lane. He could claim eight mules, but he owed $4,000 on the goods that lay smouldering in the rubble. Life in the placer camps began to wear on his earlier enthusiasm. "Next morning the world was staring me in the face, looking lovely, but somehow I did not feel very exuberant." Lane sold four of his mules and bought supplies for another mining expedition. He joined two other men and together they established operations near Shasta City. After several months, Lane managed to mine enough gold to pay off his debt and realized an additional $5,000. He took his profits and quit the mining business. Sometime in late 1851 or early 1852, the major left the placer fields and never returned.[29]

After he settled his remaining debts in the fall of 1851, Lane traveled to San Francisco, where he could book passage home. As the archetypical Gold Rush boomtown, San Francisco provided safe haven for vice and villainy. Here, Lane found a variety of establishments designed to separate him from his gold. He could have enjoyed a variety of entertainments, such as billiards, card games, theaters, saloons, brothels, and others. "The most prominent sights are the great gambling saloons," Lord recorded in February 1851. "They are as magnificent as wood and brick and labor and gold and tinsel and paint can make them. Some of them are immensely large." In this environment, Major Lane dallied. To partake of the good life in style, he bought himself a "plug hat and a dude suit." He admitted, "[I] enjoyed myself for several months."[30]

Lane probably left California in the late summer of 1852, traveling by sea. After a sojourn in Lima, Peru, he crossed the isthmus between Panama City and Aspinwall, via the Charges River and a newly constructed railroad. Sometime in the summer of 1853, Lane landed in New Orleans. He tarried for a few months before embarking for Texas. From this time, and for the next two and a half years, Lane left no record of his whereabouts. Except for the few paragraphs in his memoirs, documents on Lane are non-extant from his enumeration in the Nevada City census on November 15, 1850, until the advertisement of his grocery firm in Marshall, Texas, on February 16, 1856. During this period of his life, when the "spirit of unrest" so easily swayed him, it is unlikely that he remained in Marshall for over two years. More probably, Lane first visited towns in Texas that were more familiar to him, such as San Augustine or San Antonio, before arriving in Marshall—perhaps in late 1855.[31]

Lane's brother George had transferred his law practice from San Augustine to Marshall in the early 1840s. Its founders cut Marshall out of the deep pine forest of East Texas, and it received a charter as the seat of Harrison County in 1842, emerging as one of the most important trading and political centers of the region. George Lane was a member of a very talented group of local lawyers and jurists. Among the town's residents were Edward Clark, Pendleton Murrah, William B. Ochiltree, Louis T. Wigfall, W. R. D. Ward, Isaac Van Zandt, and others who would become important figures in Texas during the contentious decade to come.[32]

After he arrived in Marshall, Major Lane acquainted himself with the community, especially the Ward family. The patriarch, W. R. D. Ward, was a wealthy merchant, and as an active proponent of railroad construction, he was one of the founders of the Louisiana and Texas Railroad and a board member of the Southern Pacific. In February 1856, Walter Lane entered into a partnership with Ward's son, Virgil. They established a grocery firm next to the Planter's Hotel. The firm of Lane and Ward boasted that they "have now on hand, and for sale at extremely low prices, a full and complete assortment of family Groceries." The partners, however, did not remain in business long. Rumors of gold in the Gadsden Purchase lured Lane on yet another expedition.[33]

The Gadsden Purchase was a thirty-thousand-square-mile stretch of Sonoran desert in northwestern Mexico. Surveyors from the United States and Mexico could not agree on the boundary that the Treaty of Guadalupe Hidalgo had stipulated, and advocates of a Pacific railroad realized that the terrain north of the proposed boundary would hinder the construction of a southern route. As a result, the U.S. government sent James Gadsden to Mexico to negotiate a new boundary. In June 1854, the two governments formalized the Gadsden Purchase, or Tratado de la Mesilla.

Word arrived in Marshall, in early August 1856, that John C. Reid of Marion County, Alabama, had organized an expedition to the Mesilla Valley in the purchase, for exploration and possible colonization. This probably inspired Lane and his partner Virgil Ward with the idea of traveling to the region. As both were veterans of the Gold Rush, they hoped that they might discover a strike in an area rumored to be rich in minerals. On August 16, they placed an advertisement in the Marshall *Texas Republican,* alerting the citizens, "*Attention Company! Ho for Arizona!!*" The notice called for a meeting in a week's time, to make arrangements for the expedition. Gold provided a convenient excuse, but according to Lane, he decided to go because a "spirit of unrest took hold of me again."[34]

At the August 23 meeting, the participants declared that they intended "to organize a company to visit and explore that portion of our territory lately acquired from Mexico, known as Arizona." On the 30th, they issued a notice to attract potential members. "The territory of Arizona is represented to be extremely fertile and to be rich in mines of gold, silver, and copper." To intrigue those who preferred adventure, the advertisement added, "The trip will be full of novelty and interest." At a final meeting held on September 1, the group created the Arizonian Company. According to Virgil Ward, Major Lane, "a gentleman of so much experience and ability," assumed leadership, and in making arrangements, he drew upon his twenty years of organizing adventurous expeditions. The group determined that they would need one wagon and three yoke of oxen per five men, provisions for each man for six months, a horse or mule for four of the five men per each wagon, and that each man should arm himself "with a good gun and a pistol—a repeater." On October 1, with a little pomp, Major Lane gathered nineteen men at the courthouse. The local newspaper reported, "A good deal of interest and feeling was exhibited by a large number of our citizens when the company was about leaving." After a public address and flag presentation, the Arizonian Company pulled out of Marshall. They expected to augment their number five-fold at their rendezvous at Fort Graham.[35]

As with his overland experience during the Gold Rush, Lane commented little about his travels across Texas to the Gadsden Purchase. Although they crossed the southern limits of the Comanchería, the company did not encounter any Native Americans. Once they had crossed the Brazos River, the landscape was less varied than the overland route farther north. The company did not endure the hardships and toil that Lane experienced on his journey to California, but for a stretch of about four hundred miles, between Fort Chadbourne and El Paso, they traveled in greater solitude compared to the numbers that had crowded the Gold Rush trail.

For the first one hundred and seventy-five miles, the Arizonian Company crossed through some the most fertile regions of Texas. Passing out of the East Texas woodlands, they crossed over the loamy Blackland Prairie and negotiated the tangled reaches of the Cross Timbers, before arriving at the village of Fort Graham on the Brazos River. The company, however, did not find the throng of anxious men seeking to join them. Instead, they augmented their number only by eight, bringing the total to twenty-seven.

In the waning days of October, the Arizonian Company struck across the Brazos and tracked due west. As they traveled farther, the company experienced a more arid and less settled landscape. They crossed the Bosque and Leon rivers, smaller tributaries to the Brazos. In early November, the band arrived at Fort Chadbourne on Oak Creek, about thirty miles north of the Colorado River and one hundred and seventy-five miles away from Fort Graham. Here, the Arizonian Company sojourned and mustered their resolve to continue their journey. Over four hundred miles of desolate, unsettled country still lay ahead of them, and the fort provided them with their last respite.

In November 1856, the Arizonian Company sojourned at Fort Chadbourne, gathering resolve to continue their journey into West Texas. [Carl Schuchard], "Fort Chadbourne—January 1854." Lithograph in A. B. Gray, *Survey of a Route for a Southern Pacific R.R. . . . ,* 1856. Courtesy of the Texas State Library & Archives Commission, Austin, Tex.

On November 4, 1856, the company took leave of the Spartan comfort of the post. Upon reaching the Colorado River, Major Lane and his comrades followed its course upriver. "This stream is remarkably clear," Ward described, "a noble stream, winding amid steep hills and bright valleys." The company found a variety of fish, waterfowl, deer, and turkey, which the men hunted and ate on a daily basis. When they left the river, they struck northwest across the plains. They spent a day without water, until Lane located a spring. The men found plenty of water—though it was bitter and alkaline—and named the site Lane's Springs. The name did not stick.

Lane's crew also found a good supply of water at the edge of the sand hills, near present-day Monahans, but once they entered the fields of white quartz dunes, the company again entered a region lacking water. Despite the hardship, which left three oxen dead, Ward could not help but remark on the wonder of the sand hills. "Glistening in the rays of the sun [the dunes] seem to be snow drifts in the distance, so white and fine are the particles of sand, that the lightest breeze puts it in motion, and drifting from hill to another." The company encountered dunes as high as fifty feet, with a few oak trees struggling against submergence in the sand. As dunes obscured the road, they became temporarily lost.

Lane and his comrades, however, survived the sand hills and reached the Pecos at Emigrants' Crossing. They followed the river eighty-five miles to Delaware Creek, where they began a more westerly course for another forty miles. The Sierra Guadalupe loomed in the distance, acting as a beacon to the Arizonian Company. Guadalupe Peak, the highest point in Texas, inspired Ward and his companions with awe. "Its Southern abutment . . . presents truly a sublime sight, like some grand colossus reared by the hand of the Deity, to instill in the heart of man a knowledge of his inferiority, and an emblem of his own power." After paying their respects to Guadalupe, Lane's group crossed the Sierra de los Alamos and Sierra de Hueco. From these western slopes, they followed a road that led them to the Hueco Tanks, where they made camp. Arising on the morning of December 12, they entered the valley of the Rio Grande. During their journey across West Texas, they lost six oxen and six horses.[36]

On December 14, the Arizonian Company reached Jaletta on the Rio Grande and continued upriver until they camped near Fort Bliss, opposite El Paso. They remained a fortnight in order to recuperate and to obtain intelligence from Arizona, but the news that they received proved discouraging. W. P. McCall, a member from Rusk County, wrote home, "They give a very discouraging account of the country in regard to its mines. Some of them have been in the country four or five months but found no mines worth working." The news destroyed what little resolve most of the men had since their trek across West Texas. McCall admitted, "In short the account from the gold regions, was so bad that our company disbanded here."

Lane managed to convince five of the twenty-seven men to continue with the expedition. "Maj. Lane is a determined man," McCall reported, but he chose not to continue. On December 21, Lane, Ward, and the others who continued struck their El Paso camp. They decided to push ahead as far as Fort Fillmore in New Mexico, where they hoped to recruit additional members. By year's end, they arrived at the post that guarded the entrance to the Mesilla Valley. The celebrated location did not impress Ward. "[The valley] is hardly worth the discussion that its possession has elicited by the two contending governments."[37]

The men from East Texas waited at Fort Fillmore for several days and found only two men willing to join them. Lane learned that the group from Alabama, commanded by John C. Reid, had recently passed on their way to the purchase. This was the same outfit that might have inspired Lane and Ward with the idea of exploring Arizona, but they had fared worse than the men from East Texas. Upon arriving in San Antonio, the Mesilla Valley Company, as they styled themselves, disbanded when they learned how difficult the West Texas passage would be. Only six of the eighteen continued. On November 6, 1856, they fought Apaches at Eagle Springs. Fortunately for the remnants of the Arizonian Company, the men from Alabama halted at Fort Thorn, New Mexico, waiting for a military company or a mail party to follow into the purchase. Lane sent a message to them, and Reid agreed to wait and join companies.[38]

On January 19, 1857, Lane and Reid combined their companies, a total of twelve men, and departed Fort Thorn the next day. Reid described their journey as "leisurely pushing ahead." They maintained strict guard duty at night and found game and water in good supply. They crossed the tablelands just south of the Rockies—terrain that made this territory valuable to railroad promoters. The company passed under the shadows of Cooke's Peak, the Burro Mountains, and the Peloncillo Mountains. They crossed over Puerta del Dado, or Apache Pass, between the Chiricahua and the Dos Cabezas Mountains. In the Chiricahua range, they stopped to pan for gold. "We used the common pick, shovel, and pan, and ob[t]ained the 'color' often, though but little gold," Reid recalled.

On February 7, after eighteen days, the company reached the town of Tubac in the Gadsden Purchase but decided to set up quarters near the U.S. troops at Rancho de las Calabasas, about fifteen miles south. Reid called it "a spot which for months had engrossed the minds of many of ambition's votaries," describing the yearning for the elsewhere prevalent in the adventurer's imagination, but the site did not meet such extravagant contemplation. "Our expectations lessened as we drew near to, and faded into nothingness as we reached 'the land of promise.'"

The landscape may have disappointed Reid, but for many adventurers, the comradery of the expedition fulfilled another and perhaps equally important, expectation. The journey into the Sonoran Desert forged new friendships. Echoing Jasper Hixon upon his arrival in California, Reid commented, "Our new companions [Lane's company], by their kind and g[e]ntlemanly bearing so won upon us, that after a day's association they felt to us like friends and acquaintances of long standing."

Sixty miles south of Tucson and ten miles from the recently established U.S.-Mexico border, Maj. Enoch Steen, of the Second U.S. Dragoons, chose Calabasas as the site for a new fort and stationed four companies there the previous November. He named the post Camp Moore, which consisted of little more than a collection of military tents and civilian shanties, strewn along the Rio Santa Cruz near the mouth of Sonoita Creek. Reid described the picturesque location as "a bottom covered with tall, golden grass, hedged by mountains whose sands glitter like metal, divided by a meandering

When they arrived in Calabasas, Lane, Virgil Ward, and John Reid did not find gold but found instead an encampment of the Second U.S. Dragoons. While Reid described a picturesque landscape reminiscent of this engraving, Calabasas did not meet his romantic expectations. [Carl Schuchard], "Calabaza – Santa Cruz Valley – Sonora." Lithograph in A. B. Gray, *Survey of a Route for a Southern Pacific R.R. . . .*, 1856. Courtesy of the Texas State Library & Archives Commission.

stream. . . . [T]his shaded by cotton-woods, willows, and musquites [*sic*]." Reid prospected for the next several weeks but found little success. Although Arizona possessed a wealth of minerals, mining in the region required large capital investments that neither Reid nor Lane could afford.

Major Lane apparently realized this sooner than Reid. Upon their arrival in Calabasas, the remnants of the Arizonian Company, including two men from Reid's party, elected to attempt farming and ranching instead. They could realize a handsome sum if they could raise a crop of corn for the supply-strapped dragoons. Lane recalled, "We worked under difficulties, having to stand guard every night over our stock, and dig trenches to irrigate our land, as it only rained once a year." While beginning this enterprise, Walter Lane turned forty years old on February 18, 1857.[39]

In March, two men from California arrived at Calabasas. Robert Wood and Charles Tozer were associates of Henry Crabb, who had organized a filibustering expedition bound for Sonora, Mexico. They had heard that Lane and Reid brought a hundred men from the East, but the truth disappointed them when they arrived in the Santa Cruz valley. According to Lane, the men offered him a colonel's commission in their enterprise, but the Texan prudently declined. This reluctance may have seemed uncharacteristic of Lane's adventuristic impulse. Perhaps sobered by his recent fortieth birthday, the major's refusal might have been an example of a long overdue maturation—an appreciation of pragmatism over romanticism. Writing home to his brother George, however, the major explained his decision in simpler terms: "[Crabb] had only 80 men with him, and I thought that rather a small number to go in with."[40]

Despite Lane's misgivings, Wood and Tozer managed to recruit a company of about thirty men. On April 1, they elected Granville H. Oury captain and John Reid first lieutenant.[41] Lane's partner, Virgil Ward, and several other companions of Lane's and Reid's joined the venture. They marched into Mexico to support Crabb, who in late March had seized the Sonoran town of Caborca. Oury's men fought and won a sharp skirmish with the Mexicans at Pitiquito, but once the company reached the outskirts of Caborca, they discovered that Mexican forces had defeated and executed Crabb.[42] Whether Lane's reluctance to join the adventure represented a new-found pragmatism to counteract his boyish romanticism, his instincts proved correct.

In the Purchase, meanwhile, Major Steen moved his command to a permanent post at Ojo Calientes and christened it Fort Buchanan, in honor of the recently inaugurated president, James Buchanan. After the Crabb affair, Reid returned home to Alabama. Ward apparently remained with Lane's crew, to help bring in the crop of corn during the autumn of 1857. They managed to harvest two thousand bushels, which they sold to Steen's garrison at four dollars each. Most of the men, including Lane, did not care for the farmer's life. Ward and many others left for East Texas, but Lane felt little urgency to return to Marshall and obtained a job as a clerk at Fort Buchanan.[43]

Walter Lane felt at ease at the post and its male environment. He explained, "Most of [the men] being young officers, and having no wives there, to pass away the time, would indulge a good deal in wines and cards." Recognizing his past service, the officers admitted Lane into their wife-less society, much to his gratification. Major Steen invited Lane to his quarters for dinner the night that he arrived. "I found there fourteen officers, three card tables set out, a side table with all kinds of liquors and cigars," Lane described, "and we enjoyed ourselves until 3 o'clock in the morning." Every night, as Lane recalled, they reveled in this manner. Each officer took a turn at hosting a party, and when it came his turn, Lane presided over "a 'blow-out' at the sutler's, which generally cost me a hundred dollars." Thus, Lane waited out the winter.[44]

In the early spring of 1858, Major Lane took his leave of Fort Buchanan and its officers, but he did not immediately return to Marshall. He stopped in San Antonio in April and applied for his bounty warrant, a land grant for his service during the Texas Revolution. Lane probably remained long enough to visit with his old comrade, Young P. Alsbury, who later signed an affidavit for Lane's service in Henry Karnes's company.[45] Lane drifted into Marshall, probably in the summer of 1858. Although he might not have known it the moment he arrived, the middle-aged adventurer would make the East Texas town his permanent home.

• 7 •

FAMILY, COMMUNITY, AND SECESSION, 1858–61

The Texas to which Walter Lane returned in 1858 was far different than the one that he traveled to in 1836. After independence, and later, statehood, immigrants rushed in from the United States and Europe and inflated its population from an estimated fifty thousand in 1836 to over six hundred thousand by 1860. The European-American settlement expanded from the squatter communities of East Texas, Austin's colonies of the lower Brazos and Colorado rivers, and from the Tejano communities of San Antonio and Goliad. They moved into the Cross Timbers, beyond the Brazos, and into the fringes of the Comanchería. By 1860, more than one hundred counties provided local government to Texans.[1]

The past twenty years also transformed Lane. No longer the wild-eyed adventurer, the major was now a battle-tested veteran of the Texas Revolution and the U.S.-Mexican War. He had traversed the breadth of the continent, sought gold in the Sierra Nevada and the Sonoran desert, and crossed the jungle isthmus of Panama. If Lane exhibited a degree of maturation when he turned down Henry Crabb's commission in Arizona, he further demonstrated his growth as an adult after his arrival in Marshall, as evidenced by the respect of his peers. Although his attitude toward women endured, Lane would accept a compromise with domesticity. His family and new-found community ties would compel him to identify with the plight of the South and draw him into the political debate over slavery.

Lane's reputation as a soldier translated easily into respect in civilian life. Many politicians used military careers to attain greater visibility. Although Major Lane exhibited other motivations for joining expeditions, he had accumulated a considerable amount of prestige. His military service often impressed civilian men, such as Jasper Hixson, with whom Lane traveled to

California. He declared that "there never was a man trod shoeleather braver and cooler in danger than Walter P. Lane." Other men acknowledged the qualities of a warrior and of an expeditionary commander, as qualities suited for the political arena. While awaiting developments in El Paso in 1856, Virgil Ward learned that the United States planned to establish a new territory in the Gadsden Purchase. He commented to his father, "I know of no man better fitted for the position of Governor of this Territory than Walter P. Lane."[2] When he arrived in Marshall, Lane first experienced the benefits that he could reap from his martial reputation. As the events of 1860 and 1861 unfolded, however, the citizens of Harrison County needed his expertise as a soldier more than any political position he might fill.

Lane's attitude toward women and marriage also endured the twenty years since he first came to Texas. Lane was not a misogynist. He did leave a few clues that indicated that he acknowledged and admired women. Testifying to this appreciation, Lane described Antonia García, whose husband he executed, as "a beautiful woman," and later conceded that Jennie Blount of San Augustine was "a *beautiful young lady.*" While in Mexico, in command of a group of young rowdies, he sympathized with their plight. "I had been once *young myself,* and still had a taste for the *fine arts.*" In his memoirs, Lane recorded occasions when he received the kindness of women and provided ample space for the exploits of his more amorous friends.[3]

Although Major Lane may or may not have fallen in love when he was younger, in his later days and probably by the time he arrived in Marshall in 1858, he possessed very strong feelings against the institution of marriage. Lane left few records of his life before the 1860s, and obtaining an accurate measure of his attitude toward marriage at that time remains problematic. In his autobiography, Lane recalled his encounter with Antonia García when he came to arrest her husband. When she claimed that he was not home, Lane commented, "[A]s I had been atrociously lied to by *white* women, I did not give much credence to the assertions of the Mexican sister."[4] The statement might have been a more accurate reflection of his sentiment in 1887. If it reflected his disposition in 1847, however, it might have suggested that Lane had a relationship or a fondness for a woman who did not return the affection. He might have courted a girl during his residence at San Augustine. If he had experienced a romance that had soured, it could explain why he left the settled life in East Texas and headed to John C. Hays's rangers in San Antonio—complicating the explanation of his adventuristic impulse. Having been "lied to by *white* women" was a revealing remark and suggested that Lane experienced disappointment with women that contributed to his resentment and hostility toward marriage.

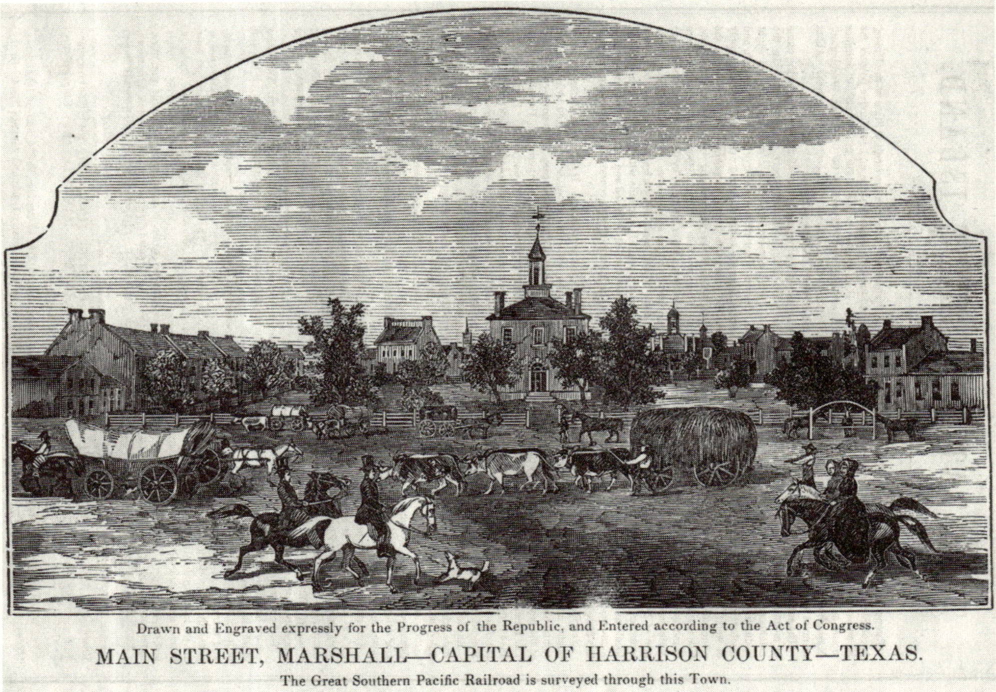

Although this engraving might not represent an authentic rendering of mid-century Marshall, it captures the domestic images—ladies and gentlemen on horseback, ox-drawn harvest, orderly arrayed fencing—that contrasted to Lane's adventurous life. Unknown, "Main Street, Marshall—Capital of Harrison County—Texas." Disbound lithograph from *Progress of the Republic,* ca. 1855. Author's collection.

In any event, Walter Lane came to Marshall as a single man, and he jealously guarded his bachelorhood. When Lane applied for a U.S.-Mexican War pension, the form left a blank space after: "The name of my present wife is," to which he filled in an emphatic, "*is no one* being still, & allways [*sic*] will, a batchelor [*sic*]." As in the case of many bachelors, Lane kept close ties to his family, and for the first couple years upon his arrival in Marshall, the major resided at his brother George's home. His reputation on the battlefield and on the expedition and his relationship to George—who had recently attained the position of county judge—provided Major Lane with his initial entry into the Harrison County community, but he could not expect to keep that membership unless he made some changes in his life. Harrison County was not the all-male environment to which Walter Lane was accustomed.[5]

If he wanted to take his place in this political, commercial, and social community, Lane needed to give up his adventurer's life and make a compromise with domesticity. He had to demonstrate his willingness to stay and place his stake in the community. During his first attempt, in 1856, Lane established a grocery firm with Virgil Ward, but they both pulled out to search for gold in Arizona. This time around, however, the major made a bolder step toward permanent residency by purchasing his own house. Although the date of the purchase remains uncertain, he apparently made arrangements, sometime just before or during the Civil War, to purchase the home of W. R. D. Ward, with whom Lane became friends during his first residence in Marshall.[6]

Situated several blocks northwest of the courthouse square, Major Lane's new home sat on an entire town block. Ward constructed the house in 1847 and 1848, at the southeast corner of present-day Wellington and Grand avenues, facing Wellington. Lane's niece, Mary Jane Lane, described the home as surrounded by gardens. "A Summer house, covered with ramblers, woodbine and honeysuckle occupied the middle space. . . . There were other walks between beds of flowers; among which were a variety of roses, lilac, single and double spirea, mock orange, bridle wreath, flowering almond, lilies, blue bottles, snow-drops, different kinds of hyacinths, jonquils, etc." The estate hardly appeared like the abode of a bachelor—even less than of an unrefined adventurer.[7]

Indeed, in order to complete his compromise with domesticity, Lane required a female housekeeper. He would not marry, of course, so he entered into an arrangement with his niece, Mary Jane Lane—George Lane's oldest child. She turned eighteen in 1860 and agreed to move into her uncle's home. She assumed more than domestic duties. Mary Jane also acted as hostess, representing her uncle in the more genteel circles of Harrison County society. She maintained the home while Walter Lane fought in the Civil War and would accompany him to the meetings of the Texas Veterans Association and other reunions later in their lives. When her uncle passed away, Mary Jane inherited his home and much of his property. She represented an anchor that moored the major to community and family. She was both a dependant and a helpmate. For Walter, the compromise worked well.

Although the Civil War significantly disrupted this process, the citizens of Harrison County welcomed him and his niece into their community. Lane's interaction with the women of the community testified to his success. During the Panic of 1873, he and his business partners turned to the widows of the town for assistance. He not only tolerated but enjoyed social encounters with the women of the town. In January 1881, for example, he hosted the Marshall's Ladies' Aid Society at his home, the first in a series of dime socials to raise money for the relief of the area poor. After a similar gathering at his home, the *Tri-Weekly Herald* described Lane as "unbounding in hospitality, and was as happy as any of the party." Three years later, he worked with the ladies of Harrison County to prepare exhibits for the New Orleans World Exposition. Of twenty committee members, Lane was the only man. Running for tax collector in 1884, Lane issued a special appeal to the ladies of the county. "[I]f he can enlist their smiles and charms in his behalf, . . . he will gain as signal a victory as . . . San Jacinto." Texas women, at that time, could not vote, but Lane hoped that they could use their influence to compel their husbands to vote for him. The announcement also revealed that Lane found humor in the juxtaposition of his war experience with the women's society that he encountered. In 1882, Lane served as drill master of the "Brown Brigade," a group of young women charged with sweeping the town. When he asked for the women's assistance in his 1884 bid for county office, he concluded with the martial order, "Attention! Ladies, fall in." With Mary Jane as facilitator, the women of Marshall accepted the general's compromise with domesticity and acknowledged him as a member of the community.[8]

Furthermore, the community of Marshall embraced Lane's bachelorhood. After attending a veterans' meeting in Waco, a newspaper correspondent commented on Lane. "A wife's kind smiles would mend his ways greatly." The Marshall *Tri-Weekly Herald* quickly came to the old bachelor's defense. "On the contrary, it is generally conceded that his ways do not specially require mending; in fact, that the harmony of his composition might be seriously jeopardized by such an experiment." After Lane informed the *Herald* that his friend and comrade of the Texas Veteran Association, Samuel W. McKneely, had married, the editor remarked, "Gen. Lane feels forsaken at being thus abandoned by his old comrade, but hopes that no domestic wars may disturb the peace and happiness of his friend."[9]

As his compromise with domesticity eventually succeeded, Major Lane tackled the more immediate problem of a livelihood. As had been his habit in the past, he turned to the merchant trade, but he did not resume his business with Virgil Ward. Instead, he teamed up with Septimus J. Taylor. During the waning months of 1858, the two men combined their resources and bought out the dry goods firm of C. E. Hynson. The new firm of Lane & Taylor purchased Hynson's existing inventory, assumed his accounts, and set up shop in his store, located on the east side of the courthouse square. On April 8, 1859, Lane & Taylor formally announced to Harrison County that they were open for business. "[We] respectfully tender [our] thanks to the former customers of the house, and hope a continuance of their patronage, together with other good and punctual customers."[10]

Styling themselves as "Dealers in Every Variety of Staple and Fancy Dry Goods," Lane & Taylor prospered during their first years in business. They advertised regularly in both Harrison County newspapers. In September 1859, Lane traveled to the East and purchased a large inventory. They began an aggressive advertising campaign, exploiting their patrons' anxieties. "THE WAR RENEWED!! GREAT EXCITEMENT! The whole Community rushing to the Store of Lane and Taylor." The *Harrison Flag* announced in March 1860 that the firm was "in receipt of one of the most attractive stocks of Spring Goods ever opened in Marshall," offering a wide array of dry goods. "[E]mbracing everything to complete the wardrobes of ladies and gentlemen," the article continued, "farming utensils, plantation goods, and a thousand other articles of utility and ornament; among which may be instanced a pretty lar[g]e supply of fine Jewelry." Lane & Taylor made a few small loans to their customers and dabbled in land speculation, with holdings in Harrison County as well as counties farther away such as Tarrant, Jack, and Hays—as much as two thousand acres.[11]

Marshall and its Harrison County hinterland provided Lane & Taylor with an environment conducive to prosperity. The community was far ahead of its East Texas rivals in transportation. Eight stage routes provided service to and from Marshall, and steamboats regularly plied Lake Caddo, about twenty-five miles to the northeast. With passage to the Red River, Harrison County benefitted from trade with Shreveport, New Orleans, and other Mississippi River cities. By 1859, the Southern Pacific Railroad facilitated shipping between Marshall and Swanson's Landing on Lake Caddo. Because the dominance of the cotton planter economy hindered the diversification of Harrison County, Marshall would achieve no more than a regional influence. These same planters, however, provided firms like Lane & Taylor with a lucrative market to peddle their wares, and the transportation facilities enabled them to sell at lower prices than their competitors in other East Texas towns.[12]

Although Lane might have compromised and made arrangements to establish a permanent home, the national crisis over slavery confounded his plans for prosperity. Before his arrival in Marshall in 1858, the major exhibited little interest in national affairs, but the crisis nonetheless gathered momentum. The short-lived national euphoria after the victory over Mexico waned, as leaders of the North and South began to wrangle over who would control the Mexican cession. The new territory promised to upset the precarious balance of power that the North and South had maintained in the U.S. Senate for almost forty years. From the ashes of the "Know-Nothing" defeat in the elections of 1856, the Republican party emerged with a platform to prevent the expansion of slavery into the new territories. Although the Republicans promised not to move against slavery where it already existed,

Southern planters, their politicians, and demagogue editors, such as Robert W. Loughery of Marhsall's *Texas Republican,* refused to acknowledge this difference and interpreted any movement of the "Black Republicans" as an effort to destroy the South. When Republican candidate Abraham Lincoln won the election of 1860, most of the Southern leadership determined that secession offered the best way to preserve their slave-based wealth. Even as Lincoln pledged time and again to protect slavery, Southerners prepared to defend their institutions with violence.

Citizens of Harrison County rarely engaged in debates over national issues, but they reacted vehemently when they perceived a threat to slavery and cotton—the two mainstays of their economy. The county included one of the largest slave populations in Texas, outnumbering whites 8,700 to 6,200. Although the leaders of the county agreed that they should defend slavery, they did not agree on the method. Most in Harrison County adhered to the Southern Democratic tactics of confrontation and conflict, while a smaller, yet persistent, number of opposition leaders argued that the South should remain in the Union and solve their differences by constitutional means. Secession, after all, was an all-or-nothing gambit. Should the South lose a civil war, they would almost certainly lose their slaves, which would destroy their economy. Marshall's two newspapers best exemplified the local debate. The *Texas Republican* championed secession, while the *Harrison Flag* counseled for union.[13]

Perhaps Walter Lane joined the conflict for no other reason than "wishing to have a finger in that pie," as he stated in his memoirs, but his adventuristic impulse did not determine on which side he would fight. Family and community determined that for him.[14] Despite their Irish origins and their childhood spent in Ohio, the Lanes were Southern sympathizers. George Lane had moved to Texas and joined the slave-based political leadership in Harrison County. The citizens elected him to lead the local government as county judge in August 1860, at which time he owned six slaves. Wade Lane was located in Louisville, Kentucky. A merchant, he nonetheless owned one slave. William Lane moved to Liberty, Missouri, and although he did not own slaves, he and his son, Walter P. Jr., joined Southern military organizations. Walter Lane's friends were also ardent secessionists. W. R. D. Ward, for example, owned twenty-two slaves and was one of the Democratic leaders in the county. In September 1860, he discontinued his subscription of the Unionist *Harrison Flag,* because "I cannot longer stand your political gyrations and unconditional submission to abolition rule." Major Lane probably never owned slaves himself. His wandering ways made slave ownership impracticable and unnecessary. The census and local tax records demonstrated that the major did not own bondsmen in 1860 or 1861, but he probably had very few misgivings about the "peculiar institution."[15]

Regardless of his sentiments on slavery and his loyalties to the South, Lane would fight on the side of Texas. Despite his life on the wing, to Texas he attached his fortunes, and when the Lone Star State joined the Southern movement, so too did Walter Lane; his feelings were clear on the subject. Although he had fought alongside many of them, he would soon view the Yankees as enemies, describing them as "deluded bigots who had invaded our soil." Written in 1862, after the Confederate defeat at Pea Ridge, the words might better reflect a moment of bitterness—or words appropriate when humoring a superior officer. Whatever their inspiration, these words illustrated how Lane would identify his role during the Civil War to come.[16]

The citizens of Harrison County were pro-active to the perceived threat of the 1860 elections, and as a member of the community, Major Lane participated in the public reaction. An early indication of trouble occurred in May 1860, at the Democratic National Convention in Charleston, South Carolina. There, the delegates could not agree upon a candidate, and when the northern faction nominated Illinois senator Stephen Douglas, the southern delegation, including those from Texas, bolted and refused to recognize him. Once the news arrived in Marshall, the "Democracy of Harrison County" called a public meeting on the 26th, "to take some action in regard to the course pursued by the Texas delegates at the Charleston Convention." The attendees resolved to support the withdrawal, declaring that the time for compromise on slavery had passed. The Democrats also called on their neighbors to meet in convention at Gilmer, to select a district attorney. They selected Major Lane as one of the delegates to represent Harrison County. The Gilmer convention, however, failed due to lack of interest.

On November 16, when news of Lincoln's election reached Harrison County, its citizens convened another meeting. A talented group of leaders, which included George Lane, passed a resolution that called for resisting the Lincoln presidency because it threatened slavery and called for a statewide convention to decide the future of Texas. Eight days later, the citizens gathered for a second meeting. The *Texas Republican* described it as "the largest and most imposing meeting ever convened in the county." George Lane addressed the meeting, along with seven other leaders. On December 15, Walter Lane appended his name to a letter to state representative Ochiltree, asking for his opinion on whether Gov. Samuel Houston would call a special session of the legislature to decide the state's stance on secession.

Across Texas and the South, similar meetings convened with similar results. South Carolina took the lead and on December 20, formally seceded from the United States. Harrison County celebrated the event. On the 29th, a public meeting adopted resolutions supporting South Carolina and appointed Elkanah Greer, Ochiltree, and George and Walter Lane to a committee to prepare a night demonstration. "After supper, the town was brilliantly illuminated, and large bonfires of pine, blazed brightly on the public square," the *Texas Republican* reported. "A torchlight procession traversed the town, and the 'anvilading' was resumed, and continued until a late hour." The citizens of Jefferson, sixteen miles north of Marshall, reportedly could hear the firing of the anvils.

Defying Governor Houston's unionist stance, the Texas legislature called for the citizens of Texas to send delegates to a secession convention. That body met on January 28, 1861. Four days later, on February 1, the delegates passed an ordinance of secession, with only 8 of 174 votes against the measure. They placed the ordinance before the Texas public, who overwhelming ratified secession on the 23rd. Harrison County citizens supported the measure, with a vote of 866 to 44. Texas officially withdrew from the Union on March 2—the last of the original seven states that met in Montgomery, Alabama, to form the Confederate States of America.

Throughout the "Secession Winter," the citizens of Harrison County regularly met to discuss the unfolding events. A jubilant mood belied the unease that many felt as war loomed in the near future. Major Lane participated in most, if not all, of the public meetings, casting his fortunes with the secessionists. The meeting of February 20 appointed Lane to a committee that selected M. J. Hall as a delegate to the Secession Convention, filling the seat vacated by Ochiltree after he accepted a seat at the provisional congress of the Confederacy. The major briefly flirted with a political career during the first week of December, when he stood as an at-large candidate for Marshall city alderman. His candidacy lasted only a week before he withdrew his name.[17]

Walter Lane attended the pro-secession rallies and sat on a few committees, but the citizens needed the adventurer's talents as a soldier more than any political acumen he might have possessed. As early as November 1860, Harrison County recognized the need for military preparedness. On December 1, Lane was appointed to a five-man committee charged with the organization of a battalion of minutemen, a term that harkened back to the patriot days of the 1770s. In March 1861, the Texas Secession Convention issued a call for a mounted regiment. Perhaps unknown to Lane, Eli H. Baxter—a Harrison County delegate—put Lane's name forward as a nominee for the lieutenant colonel position, demonstrating Lane's growing stature in both the local and state community. After two rounds of balloting, however,

Lane did not receive the post. On April 19, responding to the call of the convention, eager volunteers from Harrison and surrounding counties gathered in Marshall. They elected Samuel J. Richardson captain and, as one trooper recalled, "unanimously, and enthusiastically" named themselves the W. P. Lane Rangers, honoring the major who had "distinguished himself in many hard fought battles for Texas Independence." As flattered as Lane might have been by these gestures, he would do more than play this symbolic role.[18]

As the crisis gathered momentum, Texas governor Edward Clark issued a proclamation for additional troops in late April. He appointed Lane as enrolling clerk for the sixth militia district, which included Harrison and Upshur counties. The major acted without delay. He published broadsides and placed notices in the local papers, calling for volunteers. By the beginning of May, enough men had responded to fill the rosters of two companies. One group, which consisted primarily of volunteers from the town of Marshall, styled themselves the Marshall Guards. The other group organized at Jonesville with men from rural northeastern Harrison county and included many of the planter elite and their sons. They chose the name of Texas Hunters.[19]

On May 7, their first opportunity for action arrived. A lone express rode into town with urgent reports that the notorious Kansas Jayhawker, James Montgomery, had entered the Indian Territory at the head of some three thousand men, with the intent to invade North Texas. The citizens of Marshall immediately responded to the emergency. On the 7th, a committee of fourteen, including Lane, issued a challenge. "Let old Harrison respond to the call." In response, Major Lane took command of the Marshall Guards and Texas Hunters. On May 11, he paraded the 150 soldiers of the so-called Washita Expedition on the courthouse square, to the delight of the crowded citizens. The *Texas Republican* proudly claimed, "A more imposing body of men are not to be found." Marshall lawyer and future governor Pendleton Murrah addressed the troops. Filled with the martial spirit, anxious to prove their mettle, the East Texans marched from town, making for the Indian Territory, but they would have to wait for a fight. The reports of Montgomery marching toward Texas proved false. After returning to Harrison County, the Marshall Guards embarked for the East and eventually joined the Army of Northern Virginia as part of John Bell Hood's celebrated Texas brigade. Although the Texas Hunters would have to wait a while longer before joining the Confederate Army, they would fire the first shots of Harrison County men in the Civil War.[20]

Upon his arrival in town, Lane learned that Governor Clark had appointed him brigadier general. The rank suited the veteran soldier, who had carried the title of major for over thirteen years. His command, however, consisted of state troops—men too old or too young for active service, charged with protecting the home front. Although Lane dutifully accepted the post and organized his command, and although he established community ties and made a compromise with domesticity, he watched for an opportunity to put his finger in the Civil War pie.[21]

• 8 •

THE MARSHAL NEY OF TEXAS, 1861-62

In his memoirs, Walter Lane stated that he joined the Civil War for no other reason than "wishing to have a finger in that pie."[1] Despite the frivolity of that phrase, it reiterated the importance of adventure in Lane's life. Although family, community, and state allegiance determined on which side he would fight, the familiar pull of masculine relationships, incidents of the expedition, and a longing for renown continued to influence his decisions. Maturity might have diminished his romantic ardor, but adventure—specifically, warfare—was his sober vocation.

The problem of defining the motivation and experiences of the typical Civil War soldier has vexed historians, and in several ways, Lane's circumstances defy their efforts to generalize. As a veteran who knew well both the exhilaration and brutality of battle, Lane possessed few misconceptions that contrasted with the realities of war. That bracing probably contributed to his forbearance against the disillusionment that many of his contemporaries felt late in the war. Others resisted disillusionment by adhering to a steadfast ideology. Lane, however, exhibited only moderate interest in causes. Instead, he sustained himself on the bonds of masculine camaraderie and the quest for wartime laurels.[2]

In May of 1861, as the nation prepared to go to war with itself, Lane organized his brigade of state troops. Serving as a general in the militia, however, satisfied neither his adventuristic impulse nor his ambition, so he also worked to obtain a more active appointment. On the 26th, Marshall attorney Elkanah Greer arrived from the Confederacy's provisional capital in Montgomery, Alabama. He carried a commission to raise a regiment of cavalry to assist in Benjamin McCulloch's defense of Arkansas and the Indian Territory. Greer had lived in Marshall since about 1850, and he was an ardent secessionist, obsessed with seizing Kansas for the slavocracy. With a commission direct from the Confederate government, he promised action to any who might follow him.[3]

The Texas Hunters agreed to join Greer's regiment. On June 1, the company assembled in Jonesville, and while a brass band serenaded them, the company rode out of town and made for Greer's rendezvous at Dallas. Lane, brigadier general of the militia, joined the company as a private. Although he would later feign surprise, he had little intention of remaining at that rank. Lane remembered that John C. Hays and Michael H. Chevallié had employed the same tactic in order to win elections for field commissions on the eve of the U.S.-Mexican War, and he intended to do the same. Indeed, as he rode out of Harrison County, the *Texas Republican* already suggested Lane as the logical choice for lieutenant colonel—second-in-command of the regiment. "No better disciplinarian, no commander, or no one who will retain more fully the confidence of his men can be found," so claimed the hometown newspaper.[4]

On the evening of June 14, the Texas Hunters arrived at the outskirts of Dallas and rendezvoused with the other companies of the regiment. Most hailed from East Texas and represented the more prosperous citizens of the state. For example, Leonidas and Americus Cartwright, of the San Augustine company, were the sons of Lane's former employer, Matthew Cartwright—the seventh wealthiest man in Texas. On June 13, the men from East Texas mustered into the Confederate Army. In keeping with Greer's long-held dream of conquering Kansas, the new regiment took the designation of the South Kansas Texas Regiment.[5]

Although a private, Walter Lane was a conspicuous member of the Texas Hunters. The *Dallas Herald* noted his arrival. "Major Lane, of Harrison County, who saw much service and won a fine reputation for himself [in the U.S.-Mexican War] . . . is a favorite, not only with the men of his county, but many others. Major Lane is a fine officer, of large experience in the army, and one of the most popular men we know." On July 2, the companies elected the officers of the regiment. Lane stood for lieutenant colonel and defeated his nearest opponent by a wide margin of 575 to 276 votes. George W. Chilton, a lawyer from Tyler who fought with Lane in Christopher Acklin's company in the U.S.-Mexican War, won a closer election for major. Matthew D. Ector, lawyer and editor from Henderson, accepted the post as adjutant.[6]

Later that evening, the troopers of the South Kansas Texas Regiment gathered outside Lane's hotel room and serenaded him, "to testify their joy at his election," the *Dallas Herald* explained. "Entire good feeling prevails throughout the regiment, and all seem well pleased to have secured the services of an able and experienced officer."[7] Sgt. Samuel B. Barron of Cherokee County recalled how his fellow soldiers admired Lane. He acknowledged the qualities of Greer and Chilton, but for Lane, Barron reserved the most esteeem. The lieutenant colonel "was the life of the regiment during our first year's service," Barron wrote. "A more gallant man than he never wore a sword, bestrode a war horse, or led a regiment in battle. He was one of the heroes of San Jacinto, and a born soldier."[8] Lane must have been gratified at these expressions of manly regard in this martial setting.

Meanwhile, Greer's commander, Benjamin McCulloch, gathered his army at Fort Smith, Arkansas. He agreed to cooperate with Sterling Price to take Missouri for the secessionists, but he had to wait for his disparate units from Arkansas, Texas, and Louisiana to join him, and he urged Greer to move. The East Texans were eager to join McCulloch, but tardy supplies delayed their departure. Not until July 9 did the South Kansas Texas Regiment leave Dallas.[9]

On July 27, Greer's men arrived at Fort Smith, only to find that McCulloch had pushed forward, leaving orders for the Texans to follow. They crossed over the Boston Mountains and on August 4, reached McCulloch's camp near Cassville. The general had just returned from a heated meeting with Price. They deeply distrusted one another, but Price understood that he could not defeat the Missouri Federals without McCulloch's cooperation and reluctantly agreed to give the Texan command of their joint operation. Before Greer and Lane could locate a camp for their men, McCulloch ordered them to cook three days of rations and prepare for a forward movement. He wanted to surprise the forces under U.S. Gen. Nathaniel Lyon, who reportedly had moved south from Springfield.[10]

McCulloch placed Greer's men in advance, and Lieutenant Colonel Lane took command of the most forward companies. As they anxiously made their way toward Lyon's camp, gunfire sounded from the rear. Lane quickly rallied his men, "Turn your horses around, men, and go like h—l the other way," Barron recorded. The cavalry bounded toward the action but found no fight. The shots came from some careless infantry who were unloading their weapons. Disgusted, Lane reigned his men about and returned to the advance. When they reached Lyon's camp, the Texans found it abandoned.[11]

In the valley about Wilson's Creek, ten miles south of Springfield, McCulloch waited several days, while Price urged him to make an assault on the Federals. The Missourian placed his forces on Oak Hill, at the north of end of the valley. McCulloch arranged his men along the creek, forming an elongated and exposed encampment. A telegraph road and Skegg's Branch, a small tributary of Wilson's Creek, divided the camps. Greer's men waited in the southern end of the valley, with Thomas J. Churchill's Arkansas Mounted Rifles holding down the rear.

On the morning of August 10, the Confederates in the valley of Wilson's Creek awoke just before daybreak. They lit fires and stretched casually about their tents as they prepared breakfast, when artillery suddenly disrupted their preparations. The first shot came from the south and tore through Churchill's regiment. From the ridge to the east, another battery cast shells harmlessly through the treetops, over the South Kansas Texas, while further to the north, artillery awakened Price's Missourians. Lyon had sent Gen. Franz Sigel to attack from the south along Wilson's Creek, while he moved from the north on Oak Hill. With little more than five thousand men, Lyon hoped to catch McCulloch's ten thousand off-guard. He succeeded admirably.[12]

Greer's troopers scrambled from under the cannon fire. "The very earth trembled from the thunders of the artillery," Adjutant Ector reported. Fortunately, most had already saddled their horses. Relying on the meager training that they had received in Dallas, the officers frantically called for their men to fall into line, and Lane worked mightily to restore order. "I rode down the line, and . . . ordered the men to mount, and drew them from under fire," he recalled. A civilian from Corsicana, Roger Q. Mills, watched as Lane rallied the troops. "A smile of delight played on Col Lane's face as he rose in his stirrups and cried, 'Forward!'" Not since the battle of Monterrey had Lane endured such heavy fire, and he apparently remembered the experience fondly. At the ford where the telegraph road crossed Skegg's Branch, Lane and Greer managed to form five companies. The balance of the regiment remained separated for the duration of the battle.[13]

At Skegg's Branch, Greer and Lane waited for orders while the battle clamored around them. To the south, McCulloch countered and routed Sigel. He then ordered Greer and his five companies to support the Missourians on Oak Hill, by charging James Totten's Second U.S. Artillery on the Federal right. Once in position, the din of battle and the dense underbrush made it difficult for Greer and Lane to prepare the men for the charge. When Greer finally gave the order, only a small portion of the command heard. While bounding up the hill, Lane's mount faltered. "My horse was shot centrally through, falling dead under me," he explained. He commandeered a horse from a fallen Yankee soldier and rode after his men. The result hardly exemplified effective cavalry tactics. Although Totten did not see the Texans forming, they so bungled the maneuver that the few infantry and pieces of artillery already facing that direction easily dispatched them. Greer claimed that his charge "embarrassed" the Federals and "gave our army encouragement and enabled them to strengthen their position." Regardless of Greer's assessment, the first real action of the South Kansas Texas was an utter failure. Captain Totten looked upon the Texans with such derision that he described their cavalry charge as so "*effete* and ineffectual in its force and character as to deserve only the appellation of child's play." He concluded, "Their cavalry is utterly worthless on the battle-field." Such commentary would have made the proud Texans blush.[14]

After Sigel's defeat in the valley, the Federals enjoyed little chance at victory on Oak Hill. Any possibility disappeared when their commander, Nathaniel Lyon, fell with mortal wounds—the first Union general killed in action during the Civil War. The Federal troops withdrew from the battle of Wilson's Creek—or Oak Hills, as the Yankees remembered. For their part, the South Kansas Texas suffered six killed, twenty-three wounded, and six missing. The secessionist forces won the day, but the decisive battle for Missouri would have to wait until spring.[15]

For the next several months, the East Texans operated in southwestern Missouri. During this time, the South Kansas Texas received its official designation as the Third Texas Cavalry. McCulloch prepared to strike at Kansas, but reports that the Federals were once again advancing toward Springfield changed his mind. As he withdrew to Arkansas, he left the Third Texas with other cavalry in Missouri, to "burn all the mills and every character of property that would be of service to an enemy," as one Texas soldier explained. On November 29, he withdrew the Texans to Arkansas, directing them to locate winter quarters. They crossed through the Boston Mountains and established camp on Frog Bayou, near its junction with the Arkansas River, about ten miles east of Van Buren. The soldiers traded their weapons for the tools of a carpenter and constructed a small village of log cabins, in which to seek protection from the Ozark winter.[16]

The hiatus permitted many troopers of the Third Texas to obtain furloughs for home. Greer was one of them, and Lane assumed command of the regiment. General McCulloch also took his leave and placed Col. James M. McIntosh, of the Second Arkansas Mounted Rifles, in command of the cavalry. The first three months at Frog Bayou passed leisurely, until an urgent plea from Douglas H. Cooper, commander of Confederate forces in the Indian Territory, arrived at McIntosh's headquarters.

Many Native Americans of the Indian Territory had joined the Southern cause, but several groups joined the Union, or professed neutrality. Opothle Yahola and a band of about six thousand Creeks formed an encampment that Cooper deemed a threat—although they were probably neutral. In November and December, the Confederate colonel clashed with the Creeks.

Sustaining severe losses, Opothle Yahola withstood the assault, but he began preparations to remove his people to Kansas. Cooper, in the meantime, wrote to McIntosh and requested reinforcements.

McIntosh leapt at the opportunity for wartime laurels, and he could find no more enthusiastic supporter than Walter Lane and the boys from East Texas. On December 20, they arrived at Fort Gibson, in the Indian Territory. There, McIntosh conferred with Cooper, and the two colonels agreed on a plan. Cooper would make a circuitous route and gain the rear of Opothle Yahola's encampment, while McIntosh advanced due west. If the plan worked, McIntosh would assault the enemy's position and drive them to Cooper's waiting forces. On the 22nd, McIntosh left Fort Gibson with about fourteen hundred cavalry. Lane and his men rode in the forward position.

On December 26, however, McIntosh received reports that Cooper was drunk and incapacitated and decided to move forward without him. During the ride through the snow, the wind gusted so fiercely that the men walked alongside their mounts to find relief, and Lane feared that his men would be unable to load their weapons with their frost-bitten fingers. Capt. Daniel M. Short led his company in the forward position and sometime near noon clashed briefly with an unknown native group. After receiving the report, Lane ordered the column to halt and permitted his men to build campfires to ward off the cold. A quarter-mile away, seventeen hundred Creeks and other Native Americans held a formidable position atop a boulder-crowned hill called Chustenahlah. McIntosh arrived soon after with the remainder of his force and allowed them to join the Third Texas beside the campfires.[17]

McIntosh informed Lane of his attack plan. "Colonel, we will carry it by storm," Lane recalled. "Form your men at the foot of the hill to charge it on horseback." McIntosh intended to send John S. Griffith's Sixth Texas around the right and William C. Young's Eleventh to the left, while Lane would take the Third and the Arkansas troops and charge up the hill in a frontal assault. McIntosh promised that if Lane failed in his first attempt, the others would assist him. The lieutenant colonel reluctantly accepted the order. "All right," he remembered saying to McIntosh, "but if I do not carry the position I will be at the bottom before the re-enforcements [*sic*] can arrive." He later admitted that McIntosh's confidence flattered him, but he explained, "I would have freely forgiven him if he had dropped the mantle on some other colonel's shoulders; for, when I looked upon that hill . . . , I felt as if I was being ordered to a sudden and speedy death."[18]

Lane ordered his men from their campfires and drew them into battle lines at the foot of Chustenahlah. While the Creeks above shouted and jeered at them, Lane instructed his men to "[t]ighten girths," and warned them "that the sooner they got on the top of that hill, the fewer empty saddles there would be." When his cavalrymen were ready, Lane turned to his regimental bugler, Charlie Watts, and gave the order to blow the charge. "We went up the hill like 'shot out of a shovel,'" Lane described. "The order of the day then was, six-shooters and double-barreled guns, and the Indians running in all directions." Observing from his command post, McIntosh reported that Lane led the assault "with the irresistible force of a tornado, and swept everything before it." Once they reached the summit, the men of the Third Texas dismounted and engaged the Indians in close quarters. Surprised by Lane's quick assault, most of the Creeks managed to fire only one round before retreating.[19]

The next morning, McIntosh dispatched Lane and Griffith to pursue the Creeks. They returned when they could not find them. McIntosh estimated that Opothle Yahola lost some two hundred and fifty killed and wounded. He reported that his command lost nine killed and forty wounded. Of those, the Third Texas lost five men killed and at least twelve wounded.

Upon returning to their Frog Bayou camp, Lane received a thirty-day leave and returned to Marshall, where he could "ventilate his laurels," as he often described an adventurer's homecoming. He had not been able to enjoy such venting since the end of the U.S.–Mexican War a decade before. This time, his laurels preceded him.

Lane's performance at the battle of Chustenahlah impressed his fellow lieutenant colonel of the Eleventh Texas, James J. Diamond. While his regiment waited to join the fray, Diamond watched Lane lead his men against the Creek position. "Col. Lane . . . was wisely selected to charge the front," he wrote to his brother, "This was done under a galling fire in the most gallant manner . . . no living soldier could have done it. For prudence, coolness, and bravery, their [Third Texas] leader has no superior." Diamond's brother forwarded the letter to Charles R. Pryor, editor of the *Dallas Herald,* who printed the flattering remarks. On January 8, 1862, Lane arrived in Marshall. He presented the editor of the *Texas Republican* his own account of the battle and a copy of his official report. On the 29th, he attended a party that Joseph M. "Uncle Joe" Taylor organized for the lieutenant colonel and other furloughed soldiers. Such gaiety and ventilation, however, did not last long. On the 17th of February, a day short of his forty-fifth birthday, he took leave of his friends and family and returned to his regiment at Frog Bayou.[20]

When he rejoined the Third Texas, Lane found that Confederate authorities had reorganized their forces in the region. Pres. Jefferson Davis created the Trans-Mississippi Department and on January 10 appointed West Point graduate Earl Van Dorn commander, resolving the question of leadership that had hindered cooperation between McCulloch and Price. Under Van Dorn, McCulloch took charge of a division that consisted of an infantry brigade under Louis Hébert and a cavalry brigade under McIntosh, including the Third Texas. Lane reached his troops in camp near Fayetteville, Arkansas.

The Federals had also reorganized. Samuel R. Curtis took command of the new Army of the Southwest. He established his headquarters on Sugar Creek, along the south face of a wooded hillside called Pea Ridge, just south of the Missouri-Arkansas line. Although he could boast a force of over ten thousand soldiers, Curtis arrayed his men piecemeal across northwestern Arkansas.

Van Dorn decided to strike. With Albert Pike and his Indian units augmenting Price and McCulloch, the general commanded sixteen thousand men. On March 4, he ordered his army into action, with the goal of catching the Federals posted at Bentonville, Arkansas—an exposed position commanded by Franz Sigel, who most of the Third Cavalry remembered from Wilson's Creek. Curtis learned of the movement and ordered Sigel to withdraw to Pea Ridge.[21]

On March 6, the Rebel cavalry under McIntosh rushed forward to intercept Sigel but only managed a few brief clashes, including an intense skirmish on Sugar Creek Road, north of Bentonville. To that location, Lane led the advance companies of the Third Texas, with the remainder of McIntosh's brigade strung out behind him. In the early afternoon, he encountered a squad of Federal cavalry that fired on him. McIntosh rode up to the scene and Lane asked for orders. The general impetuously ordered a charge. Lane took Capt. Robert Cumby's company and broke through the Yankee pickets, driving them to the foot of a hill, where infantry awaited in support of their cavalry. Lane pulled back to McIntosh, who ordered yet another charge.

The resulting maneuver was as bungled as the charge at Wilson's Creek. Half of the Third Texas formed in a skirmish line, while the rest charged up the steep hill, with Lane and McIntosh leading the way. Expressing their bravado with their distinctive war whoop, the Texans rushed the summit. Lane recalled the demoralizing surprise that they found at the top. "We had got nearly to the brow of the hill, when about a thousand infantry rose up, and simultaneously the brush was pulled away from a masked battery of six pieces of artillery, which met my astonished gaze at sixty yards distance." The green troops of the Twelfth Missouri Infantry and Gustavus Elbert's First Missouri Flying Artillery blasted into the Texas cavalry. Trooper B. P. Hollinsworth admitted that the cannon fire "opened our eyes and shut our mouths." McIntosh wanted to continue the charge, picked up the regimental flag, and called for his men to follow, but Lane was more suspect of their chances for success. "I hallooed to my men: 'Fall back, or you will all be murdered!' They didn't wait for a repetition of the order but went at once, and, as Shakespeare put it, 'Stood not on the order of their going.'" Amid the confusion of charge and retreat, General McIntosh reluctantly abandoned the idea of rallying his troops and accompanied the retreating Texans back to the main body of his brigade.[22]

Having removed themselves safely from the guns, the soldiers of the Third Texas took a moment to grasp the meaning of their sudden encounter with Yankee artillery. Captain Cumby ordered a roll call. Only two men failed to answer. Trooper Douglas Cater reported Cumby saying, "I don't understand why we didn't have more men killed, we will never be in a worse place than we were this evening." Pvt. Albert Blocker agreed when he said Sigel "gave the 3rd Texas a 'black eye,'" but Capt. Stephen Hale was far more critical in his assessment. "This here regiment are [*sic*] disgraced forever!" In addition to the two killed, the Third Texas suffered nine men wounded and a collective ego bruised.[23]

Lane and the Third Texas would experience no more fighting, as the sun set on the 6th of March, 1862. Sigel continued up Telegraph Road, to the safety of Curtis's army, while McIntosh instructed his men to set up camp. They enjoyed the last food and rest that they would have for the next two days. Van Dorn brought up Price's Missourians and consulted with his lieutenants. McCulloch informed him that a rugged route, called the Bentonville Detour, would permit the Rebels to gain the rear of Curtis's position. Early in the morning of the 7th, with little regard for his soldiers' hunger and lack of rest, Van Dorn ordered his troops back into action. He led the Missourians out of camp and ordered McCulloch to follow with his division.

Van Dorn's lack of reconnaissance proved costly. Choked with thick woods and crossed by numerous creeks, the narrow Bentonville Detour did not provide adequate passage for large-scale troop movements. Van Dorn managed to reach the Telegraph Road, above Curtis's position, after sunrise but found the Yankee general waiting for him. The battle opened at about eight o'clock in the morning, near Elkhorn Tavern on the east end of Pea Ridge. When he heard the guns erupt between Van Dorn and Curtis, McCulloch was still leading his division up the Bentonville Detour on the west end of the hill, near the hamlet of Leetown. He countermarched his command to Ford's Road, which permitted a direct route toward Curtis. Traveling in a southeastern direction, McCulloch's Rebels marched toward an elevated pass, between Pea Ridge on their left and Little Mountain on their right. Ford's Road led them through a dense wood and opened briefly into a field—the Third Texas in its customary position on point. Scouts informed McCulloch that the enemy lay only a quarter-mile distance ahead of them, and he ordered a halt.

Not knowing the reason for delay, Greer sent Lane to McIntosh for orders, and while the lieutenant colonel consulted with the Arkansas general, a Federal battery surprised the Confederates with a salvo of solid shot. On their right and toward their rear, at about three hundred yards distance, three James rifles of the First Missouri Flying Artillery fired on them. The battery—the same that shut Texan mouths the day before—and the First Missouri Cavalry dismounted in support, represented the forward elements of a Union task force commanded by Gen. Peter J. Osterhaus. Posted in reserve behind the Yankee artillery, Henry Dysart of the Third Iowa Cavalry witnessed the confusion that the bombardment caused in the Rebel ranks. "I could distinguish officers rushing to and fro in wild excitement seemingly preparing for an advance on [u]s."[24]

Dysart surmised correctly. McCulloch directed McIntosh to take the offending battery, and the Arkansan called on Lane to lead the charge. Despite the fiasco on Sugar Creek Road the day before, McIntosh selected Lane, a lieutenant colonel, over Greer and the colonels of the other regiments. Perhaps Lane was simply the closest officer on the field, but more likely, McIntosh remembered Lane's handling of the difficult charge up Chustenahlah that past Christmas. Regardless of McIntosh's reasons, Lane accepted the order with relish.[25]

The lieutenant colonel rode to the front of the column, with regimental bugler Charlie Watts in tow. As he readied the brigade, McCulloch rode up and ordered the Third Texas out of line to protect the Rebel artillery. Lane and Watts remained with the Sixth, Eleventh, portions of the Ninth Texas regiments, and the First Texas and First Arkansas battalions—numbering, perhaps, fifteen hundred men and horses.[26] Barron heard Lane order the bugler, "[B]low the charge until you are black in the face." The Texans whooped and hollered over the prairie, toward the Federal battery. From Ford's Road, an infantryman from Louisiana witnessed the charge. "Like a flash of lightning two columns of the cavalry dashed out, completely surrounding [the artillery] . . . ," he recalled. "The enemy's infantry and cavalry, who were supporting the battery, fired one round and run [*sic*]."[27]

General Osterhaus watched as Lane's cavalry dashed over the field like "a wild, numerous, and irregular throng," dispersing the Missourians manning and defending the artillery. They did not have time to spike their cannon or explode their ammunition. "[I]n every direction I could see my comrads [*sic*] falling," Dysart of the Third Iowa observed. "[H]orses frencied [*sic*] and riderless, ran to and fro. [M]en and horses ran in collision crushing each other to the ground[. D]ismounted troopers ran in every direction. [O]fficers tride [*sic*] to rally their men but order gave way to confusion."[28]

The brief affair cost Lane at least twenty killed and twenty wounded and missing. He nevertheless managed to avenge the humiliation of the day before by capturing the guns of the First Missouri Flying Artillery and inflicting thirty killed and fifty-six wounded and missing among the Federals. Although they left the battery in working order, the artillerymen escaped with the horses. With no way of moving the three James rifles, the Rebels burned the pieces before the end of the day. McIntosh sent a message to Lane to reform the cavalry and withdraw, in order to form a reserve, while he and McCulloch readied the infantry for action. The colonels of McIntosh's brigade chafed under the command of a subordinate officer but reluctantly complied when Lindsey Lomax, of McCulloch's staff, confirmed Lane's position.[29]

Lane's impressive cavalry charge opened the second front, at the battle of Pea Ridge, in dramatic style. While Van Dorn and Price grappled with Curtis near Elkhorn Tavern, McCulloch and McIntosh advanced toward Leetown to seize their advantage. While the infantry moved forward, Lane and Greer remained behind with the cavalry. Greer posted the Third Texas on Little Mountain, where his men could watch the unfolding battle. Lane, with the remainder of the cavalry, waited in the woods and could only listen to the storming battle. For hours, Lane and Greer anticipated orders to join the fray.

Orders never arrived. One of McIntosh's staff members rode up to Lane and informed him of the gloomy developments on the Leetown front. Both McCulloch and McIntosh were dead—killed while leading their men. The enemy had captured Col. Louis Hébert, next in line. Without a commander, the Confederates in the Leetown section fell back from the Federal advance. Lane, Greer, and the other cavalry colonels met in a log cabin behind the lines. There, Lane turned over McIntosh's brigade to Greer, who also assumed command of McCulloch's division. Lane took the reins of the Third Texas. Greer decided to send a courier to Van Dorn, informing him of the news and asking for orders.

At two o'clock in the morning on March 8, the courier returned to Greer's headquarters with verbal orders to strike camp and march to the aid of Van Dorn and Price. Lane roused his men. In his after-battle report, he described the enthusiasm they expressed despite their haggard condition. "[T]he alacrity with which they obeyed the first summons indicated the patriotic purpose of each one to discharge fully his duty." Contrary to the sobriety usually found in such official communications, Lane added a romantic flourish. "Silently and with stern resolve did they form for battle, and many a brave heart chafed with anxious zeal during the heavy firing which occurred near Elkhorn Tavern." Through the cold night, Greer led McCulloch's division, with Lane and the Third Texas following in the rear. If they could make the connection, Greer's men might provide the difference for Van Dorn to salvage victory at Pea Ridge. As ordered, Greer arrived before dawn. Lane stationed the Third Texas about a mile and a half north of Elkhorn Tavern.[30]

They waited through the morning until midday, when Greer arrived with orders from Van Dorn to withdraw. Lane was disappointed. "I never was so astonished in my life, as here we were, three thousand men just arrived, fresh and willing to fight." Others in the Third Texas expressed similar sentiments. Cater recalled, "This seemed to our army very wrong. . . . [M]any of our troops had not fired a gun and we were ready to make a forward move . . . with every hope of success."[31]

An officer from Van Dorn's staff found Lane, who had moved his regiment off the road to permit the Rebel army to pass. The aide relayed Van Dorn's orders for Lane to deploy the Third Texas across the road "and hold your position at all hazards until our retreating forces pass through," as Lane recorded. He watched as Van Dorn's men filed from the battlefield, and when the last soldier passed, Lane posted a company as a rear picket and joined the withdrawal.[32]

At Pea Ridge, Union and Confederate forces fought the decisive battle for Missouri. Indeed, the contest around Elkhorn Tavern and Leetown might have been the most important engagement west of the Mississippi River. After Van Dorn withdrew from the field, he took his weary men back to the safety of the Boston Mountains, and the Rebels never again seriously threatened Missouri. Lane, like many of the Southern participants, tried to make sense of their failure with a variety of justifications. Some, such as Sergeant Barron, took special pains to describe the orderly manner in which the Confederates retreated from the field, suggesting that the Yankees had not really beaten them. Lane agreed in his after-battle report, "As regiment after regiment passed slowly by no indication of alarm or knowledge of defeat could be discerned." David Garrett, of the Sixth Texas, took pride in the price that they exacted from Curtis. "I understand that the Feds claim the victory, but they say God damn such victories." Lane expressed similar sentiments when he wrote, "The defeat of our army was barren of results to the enemy, as they were too badly crippled to pursue us a mile." Lane and his comrades also believed that victory would have been theirs had McCulloch and McIntosh not perished.[33]

Van Dorn, nevertheless, left northwestern Arkansas in the hands of the Federals, when he crossed over the Boston Mountains and established headquarters at Van Buren. By mid-March, the Third Texas re-entered their old camp at Frog Bayou and enjoyed several days of much needed rest and food, but when Van Dorn received an urgent message from P. G. T. Beauregard, from across the Mississippi River, he ordered his command back into motion.

Earlier in February, U.S. Gen. Ulysses S. Grant had reduced the Southern garrisons at Forts Henry and Donelson on the Tennessee River. He identified the crucial railroad crossing at Corinth as his next target, and Confederate generals Albert S. Johnston and Beauregard gathered their forces to defend that location. They wanted Van Dorn's twenty-two thousand soldiers to bolster their own fifty thousand. Perhaps, together, they could bring Grant to battle and undo the setback at Pea Ridge.

In response, Van Dorn ordered Greer to De Valls Bluff, a landing on the White River about fifty miles east of Little Rock, where they would rendezvous with a steamboat. The Third Texas sloshed through the soggy bottomlands of the White and reached their point of embarkation. There, Van Dorn ordered the Texas cavalry to dismount. They would join Johnston and Beauregard as infantry.[34]

The Texans viewed this development with dismay. Trooper Victor Rose expressed the feelings of many. "[W]e regarded this order as a breach of faith, totally at variance with our contract." Lane claimed that the other regiments of the brigade consented to follow the lead of the Third Texas. To get them to accept these instructions, Lane gathered his men, appealed to their sense of duty and convinced them to continue on foot. As promised, the other regiments reluctantly released their horses.[35]

Although Lane convinced the brigade of the need for infantry, he had not fully convinced himself. Until another opportunity arose, however, he dutifully fulfilled his obligation as an infantry officer. On April 11, the Third Texas crowded aboard the steamer *Scotland.* Overburdened, the transport swayed precariously as it chugged down the White River, into the churning waters of the Mississippi. It arrived at the Memphis wharves on the night of the 15th, but the regiment did not disembark until the next morning, when they marched through town and encamped on the outskirts at a site called Big Springs.[36]

In Memphis, the Texans learned that Johnston did not wait for them. He marched into Tennessee and on April 6 and 7, fought Grant's forces at Pittsburgh Landing on the Tennessee River. The Confederates swept through the Union position and very nearly routed them, but the death of Johnston and the stiff resistance of a few Yankee divisions enabled Grant to rally his troops and force the Rebels to withdraw. The carnage staggered those who survived Pea Ridge, where Van Dorn and Curtis lost a combined three thousand killed and wounded. At Pittsburgh Landing—or Shiloh, as the Rebels remembered it—both sides lost in excess of twenty thousand. Beauregard assumed command, reassembled his forces at Corinth, and ordered the construction of earthworks. At Pittsburgh Landing, meanwhile, Union Gen. Henry W. Halleck took command of three veteran corps and marched a massive army of one hundred thousand men toward Corinth.

After a week of drill at Big Springs, Joseph L. Hogg—a lawyer from Rusk County who replaced McIntosh as commander of the brigade of Texas cavalry—received instructions to proceed to Corinth. On April 24, he loaded his command into the cars of the Memphis and Charleston Railroad. The trains suffered a number of mechanical problems and delays, which aroused the suspicions of Lane and the other officers of the brigade.

On the morning of the 25th, the train approached to within six miles of Corinth, whence the exchange of cannon fire thundered, but instead of rushing into town, the train reversed four miles to a sidetrack. Lane allowed his frustrations to overcome him. "As I was in the front car, and could get no information from the conductor and engineer—who were northern men . . . , I became uneasy." The lieutenant colonel consulted with Hogg and his staff. Other "over-suspicious 'patriots,'" as Sergeant Barron charitably described them, had convinced the general that the Memphis and Charleston was in league with the Yankees, conspiring to keep the Texans out of battle—or worse, setting them up for capture. When he visited Hogg, Barron found him "considerably excited. . . . He was rather an irritable man, and his suspicions were easily aroused." Barron knew the conductor and vouched for his dependability, but that did not convince the general, who provided Lane with written orders to force the crew to get the train underway.[37]

Lane gathered a squad of ten men under Capt. Thomas Winston of the Texas Hunters and placed the conductor and engineer under arrest. Lane demanded to go forward. The conductor asked Lane, "Colonel, suppose we meet the passenger train, what shall we do?" Trooper Albert Blocker recorded the conversation: "Col. Lane in his off-hand Irish way, said: 'By God, Sir! if they don't get out of the way run over them! I can't and won't keep my men cramped up in these cars another night, and possibly be captured by the damned yankees!'" The crew complied and powered the locomotive down the line.

As the command once again approached Corinth, however, they met another train that refused to yield. The officer in charge, "a little major, covered with gold lace," as Lane described him, derided the conductor for not stopping on the sidetrack. When he learned that Hogg and Lane had commandeered the vehicle, he challenged the lieutenant colonel: "Good God, you don't know what you are doing!" The major explained that he was the carrier of sensitive dispatches from General Beauregard to Richmond, and his mail train was an express that must go through. His ranting did not impress Lane. "I told him to get aboard his train and have it backed double-quick," he threatened, "or I would have him arrested."

The conductor of the westbound express, A. A. Slaughter, met with the stubborn officer from Texas, hoping to resolve the situation, but Lane disappointed him. "[H]e would not even listen to me," Slaughter reported to his superiors, "but in the most peremptory manner [he] ordered me back instantly." To add bite to his demand, Lane ordered a detail of twenty-five cold, wet, and irritable Texans to escort the conductor back to his locomotive and compel him to reverse directions. Slaughter acquiesced. "We told him he need not order the men out under his threats." He returned to his train and allowed the Texas brigade to move forward.[38]

The episode revealed much about Lane's personality. Armed with a fierce rectitude, he felt few qualms about contradicting orders or challenging authority. His paranoia about the loyalty of the Memphis and Charleston Railroad, or the danger of capture, might have been genuine, but it was more likely an exaggeration to convince Hogg of the necessity of keeping the train moving. The plight of his men was probably Lane's main concern. Since their departure from the comforts of Frog Bayou, the Texans suffered from the rain and cold, crowded onto precarious steamboats and herded into creaky railroad cars. Whatever his reasons, the incident also illustrated Lane's arbitrary disposition and his disdain for pretentiousness. Once convinced of the correctness of his position, he would not yield—especially not to the threats of a staff officer, who required a fancy uniform to justify his rank and authority. Such an officer could not possibility understand the plight of real soldiers—vital men such as Lane—so the lieutenant colonel bullied those who stood against him until his men reached Corinth and disembarked from the discomforts of the Memphis and Charleston.

The night after the Texans arrived in camps, Hogg received instructions to report to Beauregard and justify why he delayed the express. He had not yet taken official command of the brigade, and he already found himself in disfavor with his commander. Unnerved, Hogg called for the lieutenant colonel who created this problem. "The general was a good deal alarmed, and told me, as I had got him into trouble, I must help him get out." Lane confidently assured him that "there would be no difficulty about the matter."

He agreed to accompany Hogg to Beauregard's headquarters and provide an explanation. When they entered the commander's tent, the Texans found the major whom Lane had offended. He seemed pleased. Flashing Lane "a malicious grin," he was certain that he would receive justice.

Beauregard was irritated by the situation, but Lane had prepared an answer. "I explained to him that if we had erred, it was from our zeal in the cause." The Texans, he continued, could hear the artillery and feared that the crew of the railroad intended to keep them from performing their duty as patriotic soldiers. Lane and Hogg delayed Beauregard's express, because "we determined to get in and participate in the battle." The excuse worked, and the general accepted their regrets for the misunderstanding, then commended their enthusiasm. As he was leaving, Lane could not miss the opportunity to taunt the "little" major. "As I passed him, . . . I winked at him, observing, *sotto voce:* 'How is that for cheek?'"[39]

If Lane knew of the suffering, squalor, and death that awaited them at Corinth, he would not have been so eager to get off the trains. Dug in behind an extensive system of earthworks, Beauregard had gathered over fifty thousand troops around the rail intersection. The wounded from Shiloh, soggy weather, bad water, scarce food, and other noxious conditions created a fertile field for diseases such as dysentery and typhoid. The Confederates at Corinth suffered thousands of deaths from these maladies. The Third Texas lost fifty of their own. On May 16, after a week-long struggle with dysentery, General Hogg succumbed, scarcely a month after he took command of the brigade.

Beauregard had to contend with another force that hindered his ability to defend the railroad crossing. On April 16, the Confederate Congress passed a revolutionary measure that reflected both the modernity of the age and the desperation of the Southern cause. Dramatic losses in the West and the looming expiration of one-year volunteers—including the Third Texas—compelled Richmond policymakers to issue the Conscription Act of 1862. The law drafted into the service white men from eighteen to thirty-five years of age for a period of three years, or for the duration of the war. Although the need for fresh troops would bolster Beauregard's forces, the law also called for a reorganization of the entire Rebel army and permitted men who did not fall within the age of conscription to leave the service. The Third Texas lost 207 veterans under these provisions.

About the 8th of May, the enlistments of the Third Texas Cavalry expired. Those who remained re-elected a new slate of officers. Colonel Greer had been dissatisfied with his lack of recognition and promotion and returned to

Texas. Although the regiment requested that he stay and assume the vacancy, Lieutenant Colonel Lane refused. "I wished to return to Texas," he explained, "and raise a cavalry regiment, liking that arm of the service best." For colonel, they ultimately chose Captian Cumby over Major Chilton.[40]

The problem of this transition became apparent, as Halleck eventually brought his blue-clad host down from Tennessee. He sent only half-hearted probes against the breastworks, while he carefully—some said tentatively—constructed his siege works. Beauregard arrayed what few healthy troops he could muster. Lane was present when the Third Texas received their instructions. "We had barely got through the election when the order came: 'Fall into line and march to Farmington,'" a small village northeast of Corinth. Lane waited for Cumby to take command, but the new colonel balked. Suffering a bout of dysentery and having just received the rank of colonel after a year's service as captain, he requested that the more veteran Lane take command. "I did at the earnest request of the men," Lane claimed, and led them out with the forces under Van Dorn.[41]

During the next fortnight, as Halleck carefully arranged his one hundred thousand men around Corinth, Beauregard decided that he could not hold the ground. To conceal his withdrawal, he sent out skirmishers to maintain Halleck's anxiety. On May 27, he ordered Van Dorn to demonstrate against the Union line, and in turn, Van Dorn dispatched the Third Texas, with Lane in command. Accompanied by the recently elected Maj. James J. A. Barker and Adj. Orlando Hollingsworth, Lane could only gather 246 healthy men.

Before dawn of the 29th, he approached the Federal lines, through a valley of dense blackjack and underbrush. Awaiting behind an abatis of felled trees, the Tenth Missouri and Seventeenth Iowa Infantry regiments, commanded by Col. Samuel A. Holmes, fired on the Texans. Pvt. Thomas E. Hogg, son of the late general, recalled, "Each man took his tree and, after discharging his firelock and re-loading in that position, would advance to the next obstruction."[42]

This mode of fighting did not suit Lane. "Finding the woods were thick, I thought I would lose fewer men by charging the enemy than fighting at long range." He took command of the right wing, while Major Barker took the left. Hogg remembered, "Lane's favorite command, 'Charge!' was ordered." Written later in life with obvious exaggeration, Hogg sought to capture the romantic appeal of battle. "In full run, the Texans with the fury of madmen, close on the lurking enemy, whose skill and power are spent in vain to check them. Over three thousand rifles are belching forth their death-fraught charges into the slim line of the brave 246—still they come!"

The Texans forced the Iowa and Missouri regiments back and took the position in front of the felled trees. For the remainder of the day, Lane held his ground, exchanging fire with the enemy.[43]

Private Cater accused Lane of acting without orders. Indeed, Lane admitted, "Our main army, about four hundred yards off . . . cursed me loud and deep." Van Dorn wanted Lane to draw the enemy from their defenses. A staff member found the Texans in the middle of battle and informed Lane, "The general wants to know why in the h—l you don't fall back and let them come." But Lane would not risk the maneuver. The felled trees lay between him and the main body of Van Dorn's forces. The Yankees, Lane assured the aide, would "kill half of us before we got through." He held his ground through the day and into the night. Nevertheless, Beauregard's gambit worked, and he safely extracted his army from Corinth.[44]

The affair at Farmington cost Lane and the Third Texas eight killed, including Major Barker, and fourteen wounded. Embittered by the losses, Cater criticized Lane's recklessness. "Col. Lane made a very grave mistake. He was brave enough to have been a good private soldier but was out of place as an officer." Few, however, agreed with Cater's assessment. John W. Whitfield, temporarily commanding the Texas brigade, recommended Lane and the Third Texas for commendation, and Beauregard complied by paying them a rare honor. On the morning of June 4, he instructed that an officer should read "General Orders No. 62" to each regiment of the army. "The General commanding," the orders announced, "takes great pleasure in calling the attention of the army to the brave skillfull and gallent [*sic*] conduct of Lt Col Lane of the 3rd Texas Reg . . . [who] charged a largely superior force of the enemy [and] drove him from position. . . . The conduct of this brave Regiment is worthy of all honor & imitation." Lane felt understandably proud of this recognition. "A general order, read at the head of each regiment of an army," he beamed, "is the highest compliment that can be paid an officer or regiment for any act of gallantry."[45]

Walter Lane soon parted with the men alongside whom he fought during the past year. He had bigger plans. Before he left them, Lane drew the regiment into formation and gave them a farewell address. Although they had been a difficult bunch to control, Lane commended them for their conduct on the field of battle. "I told them that since we had been together . . . we had made some reputation as a fighting regiment, and for God's sake to hold it." The Third Texas would later maintain their reputation on battlefields in Mississippi, Tennessee, and Georgia. Lane returned to the other side of the Mississippi River, seeking to augment his own reputation.[46]

• 9 •

PARTISAN RANGER, 1862-65

After his first year in the Confederate Army, Walter Lane looked upon his contribution to the war effort with pride. He made up for the debacle at Wilson's Creek with spectacular cavalry charges at Chustenahlah and Pea Ridge, and his performance at Corinth earned him a commendation from his commanding general. As lieutenant colonel of the Third Texas Cavalry, however, Lane was impatient with subordination to Elkanah Greer, and the dismounting of the regiment convinced him to seek opportunities for a different command. Over the next year and a half, sickness and favoritism seemed to thwart his ambitions.

The years of service with the boys from East Texas also revealed Lane's maturing ideas about manliness. Lane's fondness for masculine camaraderie had helped fuel his longing for adventure. His time with Greer's regiment created similar bonds but differed in one important aspect—age. Fifteen years before, for example, he was not much older than the rangers he commanded in Mexico, but at forty-five, he stood as a paternal symbol among the boys of the Third Texas. This was a new relationship that created another dimension to Lane's notions of manhood.

Concern for the welfare of his men illustrated one aspect of Lane's newfound paternalism. The day before Pea Ridge, he contradicted James McIntosh's order to charge into Yankee guns and spared many of his men from certain harm. During the cold and wet train ride between Memphis and Corinth, the discomfort of the his men led him to commandeer the crew and ignore the priority mission of an express. As a good soldier, Lane followed orders that risked the lives of his men and himself, but if his estimation of the potential gains did not justify the sacrifice, he had few qualms about defying his superiors, as later events would testify.[1]

This fatherly concern could also create lasting bonds of affection. At Farmington, for example, Cpl. Thomas Cellum faltered as the Texans withdrew from the field, but Lane found him and then pulled his young comrade up onto his horse. Cellum reported that the lieutenant colonel "said no boy like me should be left behind while he was able to carry me on." This act inspired the young soldier "on to better deeds then I had ever done." Perhaps seeking to earn Lane's fatherly esteem, Cellum promised that "his confidence should not be misplaced," and expressed the affection that the act forged between the two, "[B]eside my Father and mother I had the Col to love me."[2]

Assuming the symbolic role of father, the protector, might have endeared Lane to many of his soldiers, but his role as the disciplinarian, coupled with his often highhanded attitude, could draw their resentment. As a lieutenant colonel of the Third Texas, Lane attained the reputation as a martinet. During his farewell speech, he admitted that he exhibited an "arbitrary conduct" toward the regiment but refused to apologize for it. "[I]f I had done my duty as an officer, I would have carried out orders much more strictly than I had done," he assured them, and characterized the Third Texas as "the hardest regiment to control I had ever seen." Considering his experience in commanding Texas Rangers during the U.S.-Mexican War, this was a damning assessment, indeed.[3]

In the fifteen years since his service in Mexico, Lane's attitude toward discipline apparently underwent a transformation. The rangers of his battalion, while operating in Nuevo León and Coahuila, hardly represented a model of good soldierly conduct. His superiors constantly reminded Lane to control his unruly Texans while scouting, but he made little effort to comply. Maturity probably lay at the root of Lane's change in temperment.

As an officer in the Texas cavalry, Lane consistently expected adherence to discipline from those under his command. He steadfastly supported Capt. Thomas W. Winston, when several troopers—enduring intense drill—sought to remove him from rank. At their Memphis encampment, he ordered infantry practice twice a day and restricted the movement of his men between evening and morning drills. In the months to come, Lane would toss out of the service both enlisted men and officers alike for their poor conduct. His soldiers often resented Lane's arbitrary disposition, but they also admired and responded to his leadership while under fire. Most would agree with Sgt. Samuel B. Barron's assessment. "In camps, in times when there was little or nothing to do, he [Lane] was not overly popular with the men, but when the fighting time came he gained the admiration of everyone."[4]

But his tour with the Third Texas ended when he led them to Baldwin, Mississippi. There, he approached his superiors about obtaining his own command in the cavalry service. He received his salvation in a new law passed on April 21, 1862, entitled "AN ACT to organize bands of partisan rangers." Issued in the same orders that announced the Conscription Act, this law permitted the organization of partisan units with the same pay, quarters, and regulations as normal soldiers.[5] In the way letters of marque legalized piracy, the Partisan Ranger Act sanctioned guerrilla warfare. Although Confederate policy makers wanted to raise guerrillas and raiders, Lane had no intention to participate in that mode of warfare. He used the law to get back into the cavalry service and fight with the main-line troops.

On June 5, Gen. Earl Van Dorn granted Lane a colonel's commission, to raise a regiment of partisans for operations west of the Mississippi. Lane took his papers and returned home, arriving at Marshall by stage on the 17th. He advertised for volunteers but relied on co-opting existing organizations such as Andrew Neill's three hundred men at Tyler and a battalion raised by fellow Marshall merchant A. D. Burns. Adding several companies raised under his own authorization, Lane brought together an unusual fourteen companies, when normal Confederate regiments numbered only ten. He styled his new command the First Texas Partisan Rangers and appointed Neill lieutenant colonel and Burns major.[6]

Lane's regiment consisted of veteran soldiers hailing primarily from East Texas. Recruiting only men over age thirty-five, as the law stipulated, Lane enlisted recently discharged soldiers from other Texas units. Many came with him from the Third Texas. Another large portion, including Major Burns, had been members of the First Texas Infantry.[7] Although they were older men, Lane was still their senior by as much as a decade and would continue to exhibit those paternal traits that had emerged during his service with the Third Texas.

At Jefferson, less than twenty miles north of Marshall, Lane located his headquarters. He implemented a rigorous drill schedule. Trooper J. P. Johnson remembered, "They kept us in this camp . . . almost all summer. They drilled us a certain numbers of hours every day. When we did leave camp we were in pretty fair shape to tackle anything which came up." Late that summer, Lane received a plea for troops from Gen. Thomas C. Hindman, commanding Rebel forces in Arkansas. On July 15, Lane dispatched Neill and Burns, with their battalions, to meet the request.[8]

As they crossed into southwestern Arkansas, Neill learned that Hindman intended to dismount their regiment. The battalion halted in the vicinity of Fulton and refused to continue. Neill explained, "[W]e don't intend to go on foot and many of us cant do so, we have stopt till we can find out more about it," and Lane intended to "find out more about it" from the highest authority. He had left the Third Texas to avoid infantry duty, and he did not want to see his summer's work undone by a general's whim. He left Neill in command of the regiment and dashed off to Richmond, Virginia, to consult with the Confederate high command.[9]

Lane arrived at the Confederate capital in early August and called on Secretary of War George W. Randolph, who agreed to meet with the colonel from Texas. Lane convinced him that Hindman had acted improperly. To his readers in Texas, Charles DeMorse of the Clarksville *Northern Standard* informed, "The Secretary of War has decided, upon direct application of Col. Walter P. Lane, that no general has the right to dismount troops raised as cavalry or Partizans." Lane sent the good news to Neill, who on August 15 issued a call to the partisan rangers. "The regiment is under urgent marching orders. . . . Bring all the arms possible." He added with emphasis, "We have special orders by which we are not to be dismounted!"[10]

Publicly, Lane traveled to Richmond on behalf of his regiment, but he also had a personal motive. After meeting with Randolph, he called on the Texas delegation to the Confederate Congress and placed in their hands an application for one of the new brigadier general positions slated for Texas commands. Eight congressmen, including John A. Wilcox, whom Lane knew from the U.S.-Mexican War, fixed their signatures to a flattering letter addressed to Pres. Jefferson Davis. "Col Lane is an old and tried officer of great experience and intelligence," they assured Davis, and reviewed his extensive military experience, emphasizing the affair at Farmington, Mississippi. "We conceive," the delegates concluded, "that Col Lane has fairly [used] his spurs, & is entitled to the honor we ask." Despite the complimentary recommendation, Lane did not receive a promotion.[11]

Several reasons might explain why Lane failed to receive one of the appointments. Combat experience was not one of them. Of the five Texans promoted between August 23 and September 12, 1862, only William Steele, a West Point graduate and veteran of the U.S.-Mexican War, could compare with Lane in terms of military service. Seniority likely played an important role. Four of the five attained the rank of colonel before Lane. Age might also have hindered his chances. In their recommendation, the delegates described him as "old," but hedged, "Col Lane is about forty three years old," when he was actually forty-five. The five men promoted ahead of him averaged thirty-nine years.[12]

Politics, however, was probably the major factor that thwarted Lane's ambition. Although he made his compromise with domesticity, decades of living life "on the wing" prevented him from making the long-term community ties and political connections necessary for promotion. Matthew D. Ector, John Gregg, Allison Nelson, and William R. Scurry were lawyers with considerable experience in state legislatures and judgeships. In addition, Nelson was an ardent defender of slavery, having served in Narciso López's Cuban filibuster and participated in the Kansas conflict, which earned him prestige among the slave-holding elite of the South. He, along with Gregg and Scurry, had been members of the Texas Secession Convention, while Gregg also represented Texas at the Confederate provisional congress. Political appointments to military command may have been unfair and even unwise, but the men selected over Lane justified the war department decisions with credible service during the remainder of the war.[13]

Richmond might have frustrated Lane's ambition for a brigadier's stars, but at least he would not have to command infantry. By September 19, he reached the camps of the partisan rangers but found his regiment ill-prepared for action. Scattered about southwestern Arkansas and northeastern Texas, Lane's rangers suffered from lack of food, supplies, and weapons. The coming winter, a year and a half of war, and a summer of heavy recruitment and conscription rendered North Texas lean on food and supplies, with little to offer the men of the partisan rangers. Writing in early August with the Arkansas detachment, Neill complained, "I have seen some hard times already, sleeping out rainy nights[. T]he other morning I was called to breakfast and had not an article to eat but the coarest [*sic*] corn bread." Lt. William H. Barnes wrote home to his wife about how they had to sleep without tents during a typical North Texas sleet storm.[14]

The lack of arms, however, proved to be Lane's most vexing problem. He sent his quartermaster to acquire weapons from Theophilus H. Holmes, who commanded the Trans-Mississippi from Little Rock. The general answered that he had nothing to send. According to Lane, Holmes wrote, "I send you *carte blanche* orders to seize, press, or buy arms wherever you can find them." Acting on this authority, Lane recalled, "I sent details of ten men from each company to the respective counties where the companies were formed to procure arms." On October 11, in Marshall, Lt. John M. Taylor advertised in the *Texas Republican*. "All those who can possibly spare any Guns, will greatly subserve their country, their own protection and interest . . . by sending arms without delay." Taylor promised to give receipts, and by the 25th, Capt. Hec McKay left Marshall with an adequate number of inadequate weapons to supply his company. The other companies succeeded in obtaining a similar supply of shotguns and old rifles.[15]

Colonel Lane was quite pleased with himself for this feat, but he apparently did more pressing and seizing than he did buying. Upon receiving complaints from northeast Texas that Lane had taken state-owned arms, Gov. Francis R. Lubbock wrote Holmes, inquiring where the weapons had gone. If the general granted Lane authority to seize weapons in Texas, he did not mention it to the governor. Holmes responded, "I am greatly disgusted that any officer of the Confederate Government should have been guilty of so great an outrage." By that time, the partisan rangers had arrived in the vicinity of Fort Smith. Instead of requiring Lane to return the contraband, Holmes promised the governor that he would replace the weapons.[16]

Lane, however, did not make it to Fort Smith. He explained, "Being taken sick with fever and a rising in my head, I was left at a farm house in the Indian Nation for three weeks." His condition worsened; unable to continue, Lane passed command to Richard Philip "Phil" Crump of Cass County, who had replaced an ailing Neill as lieutenant colonel. Lane returned to Marshall, arriving there in early December.[17]

Under Crump, the partisan rangers significantly contributed to Hindman's victory at Prairie Grove, Arkansas. The Rebels, however, could not defeat the harsh winter. Lane had failed to adequately supply his regiment before they left Texas, and they suffered terribly. With little relief from the winter and with disease reducing their numbers, desertion began to infect the partisan rangers. While on picket duty, Capt. Alexander Earp became so concerned about the plight of his men that he permitted them to return home without orders. In early January 1863, soldiers from Lane's regiment, including sixty under Earp, filtered across the Red River, seeking comfort from the winter.[18]

The Marshall *Texas Republican* tried to place a positive spin on the ignominious affair. "These men are going back in a few days and no doubt will fully make amends . . . for this unexpected stampede," it reported, blaming the misfortune on "Hindman's mismanagement." Not experiencing the discomforts firsthand, Lane proved less forgiving. On January 15, he felt well enough to issue instructions for the "stragglers who *ran away* . . . [to] report at Gen. Hindman's headquarters, or they will be reported and treated as *deserters*." William Steele, who arrived at Fort Smith on the 8th to take command of the Indian Territory, countered that order. He witnessed the distress personally. "[T]he appearance of everything was of the most gloomy description." The partisan rangers, Steele estimated, numbered only about 150 men, and they did not have "a change of clothing nor an average blanket to the man." To relieve their suffering, Steele permitted Crump to take the remnants of the regiment to the Red River, to refit, resupply, and persuade the "misguided men who have deserted" to return to duty.[19]

Once he emerged from his illness, Walter Lane turned his attention to healing his ailing regiment. When he sent Crump to the Red River, General Steele granted him authority to offer pardons to any deserters who would return, and on February 21, 1863, Lane endorsed the policy by announcing that any unauthorized absentees would "be restored to duty without trial" if they simply reported to the regiment. This reprieve apparently only applied to the rank and file, as the colonel eventually placed Captain Earp under arrest.[20]

On March 15, Lane issued a call for all companies to rendezvous at Camp Crump, near Jefferson. This defied Steele's directive to Crump not to leave the Indian Territory. Lane nevertheless began the process of reorganizing the partisan rangers, and he brought to bear his considerable experience at organizing expeditions, instructing the company commanders to establish camps in their individual counties five days before leaving for Jefferson and to hold new elections for officers. The colonel ordered the arrest of any deserter who refused to take advantage of the pardon. He appointed a new slate of staff officers and consolidated companies, reducing the regiment to the usual ten companies. Lane also promised not to repeat the mistakes of the previous autumn. "Arrangements have been made to supply the regiment with clothes, shoes, tents, and all camp equipage necessary for the comfort of the men." By the end of March, the *Texas Republican* could report, "The gallant Col. W. P. Lane . . . has reorganized his command . . . and will be soon ready to move again to the scene of action."[21]

This reorganization aroused Lane's uncompromising nature. He reserved his harshest behavior for the dismissal of several officers. Although they left the regiment under resignations, the colonel's endorsements suggested that their departures were less than voluntary. Lt. A. R. Chandler, for example, tersely stated his request with a one-line letter. "I hereby tender my Resignation as Second Lieutenant," which Lane heartily endorsed, "Lt Chandler ran twice from the enemy—please except [*sic*] his resignation so I can get rid of him." When Capt. Z. M. P. Motley sought a disability discharge, the colonel frankly assessed, "Capt. Motley never has been able for service."[22]

That spring, Lane once again ran afoul of state officials over the issue of arming his regiment. T. A. Harris, who had succeeded Lane as general of the local brigade of state troops, complained to Austin, "I have been informed . . . that Col Lane intends [impressing] all the arms belonging to the State in this section of country, I hope that the State will vindicate herself for such an outrage." In this episode, at least, the colonel did have General Steele's explicit authority to take what he needed, but he apparently did not seize weapons on the scale he had the autumn before. He was not arrested, but neither did he completely arm his regiment.[23]

In addition to dismissing several officers and risking arrest by state authorities, the colonel defied his commanding officer. He had already contradicted General Steele's orders for the partisan rangers not to leave the Indian Territory, but as his regiment neared readiness, Lane was reluctant to join him. On April 18, Steele wrote to Lane, "No difficulty is experienced in getting there [Texas], but when it is the question to come this way [Fort Smith], a thousand obstacles are presented." By the first of May, however, the general began to understand why Lane refused to heed his calls. "I have heard that Colonel Lane is trying to get ordered in another direction," Steele informed the Confederate war department, and his fears proved correct. Lane did not want to serve in the Indian Territory, with the prospect of raiding into Kansas or biding time at some fort, especially with news arriving from Louisiana reporting battles in the bayou country.[24]

Indeed, in March 1863, preparing for a campaign against Port Hudson, U.S. Gen. Nathaniel P. Banks drove the Confederates, under Gen. Richard Taylor, out of the bayou region west of New Orleans. Taylor, the son of Lane's old commander in Mexico, Zachary Taylor, retreated up the Red River to a point north of Alexandria. On May 7, Banks occupied that town, scarcely 70 miles from the Sabine River and 140 from Marshall. The emergency compelled the recently installed commander of the Trans-Mississippi, E. Kirby Smith, to order the partisan rangers to Taylor at Natchitoches. By May 2, Lane received his marching orders and recalled all furloughs. "[T]he regiment has been ordered to Alexandria to assist in driving back the invaders," he urgently declared. By the 11th, the rangers arrived at Natchitoches, still lacking adequate arms.[25]

On May 13, Banks withdrew his forces from the Red River, to support his assault on Port Hudson. He placed Gen. Godfrey Weitzel, a talented scion of Cincinnati Germans, in charge of the rear guard. When he learned of Banks's movement, Taylor sent Lane ahead to harass the enemy, placing under his command Edwin Waller's Texas Cavalry Battalion, a company from the Seventh Texas Cavalry, and a section of Oliver J. Semmes's battery. The colonel clashed with the forward units of Weitzel's forces at Boyce's Plantation, Lloyd's Bridge, and Tanner's Lane. After a week of skirmishing in the vicinity of Alexandria, the Texans lost two killed and about seventeen wounded and captured, while Weitzel suffered less—one killed, one wounded, and thirteen captured.[26]

Lane held his men in the vicinity of Alexandria, until Smith and Taylor could decide their next move. Taylor wanted to return to the bayou country, compel Banks to relinquish his hold on Port Hudson, and possibly establish a staging ground to retake New Orleans. Smith preferred supporting the besieged Confederates at Vicksburg but reluctantly provided Taylor with three brigades, including Tom Green's Texas cavalry, Alfred Mouton's Louisiana infantry, and a collection of recently arrived regiments commanded by Lane, Joseph Phillips, Charles L. Pyron, and B. Warren Stone. General Smith organized the newcomers into a brigade.

If Lane expected to lead the new brigade, Smith disappointed him by appointing Col. James P. Major instead. Although he had fought at Wilson's Creek as a lieutenant colonel in the Missouri troops, Major served most of the war as a staff officer to Van Dorn, and his colonel's commission came after Lane's. The promotion, however, might have been a case of favoritism. He was the brother-in-law of General Green. Major, however, was an 1852 graduate of West Point and had served in Texas with the Second Dragoons. Although Smith passed over Lane and several other more senior colonels, Major would prove to be a capable cavalry officer.[27]

Meanwhile, General Taylor's immediate objective was Brashear City, which sat on the Bayou Teche, at the end of the incomplete New Orleans, Opelousas, and Great Western Railroad. Commanding the Union forces in the region, Col. Albert Stickney, of the Forty-seventh Massachusetts, arrayed his troops along the railroad, with strong points at Brashear City and the crossings at bayous Boeuf and Lafourche. Taylor settled upon a two-pronged attack, sending Mouton and Green to Brashear City, while he ordered Major east into the Lafourche region, to cut the railroad and prevent the Federals from reinforcing Brashear City.[28]

In mid-June, Major placed Lane at the head of a force that included elements of the partisan rangers and Phillips's cavalry and gave him instructions to charge into the Lafource district and take the town of Thibodeaux. Partisan ranger Barnes described the hard riding in a letter home. "[H]ave traveled every night for 8 nights in succession and only Slept while our horses eat and Slept while riding day & night." They crossed through swampy terrain before entering the fertile flats, where rich plantations once flourished. During the afternoon of the 20th, they neared the outskirts of Thibodeaux.[29]

Lane halted his riders at the bridge that led into town and issued instructions. When he shouted the command to advance, Lane's rangers stormed over the bridge and "in a few minutes," trooper Americus Cartwright wrote, "we were going at full tilt toward town. When we got there the Yankees were ready to meet us but we soon made them take to their heels." Pvt. Benjamin F. Price reported that the "cowardly Yankees . . . fired three rounds before they skedaddled, and then such a yell." Lane chased the fleeing Federals until he reached the works that they had erected at Lafourche Crossing. Sharply directed artillery fire stemmed the charge. "[W]e could not stand,"

Barnes reported, "therefore we had to retreat, and the retreat was like unto the charge without much order." Lane drew his men back to the cover of town and took inventory. They captured about one hundred prisoners—mostly the sick and wounded of the Twelfth Maine and of the One Hundred and Seventy-sixth New York. They also re-captured as many as three hundred former slaves. But most important to the partisan rangers were the stores of food and arms. Lane commandeered a thousand Enfield rifles and at last saw his regiment properly armed.[30]

After Major arrived, he led his brigade west along the railroad and on June 23 arrived at Bayou Beouf. The Yankees had destroyed the railroad bridge crossing the bayou, and on the opposite side, they had constructed a formidable fortress. The Texans seized a number of sugar coolers from nearby plantations and under cover of night fashioned a bridge across the Boeuf. Lane explained, "The coolers were ten feet long and two and a half feet wide, and, being tied end to end, made a very good crossing."[31]

Major delegated command of the assaulting force to Lane, and during the predawn hours of June 24, the colonel took three regiments, crossed over the sugar coolers, and arrayed his men around the fort. The Rebels called the earthen structure Fort Defiance, but the Yankee officers inside would not uphold the spirit of that name. Just as Lane was about to order the advance, the Union commander sent up the flag of surrender. When Major and Lane entered the fort, they discovered that the Federals had just negotiated surrender terms with Green's advance on the opposite side of the fort.[32]

The Texans learned that Mouton and Green had successfully taken Brashear City, capturing even more supplies, arms, and men than Lane had at Thibodeaux. He also captured as many as twelve pieces of artillery, and he wanted to place them on the Mississippi River as soon as possible. He entrusted that mission to General Green, who took his division, including the rangers, across Berwick's Bay, direct to Donaldsonville.[33]

There, Green reconnoitered Fort Butler, the only remaining strong point that the Union held in the Lafourche region. On June 27, he gathered his lieutenants to get their opinion. To his superior, General Mouton, he informed, "They think that an attempt to storm will be attended with great loss and no adequate benefit, even if successful." He fully agreed with their opinion, but when he failed to receive a clear reply from Mouton, he construed his orders to mean that he should move forward with the operation.

That evening, Green informed his officers of their responsibilities in the attack. He placed Lane's rangers, Phillips's regiment, and Philemon Herbert's Seventh Texas Cavalry under Major, with instructions to charge from the woods across nine hundred yards of open field and draw the Union fire from the other regiments, who would rush the fort at various points. Green hired guides to take Major's cavalry through the woods, but Lane never received his. According to official reports, he and the partisan rangers became lost.

Green, nevertheless, continued his attack in the predawn hours of June 28. From two in the morning until the sun rose, the small garrison of two companies from the Twenty-eighth Maine Infantry withstood the onslaught. Despite—or perhaps because of—Green's intricate planning, the attack was a bungled affair, and Lane's inactivity was not the least conspicuous example. When Green finally ordered his troops to withdraw, he counted forty men killed and over two hundred wounded and missing. The concerns of Green and his officers proved disastrously accurate. Phillips's regiment lost its entire field staff. Maj. Denman W. Shannon, commanding the Fifth Texas Cavalry, also perished, and Lane's commander, Colonel Major, was wounded. After he pulled back from the assault, Green received Mouton's message not to engage the fort.[34]

Lane's absence from the battle might have been the most dramatic example of him defying orders for the welfare of his men. He might have intentionally remained in the woods during the assault. In a telling letter, trooper Price believed that Lane had spared his life. "We were under orders to take the Fort at all hazard, but Col Lane knowing the utter impossibility of taking the place would not carry his men into the slaughter pen." Whatever the circumstances that prevented the partisan rangers from engaging the enemy, General Green refused to criticize Lane. "There is no blame attached to Colonel Lane for the mistake."[35]

After the disaster at Fort Butler, Green withdrew south and established headquarters at Paincourtville. As the senior colonel in the brigade, Lane assumed command in place of the wounded Major. In mid-July, Green discovered Yankees advancing down both sides of the Lafourche from Donaldsonville, and he intended to check them at Cox's Plantation. He instructed Lane to post his brigade on the east side of the bayou. Late in the afternoon, two Federal brigades reached the Rebel pickets. Their forces consisted mostly of New York, Massachusetts, and Louisiana volunteers, commanded by Col. Nathan A. M. Dudley, facing Green on the west, and Col. Joseph S. Morgan, confronting Lane on the east. As night fell, each side positioned their pickets and spent an uneasy night on their arms.[36]

At nine in the morning on July 13, the Federal troops moved forward. Amid the plantation buildings and fields of tall corn, Green and Dudley grappled with one another. Lane, however, experienced little resistance. He quickly captured Morgan's pickets. Without their intelligence, Morgan was not prepared for Lane's charge—probably carried out on foot in dragoon fashion—and Lane broke through the Yankee lines, scattering Morgan's command. Without Morgan's support, Dudley withdrew from the field.[37]

Lane won the day in his first real experience as a brigade commander, breaking through Morgan's force, which, in effect, outflanked Dudley. Perhaps unknown to Lane and Green, however, the colonel did not deserve much of the credit. U. S. Gen. Cuvier Grover—division commander—explained, "Colonel Morgan fell back without cause. . . . [He] behaved badly." Apparently, Morgan was drunk and failed to adequately prepare his men for battle. A court martial would later convict him of "[m]isbehavior before the enemy" and "[d]runkness on duty," but General Banks dismissed the court's findings and placed Morgan back on duty.[38]

At Cox's Plantation, the Federals counted heavy losses. With forty killed and over two hundred wounded and missing, Yankee casualties dwarfed those reported by Green. The Texans, according to the general, suffered nine deaths, with only about twenty-four wounded. "The great disparity of loss is most wonderful," Green exclaimed, "and can only be accounted for . . . the enemy's panic in our first impetuous charge." The First Texas Partisan Rangers, however, experienced a harsh blow when Maj. A. D. Burns fell during the charge. He died two days later. Capt. William P. Saufley of Jefferson eventually replaced him.[39]

The prisoners that the Texans captured, however, informed them of more bad news. On July 4, Vicksburg had surrendered to Union forces. Five days later, Port Hudson followed, and the men who fought Lane and Green at Cox's Plantation were recent arrivals from the latter siege. The Texans might not have understood the larger consequences of these reverses, but the immediate effect doomed Taylor's dream of retaking New Orleans. On the 12th, Smith wrote to Taylor, congratulated him on a fine campaign but then warned, "Any occupation of New Orleans can now only be temporary." He instead ordered Taylor to arrange his troops so as to defend the Red River. At the end of August, Lane took a forty-day leave. During that time, the partisan rangers under Major Saufley fought at the battle of Bayou Bourbeau, performing well in Lane's and Crump's absence.[40]

Lane, however, still smarted from his lack of promotion. On January 3, 1864, he met with J. D. McAdoo, who had recently accepted an appointment as brigadier general of the Texas state troops. Gov. Pendleton Murrah, a fellow resident of Marshall, sent McAdoo to find Lane and ask him about a similar appointment. Lane relied on his sense of duty for an answer. According to McAdoo, "[I]f it were deemed best for the public service . . . he would cheerfully take such a command," but Lane did not reveal his personal wishes. "[H]e would leave the matter without any expression of desire in the promises." McAdoo, however, sensed the colonel's dissatisfaction. "I find that he *feels* the placing of Col Majors, a junior officer, in command of the Brigade, of which Col. Lane is Sen. Col. [is unfair]." Lane accepted the commission but did not consider it a permanent appointment, or a priority over his regiment. In January 1864, when he returned to active duty, Lane found the partisan rangers in winter quarters at Virginia Point—the landside end of the two-mile railroad bridge that crossed to Galveston Island.[41]

During his absence, General Smith sent Green's cavalry to Texas, to counter Banks's attempts to invade the state. Although he failed, Banks would try again in March, when he sent a flotilla of thirteen gunboats, under the command of David D. Porter, into the Red River in Louisiana. In support, Andrew J. Smith led twenty-one veteran regiments detached from William T. Sherman's army. This movement represented the opening of General Banks's final push for Texas. He intended to march up the Red and take Shreveport—the Rebel headquarters of the Trans-Mississippi department—and establish a staging point for an invasion of Texas.

As early as February 21, Smith and Taylor recognized the massing of Federal troops as a portend of a new offensive. On March 5, Smith wired John B. Magruder to send Green's division back to Louisiana. Taylor, in the meantime, began a series of reluctant withdrawals from Alexandria, which eventually led him to the small village of Mansfield—scarcely twenty miles from the Sabine River and the Texas state line. All the while, he struggled against E. Kirby Smith's plan to hunker down and defend Shreveport against a siege.[42]

On April 6, Green's cavalry reached Mansfield. Sitting on his horse, General Taylor watched the partisan rangers pass along the street and commented, "Boys, I am glad to see you." The small town teemed with army personnel preparing for the Federal advance. The martial setting inspired inexperienced soldiers, such as Harvey Medford, with ardor for their cause. "I am very much elated with the hope of repelling the Yankees. . . . We are fighting for matters real and tangible, they for matters abstract and intangible." He did not elaborate on what he meant by "real and tangible."[43]

Sometime during the movement from Texas, Smith reorganized the cavalry arm of his army, placing General Green in command of all the mounted troops. As a result, General Major moved up to head the division. Lane took command of the brigade, which consisted of the four cavalry regiments that fought together the summer before. All had different commanders: Crump, George W. Baylor, Isham Chisum, George T. Madison, and Charles L. Pyron.[44]

On March 26, General Banks arrived in Alexandria. With his own and

A. J. Smith's divisions and with Porter's sailors, he counted over thirty thousand men. After a week, Banks put his forces into motion up the Red River and on April 3, arrived at Grand Ecore, about four miles north of Natchitoches. Unfamiliar with the terrain, he continued along the road to Shreveport, which led to the west—away from the Red River and away from the protection of Porter's gunboats. This was Banks's key mistake of the campaign. His route took him deep into what Taylor termed a "pine desert."[45] Banks, however, was unconcerned. He correctly surmised that Kirby Smith would not contest his advance until he reached Shreveport. The New England general, however, could not predict that Taylor would defy his superior's wishes.

The old Camino Real, over which Banks passed, offered adequate space for his troops, but twenty miles west of Natchitoches, he turned off the route to follow the Mansfield road, via Pleasant Hill. Here, the dense pine forest squeezed the road into a narrow path that forced Banks to extend his line of march. At noon on April 7, Harai Robinson, commanding the advance units of Albert L. Lee's cavalry division, encountered the first Rebel skirmishers—portions of the Fifth and Seventh Texas Cavalry regiments under Arthur P. Bagby.[46]

Earlier that morning, Taylor dispatched Lane and his brigade from Mansfield down the road toward Pleasant Hill. He arrived just before Robinson's men clashed with Bagby's pickets, driving them back toward Lane, who rushed his soldiers forward to a clearing called Wilson's Farm. After ordering the horses tied in the woods, he arrayed his men behind a fence. He instructed Colonel Madison "to take two hundred men, pass through the field, give them a volley, and then fall back in apparent confusion, as they would follow him and fall into our ambuscade," but Madison exhibited "more zeal than discretion," and foiled Lane's plans. "[He] pitched into regular fight with them and held them in check for half an hour." Lee reported that Madison "charged with great impetuosity," and drove two regiments back toward Pleasant Hill. Gen. Thomas J. Lucas brought up his brigade in support and forced the Texans back to Lane's position at Wilson's Farm.[47]

The Texans held their ground for several hours, as Robinson and Lucas attempted to turn their flank. Lane extended his lines over a mile. He rode upon his nervous horse, Richard III, from one end to the other, yelling instructions to his brigade. When he learned that his men were running short of ammunition, Lane decided to withdraw to the safety of Green's main body, posted four miles to the rear at a place called Carroll's Mill. Lane stationed three companies just behind a rise, as he moved the rest of his men out. "The enemy, seeing we had ceased firing, made a charge on us, yelling and whooping, thinking we were running," Lane proudly recalled, "As they came over the brow of the eminence . . . we gave them a fire in the face at thirty yards, which emptied a good many saddles and sent them back quicker than they came."[48]

The fighting at Wilson's Farm was the most intense that Lane had experienced during the Civil War. A member of Bagby's command attested, "Here one of the most desperate fights of the campaign took place. . . . For three hours the brave boys under their valorous commanders . . . held their own against treble their numbers." Private Medford accompanied Major as he rode down toward the sound of battle and found the road crowded with ambulances evacuating the wounded. He boasted, "Our brigade, Col. W. P. Lane commanding, have fought and defeated the enemy today with spartan [*sic*] courage." General Lee and the Yankees disagreed, but both sides would have to wait until morning to settle the issue. Lane's affair at Wilson's Farm cost him one hundred soldiers, but it served to alert Banks that the Rebels intended to contest his advance and provided Taylor another day to choose his ground and bring up last-minute reinforcements.[49]

At dawn on April 8, Lee roused his men and set them into motion. With the infantry under William J. Landram, Lee advanced cautiously but steadily drove back Major's skirmishers until he reached a large clearing. In the middle, an eminence rose to mask what lay behind. Landram brushed aside the skirmishers, took the hill, and then discovered Taylor's 8,800 men waiting in battle formation. Lee quickly sent word for reinforcements. He managed to gather 4,800 soldiers. When he consulted with Banks, Lee assured his commander that if he tried to advance, "we would be most gloriously flogged." Banks conceded to wait.

Taylor posted his men just inside the woods along the Sabine River-Bayou Pierre road, which crossed the Mansfield-Pleasant Hill route. The crossroads immediately in his rear, Taylor could easily maneuver his forces, arrayed in a long arc facing the clearing. Lane and his brigade took their positions to the extreme left. Directly across the field, Lucas posted his cavalry.[50]

At four in the afternoon, Taylor ordered the advance. The Texas cavalry charged on foot through the woods. "[I]t was a grand sight to see our men as they swept forward yelling like demons," Colonel Baylor recalled. Posted behind a fence and a hastily prepared breastwork of felled timber, Lucas met Lane and his men with muskets and a two-gun battery. The Texans advanced to within twenty yards of the Union position before they stalled. Riding alongside Major, Private Medford observed, "The strife of this battle is terrible. Many of our men are falling. The whole heavens are replete with destructive missiles. There is not a safe place anywhere upon this battlefield." From the opposite side of the field, a Yankee soldier observed, "Dead and wounded Confederates lay in win-rows." After the failed charge, Lane exhorted his men to continue, but even the veteran colonel found the intensity of Yankee fire disconcerting. "I must acknowledge to being a good deal demoralized during this *scrimmage,* for . . . I had six ball holes through my coat, two of which drew blood."[51]

After several stalled advances, Major's division, including Lane's brigade, turned the Yankee right flank, while the Texas and Louisiana infantry broke through the center, sending Lee's men flying to the rear. U.S. Gen. William B. Franklin came up with fresh infantry and momentarily bolstered the Union line, but Lee's men were in full flight. With another charge, Lane led his men forth. While his brigade rushed forward, a minnie ball caught the colonel in the hip and knocked him to the ground.[52]

The fighting continued down the Pleasant Hill road. Although Gen. Alfred Mouton lay dead on the field, the Confederate infantry pursued Lee and Franklin to a clearing called Pleasant Grove, where the Union set yet another line. Green's cavalry failed to support their comrades. Instead, they plundered Lee's supply train, and the Yankees checked the Rebel advance. Taylor and Banks clashed again the next day at Pleasant Hill, and although the Federals held their ground, Banks decided to withdraw back toward Alexandria. Once Porter's gunboats safely passed the rapids, Banks continued to Simmsport. The Red River Campaign represented Banks's third and final attempt to invade Texas. Pvt. W. A. Lanier, of Lane's rangers, proudly declared, "Gen. Banks never got to cut the Texas wheat."[53]

While his comrades chased Banks down the Red River, Lane returned to Marshall, and at his brother's home, his nieces, Mary Jane and Louisa Paye Lane, attended his wound. Sometime during the summer, his brigade arrived at the outskirts of town en route to the Rio Grande. Lane was still unable to leave his home, so the soldiers sent his nephew, Walter, Jr.—recently released as a war prisoner—to retrieve the colonel's horse, Richard III. Demonstrating their feelings toward Lane, the brigade gave "Old Dick" a cheer, which the colonel could hear from his bed. After two years of service with the adventurer, these men had experienced both the harsh and the kind paternalistic personas that he projected. Their warm regards suggested that they accepted and appreciated both. Instead of going to South Texas, however, Confederate authorities recalled the brigade to Louisiana.[54]

Although Lane appreciated the brigade's expression of affection, he still sought an official acknowledgment of his sacrifice, experience, and abilities. In July 1864, E. Kirby Smith asked his lieutenants for recommendations to fill several vacant brigadier positions. Despite the feelings Lane might have had toward him and his appointment the year before, Major provided the colonel with an impressive reference. On the 20th, the general testified, "Col. W. P. Lane has been in the service since the opening of the war . . . and has [proved] himself worthy of this position on many battle fields." Major reminded Smith that Lane had received a special commendation from P. G. T. Beauregard, after the engagement at Farmington, Mississippi. He mentioned Lane's service in Louisiana and noted that the colonel was wounded at Mansfield while leading his men. Major assured Smith that General Green, who had fallen in battle at Blair's Landing, had implicitly trusted him. He added, "I know that his wish was to have Col Lane promoted."[55]

Acting on Major's recommendation, General Smith also endorsed Lane's promotion. In passing the letter to the president, he noted "I would respectfully recommend the promotion of Coln Lane as being next to Coln [William P.] Hardeman the most deserving of the Texas Colns." Although among a select few, Lane was yet again the second choice. A war department official examined the data and further declared, "[Xavier B.] Debray, Hardeman, and Lane are pronounced superior cavalry officers—the best brigade commanders in the Trans-Mississippi." The bureaucracy—especially one of a beleaguered government—was slow to process the promotions. On December 23, Richmond informed Smith that the president would nominate Lane, along with Hardeman and Thomas Harrison. This was good news for the colonel, but he would still have to wait for an act of Congress, and the war might end before that occurred.[56]

According to his niece, Lane ended his recuperation at Marshall prematurely. "[L]ong before the healing of [his] wound, he mounted the magnificent 'Richard the 3rd' . . . and was off to join his command." Perhaps his eagerness stemmed from the opportunity to lead a division. Smith dispatched Lane's and Hardeman's brigades to the vicinity of Camden, in southern Arkansas and placed Lane in command of both. By August 12, Lane reached his division, waiting on the Tensas Bayou in northeastern Louisiana, and moved into southwestern Arkansas. For the remainder of the summer and fall of 1864, he and his soldiers remained idle, variously stationed at points between Monticello and Washington. When Sterling Price returned from a raid into Missouri, Smith ordered John A. Wharton's entire cavalry corps, including Lane's division, back to Texas. On December 1, Lane and his men passed through Marshall and established winter quarters in the vicinity of Crockett.[57]

During the winter of 1864 and 1865, the war news that reached Texas was gloomy for the Confederacy. The Texas legislature, nevertheless, denounced the idea of reunification, and communities across the state held mass meetings to voice their support for continuing the war effort. When Lane and his division marched through Henderson County, the local reporter interviewed a number of the soldiers, asking them of their opinion on the issue of surrender. "We . . . found them without exception, opposed to any peace, save upon condition of our being acknowledged as a separate and independent nation."[58]

Meanwhile, in preparation for the campaigns of the next year, Kirby Smith reorganized his cavalry. By March, he removed Lane from the division and placed him in command of a new brigade that included George W. Carter's Twenty-first Texas Cavalry, Madison's, and Edwin Waller's cavalry regiments. Lane's old regiment, the First Texas Partisan Rangers, joined William P. Hardeman's brigade.[59]

In an order dated February 1865, Smith referred to Lane as brigadier general. Due to the distance from Richmond, a number of Trans-Mississippi colonels received their promotions directly from Smith, but a few never received their confirmations. Fortunately for Lane, he still had friends working on his behalf at the Confederate capital. Supporting Jefferson Davis's nomination of Lane, Missouri representative Thomas L. Snead testified to the Texan's merits. Snead had served as adjutant general on Sterling Price's staff and remembered Lane's service in Arkansas and Mississippi. He wrote on the 11th, "I know that he was one of the most gallant, experienced, & skillful officers in that army & . . . was on more than one occasion selected to conduct important operations." On March 18, the Confederate Congress at last confirmed Lane's promotion to brigadier general. At the end of they day, the congressmen adjourned and never reconvened. Sixteen days later, the capitol fell to the Union.[60]

By the end of March, Lane learned that the Southern congress had confirmed his promotion. He did not have long to enjoy it. The somber news of the fall of Richmond and Robert E. Lee's surrender arrived in Texas by mid-April. On the 21st, General Smith officially announced it to the Trans-Mississippi and implored his soldiers, "Stand by your colors—maintain your discipline." With headquarters at Brenham, Texas, General Lane received the news in a dispatch from Magruder. Lane ordered his brigade to the parade ground the next day. "Feeling that it was not only my military, but religious duty to make them a speech on this occasion, I laid awake until 2 o'clock concocting it." The general wanted to inspire his men to heed Smith's call and "stand to their colors." Unfortunately, he did not write it down. At eight the next morning, Lane stood before his men. "I pulled off my plumed hat and gave it an oratorical flourish. . . . Just at that moment the speech took wings unto itself and I could not recollect one single word of it. . . . I sat there and looked at the soldiers, and they looked at me in astonishment at my not going on." Finally, the old soldier dismissed formalities and approached his soldiers with his more familiar, personal manner. "After explaining the situation to them, they all promised they would stand by their flag until they were regularly disbanded. All of which they did." Soon after the speech, Lane moved his brigade to an encampment between the Brazos and Little Rivers. There, he waited to hear from Magruder if the Confederacy yet lived to continue the fight west of the Mississippi.[61]

Although the general remembered differently, many of his men did not "stand by their flag." In the Twenty-first Texas, trooper William P. Zuber witnessed how his comrades reacted to Lane's news. "To my chagrin, I found the men of our regiment broken in spirit and utterly ineffective. . . . They had lost hope, expecting the conscript law to hold them in service indefinitely." Although he had hoped to inspire his friends by example, Zuber soon applied for his own discharge. Having received the approval of his company and regimental commanders, he approached Lane, who refused to sign, claiming that he did not have the authority.[62]

Throughout May 1865, as gloomy tidings from the East portended the end of the Confederacy, half the men in Lane's brigade mustered themselves out of service. Many other Texas regiments resolved to go home by companies and await word. Company A, of the First Texas Partisan Rangers, returned to Marshall en masse. Other units, such as a garrison at Galveston, simply quit. On the Little River, Lane probably took the same attitude as the commander of the Twenty-first Texas, Maj. Benjamin D. Chenoweth, who "became weary of waiting for us to take absence without leave," as Zuber remembered. One morning, Chenoweth ordered the remaining men to take up the march. "We obeyed . . . with the major taking the lead toward Bryan. I was nearly the rearmost, but gradually the major dropped back till he became the rearmost. Then he dropped completely out of sight." The leaderless band continued east as, one by one, a soldier would drift to the rear and disappear. By the time he reached Bryan, Zuber found himself riding alone. The Twenty-first Texas and what was left of Lane's brigade determined for themselves that the war was over and vanished into the landscape.[63]

Back in Marshall, editor Robert W. Loughery blasted those men who left the ranks. "Three hundred thousand soldiers East of the Mississippi and at least fifty thousand under arms, in this department, have concluded, as if by preconcertion [*sic*], to abandon the contest." Not afraid of exaggeration, Loughery described the conditions in Texas. "Three weeks ago there was a large army, well organized, thoroughly drilled and disciplined, abundantly provisioned, and with an immense accumulation of ordnance stores. They met disasters manfully. . . . With no enemy nearer than two hundred miles, the soldiers determined . . . [not] to wait for a formal surrender."[64]

While riding through East Texas, General Smith witnessed the abandonment of his department. On May 13, he summoned the governors of Texas, Louisiana, Arkansas, and Missouri to Marshall. He wanted their opinion of the possibility of continued resistance. They unanimously agreed that Smith should seek surrender terms. Accordingly, the commander of the Trans-Mississippi met with U.S. Gen. E. R. S. Canby at New Orleans, and on the 26th, the same day that Loughery issued his diatribe against the deserting soldiers, Smith formally surrendered his army. The Smith-Canby agreement included Lane and his brigade.[65]

With the Confederacy destroyed, a number of questions confronted Lane. Would the victorious Federals punish former rebels, like himself, as traitors? As a forty-eight-year-old man, was adventure a realistic option for escape, as it had been in his younger days? If he returned to Marshall, could he salvage the ties of family and community that he began to build before the war? In the summer of 1865, General Lane faced an uncertain future.

• 10 •

CITIZEN LANE, 1865-87

Although he wrote it in 1887, Walter Lane concluded his autobiography with the end of the Civil War. This choice suggests that he deemed the intervening twenty-two years as unworthy of recollection. Perhaps he did not wish to dwell upon his business failures or political disappointments. Perhaps he felt that redeeming white rule in Harrison County, nursing Marshall through an epidemic, enforcing federal law, or doling out drought relief did not belong in a document dedicated to adventure. Indeed, Lane had made his compromise with family and community, and he would stand with them and confront the uncertainty created by the collapse of the Confederacy.

On June 17, 1865, about the same time Lane would have returned, Lt. Col. Lloyd Wheaton and the Eighth Illinois Infantry arrived in Marshall and inaugurated Federal occupation of Texas. He announced the beginning of Reconstruction and ordered the seizure of all public property. He did not explicitly declare the end of slavery, but two days later, Gen. Gordon Granger landed at Galveston and issued his "Juneteenth" proclamation—the 19th being the day that many freed people of Texas and their descendants celebrated their emergence from slavery. Rather than defying occupation, the citizens of Harrison County acknowledged the war's end and agreed to cooperate with Wheaton. While they expressed their compliance, the citizens hedged their hopes for the future. In regard to the freed people, they promised "to care for them as we have been accustomed."[1]

But the times were different. When Lane arrived in Marshall, the *Texas Republican* did not celebrate his homecoming, as it had when he passed through the previous December. He did not arrive at the head of defiant troops, pledging to fight to the last. Instead, he came alone to offer his surrender under the terms of the Smith-Canby accords. On June 24, the general signed his parole, administered by Capt. Daniel Sayer of the Illinois troops.[2]

By August, Lane began the bureaucratic process to regain his U.S. citizenship by applying for a presidential pardon. As a general in the Confederate Army, he did not qualify for the general amnesty offered by Andrew Johnson, who had ascended to the presidency after the assassination of Abraham Lincoln. On the 18th, Lane signed his oath and sent the application to Gov. Andrew J. Hamilton, explaining that "at the time of Secession it was not only not considered a crime, but a duty to support the State in the defense of that doctrine"—a far different explanation than his later claim to an adventuristic impulse. Regardless of his motivations, Lane understood that the end of the Civil War had made such a stance illegal. He assured the governor that since returning to Marshall, he had quietly entered civilian life and pledged his fealty to the United States and its constitution. The general concluded, recognizing Hamilton's and Johnson's magnanimity, "I am more and more resolved as time developes [*sic*] that the South is by the principles of your administration obtaining under the circumstances all that can be reasonably asked."[3]

Lane's application received the endorsement of the recently installed county officials, as law required. Judge J. B. Williamson testified, "[Lane] is a good citizen, so far as he can be, ready and willing to obey the laws and support the Government." Chief Justice Davis B. Bonfoey added that he had known Lane for sixteen years and emphasized the general's former service during the Texas Revolution and the U.S.-Mexican War. County clerks Alexander R. Woodall and Dr. William Evans further testified, "[W]e have Known Mr. Lane for many years and certify to his unimpeachable character and standing in the community. . . . His character during the late hostilities was that of a brave chivalrous officer and unconnected with petty annoyances or cruelties to prisoners." On February 21, 1866, Governor Hamilton approved Lane's application and forwarded it to Washington, D.C.[4]

While seeking to restore his citizenship, Lane also sought to restore his fortunes. He once again turned to the mercantile trade, joining the Ward family in a new partnership. In August 1866, with W. R. D. Ward—the patriarch—and his son, Albert G. Ward, and son-in-law, Albert G. Turney, Lane formed W. R. D. Ward and Company. The firm sold wholesale and retail groceries. Using Ward's influence with railroad concerns and owning part interest in W. F. Rapley and Company in Shreveport, they enjoyed a distinct advantage over most of their competition. In Shreveport, at the recently established terminus of the Southern Pacific Railroad, the Ward and

Rapley companies bought shares in a wharf boat that brought goods up the Red River from the Mississippi.

With a storefront located on the south side of the courthouse square, Lane served as operating partner. On August 23, he explained to their patrons that with easy access to the Mississippi, "we are prepared to Receive and Forward freights consigned to us, at less cost or fire risk to the shipper, greater dispatch, with less exposure to wet and mud, than any other house in the city." The general assured low costs and sound business practices. "We are prepared and are determined to sell our entire stock at *Shreveport prices or less,* including transportation. For it is a well established adage, that 'Goods properly bought are half sold.'" Ward and Company hoped to reap some of the prosperity that blessed Harrison County in the immediate post-war years. On February 18, 1867, while engrossed in his familiar role as a merchant, Walter Lane celebrated his fiftieth birthday.

Despite the auspicious start, Ward and Company suffered two setbacks before the firm reached its second anniversary. On March 27, 1867, a fire broke out on the square, costing Ward and Company $2,500 in damages. On April 2, south of Henderson, two men robbed and killed W. R. D. Ward and his traveling companion. Despite the fire and the loss of their senior partner, the company continued to operate under the same name. In the three years following the end of the Civil War, General Lane prospered and re-established community ties with Marshall and Harrison County.[5]

Reconstruction, for some East Texans like Lane, was not as bad as they first feared, but at the national level, radical Republicans in Congress vehemently protested against President Johnson's leniency toward the South. They looked at communities like Harrison County and saw former Confederates returning to power. Certainly, many were moved by the spirit of vengeance—wishing to punish the South for its crime of slavery, secession, and civil war. Most, however, expressed genuine concern that four years of destruction did not resolve the issues that had caused the war. During the mid-term elections of 1866, the radical Republicans won a majority in Congress and then initiated their own version of Reconstruction. In March 1867, they passed the Reconstruction Act, which placed the South under military rule, and decreed that they would not re-admit any former Confederate state until it drafted a new constitution and ratified the Fourteenth Amendment, that ostensibly guaranteed black, male suffrage. Not until April 1870 did the citizens of Texas ratify a new constitution. Military authorities turned over the government to Gov. Edmund J. Davis, and the state rejoined the Union in control of the Republicans.

In Harrison County, the first sign of trouble for the white elite occurred with the voter registration of 1867. Those who had taken an oath of allegiance to the United States and took part in the rebellion, were disqualified from voting and holding office. Even without this provision, Harrison County blacks greatly outnumbered whites. With the rolls complete, the 2,500 black voters of Harrison County overwhelmed the fewer than 900 white voters.

In response, on June 2, 1868, Harrison County Democrats organized the Conservative Club. The association sought to destroy the Republican basis of power with the black community by claiming it as their own. On July 20, the Conservative Club of the Marshall precinct elected officers, including Walter Lane as treasurer—a clear indication of his loyalties. They intended to use a two-pronged strategy—friendly persuasion and economic coercion. They passed a resolution, stating "That he who is not with us is against us, and that each and every member . . . pledges himself not to give employment, aid, or assistance in any manner to any man, white or black, whose name is not enrolled as a member." If they expected to earn a living, Harrison County blacks would have to join and vote as the club directed. This strategy intended to gain control of both the votes and labor of former slaves.[6]

But the puzzle of regaining the control of freed people's labor continued to vex cotton producers. They ultimately turned to arrangements such as tenant farming, sharecropping, and crop lien—variations of a system designed to couple free labor with a planter and merchant capital. A small farmer could work a plot with equipment and seed, provided by a planter or financier. The two parties would then split the proceeds of the crop, or the farmer would pay rent with his produce. The practice emerged in East Texas by early 1867, and because Marshall had no banks at this time, merchants supplied most of the capital for Harrison County sharecroppers and crop-lien farmers.[7]

Ward and Company participated in this new system. In 1869, they made their first tentative steps, but by the spring of 1871, crop-lien was a regular part of their operations. Between February 1871 and August 1873, the firm entered into 54 contracts, totaling $4911.18. Most of their patrons were former slaves. Of the 48 identified farmers, 40, or 83 percent, were freedmen. The company tended to lend larger amounts to their white patrons, who received an average of $154.64 to black farmers' $78.73. This imbalance certainly reflected a racial bias, but it may have also represented a bias in favor of landowners, whom Lane and his associates judged as better credit risks.[8]

While Ward and Company continued to operate profitably, General Lane also personally prospered. He dabbled in other areas, such as insurance. In October 1868, he announced the opening of an agency representing the James River Insurance Company of Montreal, Virginia. Advertising in both Marshall and Jefferson papers, the general promised, "Special attention given to insuring, at low rates, dwelling houses in town and the country." In 1870, he only claimed $200.00 of real and personal property, but Mary Jane, who lived with her uncle, still held the deed to their home, valued at $6000.00—well above average for white Harrison County households. During this time, Lane also bought and sold several Marshall town lots.[9]

In May 1873, however, W. R. D. Ward and Company began to exhibit signs of financial distress. On the 9th, Lane assumed the title to his home from his niece and mortgaged it. On behalf of the company, the general borrowed $1500.00 from Julie B. Hall—widow of wealthy planter Montreville J. Hall. This was enough to cover the $1300.00 the company loaned to local farmers in 1873, but two months later, on July 5, Lane and Albert Ward obtained another loan of almost $2500.00 from Mrs. Ann C. Burnham—the widow of Ariel M. Burnham, merchant and Lane's former quartermaster. The partners stated that they would use the money "for the purpose of . . . carrying on our said business." For security, they used their entire stock and any future additions but reserved the right to continue to sell their merchandise in the usual manner. On March 12, 1874, Lane could not pay Hall's note against his home, so he borrowed $1500.00 from Ann C. Burch, again using his house as collateral. Two days later, however, he collected on a loan that he had made the year before, paid off Burch, and cleared the title to his home. Lane and his partners left no explanation as to why they sought help from the widows of the county. Perhaps they did not want to obligate themselves to their fellow merchants, who were their competitors. Perhaps the other Marshall businesses also felt financial strain.[10]

Indeed, the problems that plagued Ward and Company might have been symptomatic of a weak national economy. The Panic of 1873 sent the United States headlong into a depression, and few areas in the country were immune to the economic downturn. Although the initial plight of Ward and Company might not have been related to the national crisis, it doomed whatever chances the partners had of rectifying their financial straits.

In the autumn, at the height of the panic, Marshall faced another, more devastating crisis. In late September, local physicians diagnosed the first case of yellow fever. The disease first appeared in New Orleans. Mosquitos carrying the virus were likely hidden away in the cargoes that plied the Mississippi to Memphis and the Red to Shreveport, where the disease emerged in August. The infected *Aedes aegypti* probably arrived in Marshall aboard the Southern Pacific Railroad. The unfortunate victims not only suffered

A note on the reverse of this photograph dates it to 1873. That was a troubling year for Lane. His partnership with W. R. D. Ward and Company failed, he helped nurse Marshall through a devastating yellow fever epidemic, and he helped white conservatives confront Harrison County's black majority at the polls. Thanks to Christian Dovel for digital retouching. Unknown, Walter P. Lane photograph, ca. 1873. Courtesy of the Harrison County Historical Museum, Marshall, Tex.

influenza-like symptoms but also a frightful "black vomit," a viscid mix of digested blood and mucus. The disease struck at the liver, producing the jaundiced appearance that inspired its name.

Uncertain of how to prevent or treat yellow fever, Marshall residents were helpless as the sudden outbreak paralyzed their town. On October 1, the *Panola Watchman,* in neighboring Carthage, recorded eleven deaths within two days at Marshall. Those who had the means abandoned the town. In addition to the health crisis, the epidemic also threatened the town's economy. As was typical in cities where the disease appeared, local leaders tried to minimize the perception of danger. On October 1, Lane and several other community leaders wrote to the widely circulated *Galveston News* and dismissed the outbreak. They explained that the few cases in their town were the result of people fleeing Shreveport "with the disease [already] in their systems." They suggested that most of the victims suffered from a less dangerous fever and assured, "We have never had, and have not now, any epidemic. Our city is very healthy. There is very little sickness of any kind, and none serious." By October 29, the *Watchman* observed, "Business is entirely suspended; few stores are opened. The town is almost deserted."[11]

To deal with the epidemic, town leaders formed an emergency relief committee, with Rev. Andrew E. Clemmons as chair and Lane as treasurer. Mary Jane remembered that when Clemmons exhibited symptoms of the fever himself, he urged Lane to leave town. "General, your life is very precious to us, take all the precaution you can." According to his niece, Lane refused. "He answered as he was an 'old bachelor' he preferred seeing others getting their families out of reach of the terrible scourge." While other businesses closed down, Lane kept the store of Ward and Company opened and provided the sick with food and clothing.

By October 27th, the community had suffered sixty deaths, but that night, Marshall experienced an early frost. The residents hoped that it would curtail the disease. Although they did not understand, their instincts proved correct. The cold weather killed the infected mosquitos, and the yellow fever released its grip on the East Texas community. Fortunately, the late arrival of the disease spared Marshall the ghastly numbers of deaths that places such as New Orleans and Shreveport experienced during the 1873 outbreak. Even so, sixty dead represented three percent of the town's 1,920 citizens enumerated in the 1870 census.[12]

Racial tensions, however, persisted in Harrison County. Military Reconstruction had ended in Texas in April 1870, and much of the state returned to the white-dominated Democratic Party, which took control of the legislature. They arranged for new elections in December 1873 in a bid to oust

Republican governor Edmund J. Davis, who represented the last vestige of statewide Reconstruction. At the polls in Marshall, the frustrations of white voters nearly erupted into violence.

On election day, December 3, 1873, the Republican-controlled officials opened the polls early. When they arrived to vote, the white citizens found their way impeded by black men crowding around the polls, casting their own votes. The Democrats waited for the crowd to disperse, but by early afternoon, the white population convinced themselves that the Republicans were deliberately barring them from voting. The *Iron Age,* a partisan Democratic newspaper in Marshall, supported that notion. "[A]mong the crowd some of the colored men declared that they had possession of the polls, and intended to keep it, and prevent the whites from voting."

The Democrats hastily organized a meeting to consider their options. They appointed three delegates to "demand the exercise of their [voting] privilege." The three men appointed were all former Confederates—Jonathan D. Rudd, an up-and-coming party member who had served as lieutenant in the Texas cavalry; Alexander T. Hawthorne, a general from Arkansas who moved to Marshall after the war; and General Lane. According to Mary Jane, the three men confronted Sheriff Stillwell H. Russell and demanded him to clear the polls for the white men to vote. The sheriff promised to do so in half an hour, but Lane and company were not satisfied, believing that the Republicans would close the polls before that time. Lane reportedly challenged Russell's promise: "No, right now! Do you understand that it is necessary for this to be done without delay? And if it comes to trouble it will not be with the negroes, but with their white leaders and YOU will be the first to be dealt with!" The *Iron Age* reported a similar, even more threatening, conversation: "[The Democrats] would not be responsible for the consequences, and blood would flow." Under these assurances, the sheriff agreed and addressed the black congregation from the balcony of the courthouse, ordering them away from the polls.[13]

Although the white Democrats managed to cast their votes, they failed to carry the election for their candidates. Supported by the black majority in the county, Republicans retained control of the local government and returned their delegation to the state legislature. The Democrats statewide, however, soundly defeated their opponents. Although the state still needed a new constitution, the installation of Richard Coke, a former Confederate, as governor marked the end of Reconstruction in Texas, but not for Harrison County. The election of December 1873 further demonstrated the impotence of the white vote in the county.

In the spring of 1874, however, the white elite of the county realized that they could nominate and support Democratic candidates for statewide and national elections. Lane's military career and his role in clearing the polls for the white vote convinced local party leaders of his potential for some high office, but they needed a larger forum with which to inform those outside of Harrison County of the general's merits. The Dallas *Herald*—perhaps unintentionally—came to their aid.

With its April 1 issue, the *Herald* published a biographical essay about Walter Lane. Written by John Henry Brown, the article recounted the general's military exploits, touching on his experience at San Jacinto, the Surveyors' Fight, and the U.S.-Mexican War, but focused on his Civil War career. Brown intended that this article would be the first in a series to appear in the *Herald*, "to be used by future historians," but by spicing his narrative with flourishes that testified to Lane's bravery and honor, he also seemed to anticipate Lane's bid for political office. The author noted the general's "noble and brave heart . . . bemoaning the desolation of the once great county of his residence where the poor, ignorant negroes are largely in the ascendant." Although Lane was a bachelor, Brown pointed out the general's strong community ties. "General Lane . . . has always occupied high social position and dispensed a generous hospitality." Brown also noted Lane's recent business failure. "[W]e regret exceedingly to learn of late, that reverses have come," but assured his readers that during the unfortunate Panic of 1873, Lane conducted himself "in such manner as in no wise to lessen, but rather to augment, the firm hold he has ever had upon public confidence."[14]

Whatever Brown's intentions were, the flattering notice helped to draw attention to Lane and his long military career. With national elections looming in November, local Democrats sought one of their own to represent East Texas in Washington, D.C. On June 25, several citizens of Marshall wrote to General Lane and requested permission to nominate him as a candidate for Congress. Lane conceded. He promised that "should the position be granted me I will discharge the duties incumbent upon me faithfully and earnestly."[15]

Other Democratic candidates emerged. They were all former Confederates. Charles DeMorse, the highly visible editor of the Clarksville *Northern Standard*, was a veteran of the Republic of Texas army, served as colonel during the Civil War, and was an active Democrat, but possessed little ambition for office. Two men from Jefferson also challenged Lane. Dr. Albert G. Clopton participated in the Secession Convention and served briefly as major of the First Texas in Virginia. David B. Culberson, former lieutenant colonel in the Southern army, was a lawyer with extensive experience in the state legislature, presently serving as senator. He emerged as Lane's chief rival.

Lane probably did not stump for himself during the campaign. He admitted that he was not much of a speaker. The *Iron Age* agreed, "Gen. Lane is no orator," but added, "he is an experienced business man, and would make a most useful and able representative."[16]

Local Democrats rallied around Lane's candidacy. They instructed its delegates to the state convention to vote for the general "first, last, & all the time." In August, *Iron Age* published several flattering notices that the Carthage *Panola Watchman,* Dallas *Herald,* and probably other newspapers in the region reprinted. Lane possessed little political experience and even less political clout. He had to rely on his war record if he wanted the nomination, cashing in on any prestige he might have accumulated during his career as an adventurer. Accordingly, the *Iron Age* emphasized Lane's military exploits, presenting him as a Texas hero. "His history is part of the history of the Lone Star State. For her honor he has periled his life and shed his blood. On his body he bears honorable wounds." A correspondent to the Dallas *Herald* enthusiastically supported the Marshall candidate. "General Lane is a man of fine mind and exceedingly quick perceptions. Of perfectly irreproachable integrity, and without one blot or stain upon the escutcheon of his name and fame."[17]

On September 3, 1874, the Democrats gathered at the state convention in Galveston. General Hawthorne, the Harrison County delegate, placed Lane's name on the nominating ballot. Lane and Culberson emerged as the leading candidates. After several ballots passed without a majority, Culberson maintained a slim lead over the general, whose supporters would not relent. On the twenty-fifth ballot, Culberson received ninety-eight and a half votes to Lane's seventy-three and a half. The general enjoyed significant support at the convention, but Culberson was the slight favorite. Reluctantly, Hawthorne withdrew Lane from contention, "rather than he should stand in the way of peace and harmony," a correspondent reported. The supporters of Clopton had already withdrawn his candidacy, and those who voted for DeMorse matched Hawthorne's gesture. On the twenty-sixth ballot, the Galveston convention unanimously nominated Culberson.[18] In the general election, the Jefferson lawyer easily defeated his Republican opponent and took his seat in the U.S. House of Representatives. Although Lane might have been disappointed, Culberson was an able representative. His constituents returned him to office nine times. He served for over twenty years, resigning in 1897.

With the failure of Ward and Company and his inability to secure the Democratic nomination for Congress, Lane needed some means to earn a living, so he turned to insurance. He had served as an agent of the James

River Insurance Company as early as 1869, and after closing his grocery firm in 1874, he joined forces with Charles H. McGill, an insurance agent from Jefferson and fellow Irish native. The Lane and McGill Insurance Agency opened an office in the upper floor of the Twyman building in Marshall and represented several different companies. In May 1875, merchant A. Kahn wrote a note of appreciation to the agents. "The prompt and honorable dealing of this Company should recommend it to the favorable consideration of the public." The firm offered policies that covered fire, death, and accidents, and from September 1876 to January 1877, they ran an advertisement targeted at the local cotton growers. "Insure Your Cotton and Cotton Gins," the agents warned. "We are now insuring this kind of property, in our best Companies, at reasonable rates, and for any length of time desired. No prudent man will expose the labor of the year to such a hazard, when he can so readily protect himself."[19]

While he attempted to resurrect his business prospects, Lane continued his participation in the local Democratic party. He represented Harrison County at district conventions in Carthage and Longview. In August 1876, Lane authorized the *Herald* to announce his candidacy for mayor of Marshall but withdrew his name a month later, thanking those "who promised him support." Looking forward to the elections in November, the general joined his Democratic colleagues and established the Harrison County Tilden and Hendricks Club, supporting the national ticket of Samuel J. Tilden and Thomas A. Hendricks. As expected, the black majority of Harrison County voted for Republican Rutherford B. Hayes.[20]

Lane was personally interested in the outcome of the election. In January 1877, while it appeared that Tilden would prevail, the *Tri-Weekly Herald* claimed that Lane would receive an appointment as U.S. marshal. Hayes won the election, however, and he appointed former sheriff Stillwell H. Russell instead. A resident of Marshall since before the Civil War, Russell had steadfastly adhered to his unionist convictions. During Reconstruction, he was one of the leading Republicans in the county and served as sheriff since 1872. Both the *Tri-Weekly Herald* and the recently established Marshall *Messenger*, however, approved of his appointment. The *Messenger* expressed its confidence: "We know that Col. Russell will not make his office an engine of oppression." By January 1878, as many as forty applicants sought deputations, and in late March, Russell made his appointments. He named six deputies, including sixty-one-year-old General Lane as his chief deputy.[21]

In April 1878, Lane embarked on his first mission as chief deputy marshal, traveling to Dallas to investigate a rash of train robberies. A band of outlaws who included Sam Bass attacked the Houston and Texas Central

Lane probably sat for this photograph in 1876, the year it first appeared in W. W. Heartsill's *Fourteen Hundred and 91 Days in the Confederate Army.* In 1890, Lane sent this uncropped version to Henry A. McArdle, to assist the artist's completion of his painting *The Battle of San Jacinto* (1898). To McArdle, Lane noted, "I send you an 'Old photograph' the farthest back I have." Unknown, "Walter P. Lane portrait, McArdle San Jacinto Companion Notebook." [Photostat?], ca. 1876. Courtesy of the Texas State Library & Archives Commission, Austin, Tex.

twice, in February and March. On April 4, they held up the Texas and Pacific at Eagle Ford west of Dallas, robbing the mail—a federal offense. When Russell and Lane arrived in Dallas, the marshal organized several posses and sent a younger deputy in pursuit of the train robbers, who were hiding out in the Cross Timbers between Denton and Lewisville. Many believed that the citizens of Denton County sympathized and abetted these outlaws.[22]

In order to properly motivate Denton County officials, Russell sent his chief deputy, Walter Lane. According to the Marshall *Messenger,* Lane confronted Sheriff William F. Egan and "informed this cowardly or criminal official that if he did not, in two hours, begin summoning men to arrest these train robbers, or drive them out of the county, he would have him arrested and placed in the Dallas jail." Thomas E. Hogg, chief justice of the county, objected to Lane's harsh treatment of Egan, and he knew the general's arbitrary nature well. He had served with Lane in both the Third Texas and the partisan rangers. In a letter to his former commander, Hogg admitted that the outlaws did have friends in the county, but the majority of the citizens were against them. He explained further that county officials had no warrants with which to arrest Bass and his gang. "They have molested no one here, and the citizens nor officers have not felt like attempting the capture of an armed and desperate body of men on mere vague rumor." Hogg made a good point, and Russell agreed that no one had authority to make the arrests. He sent Lane home, while he traveled to Tyler to obtain the proper indictments.[23]

With full-time employment, Lane decided to dissolve his partnership with Charles McGill. On April 22, 1878, he announced his retirement and asked their patrons to continue with his partner. Lane, meanwhile, began his busy work in the marshal service. In May and June, he investigated a case in Clarksville for the bankruptcy court, pursued whiskey bootleggers in Rusk County, and escorted an accused post office robber to Austin. On July 9, however, an unidentified group of Texans wrote to U.S. Atty. Gen. Charles Devens, complaining about Lane's conduct, but no details of the affair survived. Devens forwarded the letter to Russell and ordered him to take action on the matter, but whatever Lane's transgression might have been, he continued in the service until the end of the year.[24]

While Lane tended to his duties as chief deputy, Harrison County Democrats prepared to contest yet another election. Looking toward the state elections in November 1878, white politicians organized the Citizens' Party in September, calling for "good and true men of both colors as candidates for the various county offices." The Citizens' Party narrowed the voting margins but once again lost the election. They discovered, however, that the ballot box for the third precinct lay outside its limits, invalidating a thousand, mostly black, votes. The recount declared victories for the Citizens' Party candidates, including George Lane, the chief justice-elect. They obtained injunctions and physically took over their offices. On November 22, 1879, the *Messenger* triumphantly declared "Harrison County redeemed," but their legal troubles were not over, as each party filed lawsuits. The struggle for chief justice proved to be the test case. On December 31, the district court—Democrat A. J. Booty presiding—ruled for George Lane over J. B. Williamson. The Republicans appealed to the state supreme court, but the justices refused to hear the case, claiming that contested elections did not fall within their jurisdiction, handing a tenuous, yet lasting, victory to the redeemers.[25] As the Harrison County example illustrated, the specific experiences of Reconstruction might have differed from county to county and from state to state, but throughout the South, the former white elite succeeded in re-establishing the political, economic, and racial hierarchies that they had enjoyed before the Civil War.[26]

Walter Lane, meanwhile, played a small role for the opposition. During the election, several black voters in Elysian Fields, in the southern part of the county, claimed that the officials at the polling box refused their ballots. After hearing the complaints, U.S. Dist. Atty. Andrew J. Evans issued arrest warrants for five men. He charged them with obstructing voters during the election, violating the act of 1870, which enforced the provisions of the Fifteenth Amendment. The duty of serving the warrants fell to Lane. In early December, he gathered a small squad and, without incident, apprehended the five Elysian Fields prisoners, as they became known.[27] This act was probably Lane's last as the chief deputy marshal—at least, his last publicized act. The local papers, that dutifully chronicled his career, were silent on when and why he left the service. Perhaps the grievances filed against him in July had compelled him to resign. Perhaps he did not like serving warrants against those with whom he sympathized. Perhaps he counted on receiving an appointment as state adjutant general.

On December 14, the *Herald* proudly announced that General Lane was a candidate to receive that post. "[H]e will do more to arrest criminals and to put down crime, than any man that has ever filled it," the *Herald* promised. The appointment, however, was far from certain. Although laudatory of Lane, the Galveston *News* suggested the next adjutant general should come from the frontier section of the state. The *Herald* responded, "Our contemporary forgets that this distinguished gentleman has spent over half his life on the frontier; that the best portion of his military reputation has been dearly earned in defense of that section of the State." The Henderson *Beacon* and the Dallas *Herald* endorsed Lane, prompting the Marshall newspaper to declare, "The east demands the place for Gen. Walter P. Lane." Unfortunately for Lane and his East Texas supporters, Gov. Oran M. Roberts instead chose Maj. John B. Jones, of the Texas Rangers. After the announcement, the *Herald* spoke with Lane in town and reported, "He takes his defeat quietly, and without apparent disappointment."[28]

The governor, however, offered Lane another position. The Constitution of 1876 had set aside three million acres in the Panhandle, to fund the construction of a new capitol building. On May 17, 1879, Roberts asked Lane to supervise the surveying of this public land. "It is an office of considerable responsibility and labor, which will require firmness and discretion in controlling so important a work." The appointment mollified the disheartened Marshall press. The *Messenger* reported, "Every man in our community, or who knows the General, will be pleased." It seemed to have mollified Lane as well. On May 30, he asked Roberts to "*send me my commission* so that I can *show it round for granduer* [*sic*]." Perhaps reflecting on fond memories of past adventures, the sixty-two-year-old Lane enthusiastically organized an expedition. He informed Roberts, "Some twenty young men here (of good family, and their fathers [*sic*] old friends of yours and mine) are anxious to go as workmen." The general wanted to know whom the surveyor would be, when, and from where he planned to leave. He requested and received from Adjutant General Jones a Winchester carbine and a pistol. Lane also wanted a squad of four armed men—perhaps Texas Rangers—as an escort, a request that Jones apparently denied.[29]

In early July, Lane traveled to Denison, Texas, to rendezvous with J. C. Munson, the surveyor. On the 12th, however, the general informed Roberts, "He did not encourage me much about the expedition." He learned that he would have to pay for the expense of the expedition and then seek reimbursement later. Munson claimed to have surveyed in the area before and was not confident that the state could get the price for which it hoped. "So you see Governor it will be impossible for me to go, as I have not got the 300$ [*sic*] in the first place, and in the second I might not get it back, for a year or more." As a result, Lane resigned. Hoping to secure another appointment, Lane sent the letter to former governor Francis R. Lubbock. He asked him to deliver it to Roberts and use his influence, to obtain for Lane the position of assistant inspector of the state penitentiary. "I assure you very dear friend I am entirely out of employment & out of money in very old age & I do trust you will do all you possibly can to get me the inspectorship." His hoped-for appointment was not forthcoming. Although he quit the supervisor position, he kept the Winchester and the pistol that the adjutant general supplied him.[30]

After resigning, Lane found no employment for several months. In December 1879, when the treasurer of Harrison County died, the commissioners court selected the general to fill the void. "It is an appointment that will be generally acceptable, as Gen. Lane is a universal favorite," the *Herald* approved. In the meantime, local whites feared the return of Republican control of their county. The victory that the Citizens' Party experienced in the election two years before hinged on a technicality. If they expected to maintain their place, the local Democrats needed to wage a vigorous campaign. On May 18, 1880, Lane placed his name before the public as a candidate for country treasurer. In 1878, when the Citizens' Party organized, Lane was too busy with the affairs of the marshal's office to participate. Now, as a candidate, he placed his stake with their future.[31]

Soon after his announcement, Lane took part in electioneering throughout the county. With other members of the party, Lane promised to procure funds to build a bridge in the cypress section, attended a barbecue at Jonesville, and organized local clubs. The *Herald* reported, "Each meeting was well attended by white and colored voters, and good clubs were organized and set to work. The country was thoroughly canvassed and worked up." The white elite were determined to prevent the radicals from retaking the courthouse, and Lane was an active member of their cause.[32]

In November 1880, General Lane won his first political election. He defeated his Republican opponent with the same wide majorities enjoyed by the other hopefuls on the Citizens' Party ticket—a victory obtained through mass intimidation.[33] He settled into a new career that he hoped would sustain him through the remainder of his retirement. In June 1882, Lane announced his bid for re-election. In July, the general attended the Democratic convention in Van Zandt County, and he served as chairman pro tem at a Citizens' Party meeting in October. Responding to the problems of the 1880 election, the party established rules that severely restricted blacks from participating in their primary, so that at election time, no one ran against Lane for the position of treasurer—black and Republican voters had no candidate to support. Lane opened an office on the square and for at least another term, the general would have employment. His personal finances, however, still suffered. On March 14, 1883, he borrowed almost $400.00 from the Garrett and Key bank and once again mortgaged his home for security.[34]

Meanwhile, in the summer of 1883, the tension between Harrison County blacks and whites erupted in a brief moment of violence. On August 18, the *Tri-Weekly Herald* published troubling headlines, such as "Secret Negro Meetings. Very Suspicious—Should be Investigated." The editor had learned of rumors about the black men of the county meeting south of Marshall to organize a military company. He asked, "Why is it they are arming themselves with shot guns . . . and hold their meetings at night, and with closed doors, making it still more suspicious by its secrecy?" The *Herald* asserted the right of the white citizens to know what their intentions were, and for the benefit of both white and black, the editor wanted an investigation. He suggested that black citizens were more worried than their white neighbors but warned, "The colored people will do well to withdraw from such an organization, and not connect themselves with it; but, instead, to apply themselves to their farms and crops, and look after their own private business and the good of their families."

Despite these warnings, the meetings continued. On September 1, Lias Tillman arrived in Marshall and informed the local press that he had state authority to raise a company. The *Herald* suggested sending the company to the frontier and reiterated its advice for "negroes" to return to their farm work. That evening, the white community discovered that one hundred black men were meeting at a house in Happy Hollow, south of Marshall. Mary Jane Lane rather dramatically recalled the reaction. "Almost immediately was heard the steps of a rapidly ridden horse coming to the house, and a call for General Lane to come at once, which he hurriedly answered." He traveled the several blocks up the street to the courthouse and found the alarmed whites gathering. They quickly formed a committee, including Lane, to ride down to the house and investigate the meeting.

Upon reaching Happy Hollow, the committee indeed found a meeting in progress. The *Herald* claimed that the white men entered the "house in most peaceable and orderly manner and waited on the company, asked the nature of their meeting." A white man by the name of A. M. Gregory admitted that they were creating a military company, and he was charging each prospective soldier a dollar to enlist. They wanted to organize a defense against white violence, pointing to an episode in which a police officer killed a black citizen. Lane denied this charge and according to his niece, offered an emphatic warning to the congregation. "God Almighty has made you black, and that is old Master's business. This is the white man's country, and must remain so. If it is your intention to raise a race riot, I am afraid there will not be a blessed negro left in Harrison County."

The committee forced Gregory to return the money he took, ordered him and Tillman out of the county, and suggested the rest should disperse and return to their places in the cotton fields. When they returned to the courthouse, the citizens meeting there approved of the committee actions. They organized another group to go back to Happy Hollow and watch for further movements, but upon arrival, they were fired upon. "[T]he entire community was thrown into feverish excitement," the *Herald* reported. In response, Lane assembled some eight hundred men on the town square and implemented a makeshift police patrol, armed with firearms supplied by a local drug store. Returning to the scene of action, a patrol found no dead, but two black children were injured. The *Herald* argued that they were shot by stray bullets, fired by the presumed black assailants. Lane's men arrested several black citizens but soon released them once they determined their non-involvement.

General Lane led the effort to quell the unrest. "The citizens are well organized, and are determined to do everything in the bounds of law to break up this disturbing element in the county," the *Herald* reported. The next day, September 2, as his militia patrolled the neighborhoods, Lane and several other leading white citizens sent a telegram to Gov. John Ireland and Adj Gen. Wilburn H. King. "There is great indignation here and we deem it advisable to inform you of these facts and if possible help us to put a stop to the organization of such militia companies." The *Herald* took special pains to point out that these troublemakers represented only a small minority of the black community. "The little affairs that have been started by a few hot headed, bad negroes, who want to bring themselves in notice." Former black legislator David Abner, and county official S. H. Smothers, met with Lane and former county judge W. T. S. Keller and, according to the *Herald*, "pledged themselves to control the young negroes." Governor Ireland wrote back to Lane and informed him that the adjutant general planned to visit Marshall and investigate the matter.

On September 4, King arrived. Lane and state senator William H. Pope escorted the official as he investigated the affair. When he reported to the governor, King characterized the situation as "prudently and wisely managed by the whites," confronted by "the insolent conduct and threats of some of the negroes." He recommended a stronger militia, to meet the threat of Texas blacks who had expressed a "determination . . . to force themselves forward offensively, and to claim social as well as legal rights."[35]

The affair of September 1 provided a glimpse into Walter Lane's attitude toward African Americans. He never owned slaves, but his brothers had, and Lane fought alongside those who sought to preserve the institution of slavery during the Civil War. His niece Mary Jane, ever her uncle's admirer, claimed that Lane "was a real friend to the negro. Many of both races had come to him for advice and help in their troubles, for whose interest he did not spare his best efforts and tender sympathy." Lane dealt with black farmers as a partner of W. R. D. Ward and Company, loaning them money to assist in making their crops, but the firm tended to advance them less than their white counterparts. Several black servants worked and lived in the general's household. In 1870, the census listed a twenty-one-year-old female, named F. Jennison, as a cook and in 1880, listed Henry McElroy, twenty-eight, and Heywood White, ten, as servants. Mary Jane also recalled Aunt Lizzie, Polly and Uncle Seaborn, who were "devoted to him [Lane] and through a long term of years he was faithfully served." Seaborn and Henry lived with the general and his niece for over ten years, but Mary Jane referred to them by only their first names, suggesting that—in her mind—they did not warrant the dignity of surnames.[36]

Lane rarely expressed racist views—at least, not in any explicit manner. In his memoirs, which he would write in a few years, he recalled forgetting a speech to his troops. He flippantly remarked, "I would not have taken a 'little nigger' for it. (That is at the present price of negroes)." The letter that he and several others wrote to Ireland and King referred to the troublesome blacks as "creatures," but the community in which he lived and defended was much more explicit in their views toward race. Mary Jane Lane referred to "the ignorant negro" as pawns to maintain "Radical injustice" in the county. Aunt Polly and Uncle Seaborn might have taken exception to Mary Jane's characterization of the local black population. Regarding the affair of September 1, the *Herald* commented, "The white race is by nature, education, knowledge of the laws and principles of this government, and by property, financial and business interest, the superior of the negro race, and as long as the government exists the anglo saxon race will control it over every other race, be they Africans, Chinese, Indians, or what not."[37]

Walter Lane clearly sympathized with the view of the *Herald*. He believed in the superiority of the white race and actively worked to reestablish white control of the county. "This is the white man's county," he reportedly warned black men at Happy Hollow. As early as 1868, he joined the local conservatives and participated in their ten-year campaign to oust the radicals who claimed the loyalty of the black community. His actions in clearing the polls in 1873 and at Happy Hollow in 1883, indicated his willingness to use violence to assert white domination. Lane may well have been a friend to individual "negroes," as his niece claimed, but his friendship was predicated upon his superiority and their keeping to their proper places in the cotton fields and the servant quarters.[38]

The actions of the Harrison County white elite contributed to the larger movement toward the political, economic, and social exclusion of Texas blacks. Harrison County showed the way for the other so-called "negro counties" of Texas to take the courthouse. The case of *J. B. Williamson vs. George Lane* demonstrated the court's unwillingness to overturn county elections and set the precedent for the state at large. The Citizens' Party—and its forerunner, the Conservative Club—represented an early incarnation of the white primary. General state elections were more often formalities, as Democratic candidates usually defeated their Republican counterparts with large majorities. The real elections, then, occurred during the Democratic primaries, which often excluded black voters. White policy makers used events, such as the disturbances of 1883, as excuses to pass laws designed to segregate blacks from whites. Soon, a long list of legislation institutionalized Jim Crow in Texas, segregating blacks from whites in all types of public forums, such as education and transportation. Walter Lane played an important role in reasserting white dominance in Harrison County, where the white elite learned the lessons that would render Texas blacks as second-class citizens throughout the state—lessons that would remain largely unchallenged until the 1950s and 1960s.[39]

Despite his conspicuous role in the Happy Hollow affair and because of a reduction in the tax rate, the county commissioners lessened Lane's responsibilities and his salary as treasurer. In June 1884, he announced his candidacy for county tax collector, explaining that "he has not left the office [of treasurer], but the office left him." On September 13, he received the Citizens' Party nomination unopposed. During the elections, the tax collector's office was the only county post contested by a non-member of the party, but Lane soundly defeated Roe Womack by 2,825 to 416 votes.[40]

In compelling Harrison County citizens to pay their taxes, Lane exhibited his familiar impatience with shirkers. On March 26, 1885, he declared, "Tax payers who have not paid their taxes on or before April 4th will be advertised. Can't wait longer. I promised to send a postal to several parties. Let them consider they have received them." Three months later, he acted on his promise, publishing a list of delinquent tax payers. On August 15, Lane tried a different tack. "Taxpayers! Pay your taxes and *laugh* at [the] grand jury." In addition to publicizing delinquent lists, he also offered a schedule to meet with tax payers throughout the county. In June 1886, he moved his office to the south side of the courthouse square, "first door east of the engine house," and geared up for another season of campaigning.[41]

The Citizens' Party, however, disappointed the old veteran. When they gathered for the primary election on September 3, 1886, they chose F. Y. Hall. Lane lost the primary by a vote of 817 to 729. The local press did not mention why Lane failed to retain his position. When a delegation of both white and black voters approached Lane about running against Hall—or at least, voting for him "as a compliment"—he refused. "I have sworn to support the nominee of the citizens' ticket and I shall do so." The *Messenger* praised the general for his loyalty, but Lane took the defeat as a personal affront. To help assuage his hurt, Lane indulged in that old adventuristic impulse. On October 8, he rather petulantly declared, "I wish to sell my residence, as I intend to 'go West and grow up with the country.' Terms easy. If we can't agree on price, I am willing to *leave* it to *men*. Come and see me." When the county held its general election in November, the general received no complimentary votes.[42]

Lane did not leave Marshall, but he received an opportunity to tour West Texas while performing another public service. During the 1880s, Confederate refugees and Midwestern hardscrabble farmers migrated into the region west of Fort Worth, seeking better fortunes on the unpredictable landscape. In 1886, a severe drought devastated the region, forcing many to abandon their farms. On January 31, 1887, the Texas legislature appropriated $100,000 to aid the affected farmers who chose to stay, and Gov. Lawrence Sullivan Ross appointed General Lane, Judge H. R. Teague of Kaufman County, and William Ferguson, editor of the San Antonio *Evening Times*, to a committee to disburse the drought relief.[43]

On February 12, Lane and the committee arrived at Cisco, in Eastland County. Here, in the heart of the drought region and at the junction of the Texas Pacific and the Texas Central railroads, they established their base. In addition to state funds, the committee dispersed seed and cash raised by the Dallas *Morning News* and the Fort Worth *Gazette*. To better cover the area, they traveled separately. Lane visited Albany and Roby, but when he reached Midland, he encountered resistance. The general telegraphed the *Gazette* from Sweetwater and reported, "The County Judge was indignant at my coming to his county on my mission—said 'no drouth sufferers here.'" The Abilene *Taylor County News* believed that the ranchers of Midland County discouraged the relief effort in order to drive out the farmers, who fenced in the open range of West Texas. After briefly witnessing the struggle between ranchers and farmers that would attain mythic status in the literature of the American West, Lane left Midland without issuing funds.[44]

After a month, the committee concluded its work, and on the 14th, they met in Austin and filed their report. They estimated that the drought lasted in some areas as long as eighteen months, afflicting 28,750 people. They visited 34 counties and disbursed funds at $3.25 per person, drawing a total of $93,462.50 from the state relief account. Although Lane and his fellow committee members believed that lack of preparation contributed to the crisis, they also believed that the relief effort served a larger good. "Those who have remained are mainly farmers whose all is invested in their farms, with a determination and heroism rarely equaled, they have clung to their homes, they mean to remain in the country, and it is the advantage of the State to have them remain."[45]

In the decades after his last military duty, General Lane experienced many disappointments. For twelve years, between 1866 and 1878, he enjoyed modest success as a grocer and insurance agent but did not achieve lasting economic security. He failed to translate the prestige that he accumulated as an adventurer and Civil War soldier into national or state-wide office. He lost the nomination as U.S. congressman, failed to obtain the office of state adjutant general, resigned as supervisor of surveys, and served a month on drought relief. His brief stint as deputy U.S. marshal ended under unexplained circumstances. Locally, General Lane succeeded in becoming one of the most visible citizens in Harrison County, especially during the yellow fever epidemic and the Happy Hollow affair. He supported white redemption of the county, and the voters rewarded him with county offices. In 1886, they even took that away from him, but two years later, they rectified this slight when they returned Lane to the county tax collector's office, which he would hold until his death.

Business, politics, and race relations, however, did not completely define Lane's post-adventurer life. As the nineteenth century waned, many Texans began to reflect on their past and draw meanings from their history. It did not pay much, but if Lane should achieve a lasting renown, it would come with his place in the shared memory of Texans. As a practiced storyteller, Lane eagerly contributed to the shaping of Texas history, lore, and myth.

• 11 •

RECOLLECTIONS, 1874–91

For *Walter Lane, the decision* to retire from the adventurer's life was not a conscious one. Joining expeditions was very much a younger man's business, but the old general occasionally felt that familiar yearning for the elsewhere. In 1877, at age sixty, Lane wrote to the state adjutant general, offering his services for the field, if the occasion required.[1] In 1886, when he did not receive the Citizens' Party nomination for tax collector, he threatened to sell his house and move west—a few months shy of his seventieth birthday. Although he may not have accepted it, Lane was too old to endure an adventurous life. In order to exorcize those old demons, he met with his fellow veterans and retired adventurers, to wax romantic about the days of San Jacinto and the harsh years of the Civil War. Instead of performing feats of manliness, veterans would swap tales of past exploits, which testified to their manliness. Lane attained a reputation as a storyteller, placed his recollections in print, and contributed to the creation of Texas lore.

In September 1872, some thirty veterans of the Texas Revolution gathered at the Navarro County Fair in Corsicana, and they called to their old comrades to meet at the state fair in Houston. The reunion attracted "the largest collection of the old veterans since the battle of San Jacinto," a report boasted. General Lane attended the meeting, and his comrades placed him on a distinguished panel to review a pre-drawn constitution. The next day, the veterans approved the bylaws and proceeded to elect officers. They selected Francis W. Johnson president and William J. Russell first vice-president. Both men had participated in the so-called Anahuac disturbances in 1832 and fought during the siege of Béxar in 1835. For second-vice president, the group elected Walter Lane.[2]

Although Lane insisted on calling the group, "the San Jacinto Veterans," membership in the Texas Veteran Association included all soldiers and sailors, as well as appointed and elected officials of the old republic. By design, it was largely a male organization. Jerome B. Robertson recognized this fact when he introduced a resolution to "the surviving pioneer women." He reminded his comrades that the ladies "were sharers in the trials and privations of that period, and whose patriotism was equal to the occasion." Although the veterans adopted the resolution with its "kindest regards and remembrances," its inclusion demonstrated the veterans' intention to maintain a masculine environment.[3]

Like other veteran groups, the Texas association served a practical function—namely, lobbying lawmakers to grant pensions to former soldiers. For Lane, however, visiting with his old comrades was the primary draw.[4] One of the stated objects of the association was sponsoring state and local gatherings of veterans, for "a more intimate acquaintance and intercourse for mutual assistance and pleasure." In 1874, at the second annual meeting in Houston, Lane met his old comrades Robert K. Goodloe, Young P. Alsbury, and William Crittenden. In the intervening four decades, he had sporadically encountered these men, but under the auspices of the Texas Veteran Association, they could look forward to a more regular fellowship and reminisce about more vital days. As a reporter at the 1886 Dallas reunion noted, these reunions "made the old men feel as young."[5] The events also reinforced the old bonds of manly affection. As one of his closest companions, Mary Jane witnessed the warm expressions of friendship that passed between the general and his friends. She observed the moments when "the old veterans and his [Lane's] *comrades* in the various relations of his life would meet him. With the former, it is with the tenderest love, as if perhaps it might be the last time they would ever see him this side of the grave, with the latter, it is a comingled [*sic*] feelings of great love respect and admiration."[6]

In addition to the old, Lane formed new friendships. As an officer, he corresponded regularly with other leaders of the association. For example, the general exchanged letters with Moses Austin Bryan for over fifteen years. At first, the two communicated with the cordiality of businessmen, but expressions of friendship later emerged. In 1885, while preparing for one of the reunions, Lane encouraged Bryan, "Work up fast and let us have a good time." When Bryan claimed that he would not attend, the general emphatically implored, "It wont [*sic*] do. You must come." A warm relationship developed between Lane and John Henry Brown, after the latter expressed an interest in the Surveyors' Fight. In 1881, Mary Jane Lane wrote to Brown on her uncle's behalf. "Uncle more than appreciates it [Brown's regards], as I never knew any one whose heart was more keenly alive to a voice of affection and love." Lane thought so highly of Brown that he dedicated his memoirs to the historian. Of his new friends, Lane was perhaps closest to Samuel W. McKneely. A resident of Point Coupee, Louisiana, he would customarily arrive in Marshall several days early and accompany Lane to the Texas veterans' reunions. He was Lane's best friend outside Marshall.[7]

While these gatherings provided male comradery and a forum for recollections, they also recreated other aspects of the expedition. Lane often quartered with two or three other officers, in a hotel room with two beds. The arrangement was reminiscent of nights spent on the campaign—either outside, next to a campfire, or in the bed of an ousted Mexican general, such as the one Lane occupied with Samuel Walker during the battle of Monterrey. His home was often a rallying point for veterans as they prepared to travel to their various reunions, simulating rendezvous of old. They prepared knapsacks and other arrangements and departed on expeditions to Texas cities in the comfort of railroad coaches.[8]

Lane so enjoyed the experience at the first reunion in 1873, that as soon as he returned to Marshall, he organized another one. Although the Civil War was not yet a decade old, Lane joined a group of Marshall veterans and invited the survivors of the Third Texas Cavalry to the Harrison County fair. By October 1881, the reunion expanded to all of the regiments that had fought in the brigade, and Lane continued to participate, attending meetings at Sulphur Springs and Terrell. In March 1879, a larger gathering of former Confederates met in Galveston. The attendees selected former generals Lane, Richard M. Gano, and John S. Ford to a committee, to consider the possibility of establishing a formal association, called the Confederate Soldiers' Historical Association of Texas. The organization apparently did not survive its inception, but Lane did attend meetings of "ex-Confederates" at North Texas locales in 1883 and 1884. He did not join the nationwide United Confederate Veterans—established in 1889—although the local veterans named the Marshall chapter in his honor.[9]

Meanwhile, Lane regularly attended the reunions of the Texas Veteran Association. He traveled to Bryan (1878), San Antonio (1880), Palestine (1881), Waco (1882), and Belton (1883). By the San Antonio reunion, the veterans established April 21—the anniversary of San Jacinto—as their regular meeting date. Also during this time, the exclusively male organization made concessions to whom John Henry Brown referred to as "the dear old mothers of our early Isreal [*sic*]." As the organization consisted of old men with wives, children, and grandchildren, the reunions evolved into family events. This did not trouble Lane, who had made his compromise with domesticity

In March and April 1879, Lane traveled to Galveston and attended reunions for both Confederate and Texas veterans. P. H. Rose, Detail of "Veterans of San Jacinto, 1836–1879." Photographic montage, 1879. Courtesy of the Center for American History, University of Texas at Austin.

decades before. At the 1880 meeting, the veterans decided to confer honorary membership to deserving women, and Mary Jane, who often accompanied her uncle on these trips, received her credentials at the Palestine reunion.[10]

After William Russell died in 1881, Lane assumed the post of first vice-president, and when President Francis Johnson became ill while traveling in Mexico, the general presided over the 1884 Paris meeting in his absence. A few days before the veterans met, Johnson died. Until the association elected a replacement, Lane had to perform the duties of president, assuming the responsibilities for making arrangements with the host city of the next reunion, securing speakers, and seeking permission from the railroads to pass the veterans without charge—in addition to organizing the effort to retrieve the remains of their deceased president. Lane soon ran into problems.[11]

In early February 1885, General Lane wrote to C. N. Buckler, mayor of Sherman, informing him that the Texas veterans wished to meet in his town that April. After a couple of weeks without an answer, the mayor finally replied. He declined to receive the veterans, on account that his town was already planning to entertain a stock raisers association during that same time. On the 17th, Lane urgently wrote to Moses Bryan. "Now what shall we do[?]" The other officers agreed that postponing the meeting was their only option. Perhaps they could meet at the San Jacinto battleground, Lane suggested, or meet in Austin to bury Johnson's remains.[12]

When the state press learned of Sherman's rebuff, it came to the defense of the Texas veterans. The Austin *Statesman* noted, "Gen. Lane sent back a dignified, yet cutting reply, to this very inhospitable communication, in which he intimated that there were other towns in Texas that would be glad to welcome the veteran heroes of '36." The Sherman newspaper took exception to the rough handling and complained, "Gen. Lane has done our people an injustice which he ought, at the earliest possible moment, to correct." A local booster named William N. Ramey wrote to both Lane and Bryan, asking them to reconsider and arguing that they should not punish the citizens of Sherman for the actions of Mayor Buckler.[13]

These protests failed to move Lane, but on March 20, Buckler wrote to the general and explained that a misunderstanding existed between the two of them. He thought that the veterans wanted to postpone the meeting "on account of hard times." The mayor promised, "I had not the slightest intention of being discourteous toward the veterans or of doing any thing that I thought was not agreeable to them." He informed Lane that he had already called together the town leaders and planned "to give you a Royal entertainment." In addition, he offered to help raise funds for the expense of returning the body of Francis Johnson. Lane conceded. "The Sherman people are so . . . anxious for us that I for one am willing to go." The other association officials agreed, and they announced that the meeting would go forward as planned. At the meeting, the veterans formally elected Lane to the office of president.[14]

Organizing the important 1886 reunion was Lane's first duty as president. It would mark the semi-centennial of Texas independence. Boosters from Flatonia, Waco, and Dallas wrote Lane, inviting the Texas veterans to meet in their cities. John Henry Brown, on behalf of Dallas, wrote "as one of the junior Veterans of the olden band, . . . allow me . . . most cordially and earnestly, to invite the Association." The veterans selected Dallas for the honor and in January 1886, Lane asked Brown to deliver the annual address. "I select you *firstly,* [*sic*]" the general assured, "as the best Historian of Texas and secondly as being the most prominent man in [Dallas]." Brown accepted the charge.[15]

On April 18, 1886, Lane arrived in Dallas two days before the opening of the reunion. He took up quarters in the St. George Hotel. On the morning of the 20th, the veterans gathered at the Dallas Opera House, where Lane presided over a business meeting. The topic that dominated the day was the inability of the association to raise the money necessary to retrieve Johnson's remains.[16]

On the morning of the 21st, Lane awoke early and walked the streets, shaking hands with the hospitable citizens. At nine o'clock, the parade began, escorting the veterans to Shady View Park, where John Henry Brown addressed the crowd. The "Native Texans of Dallas" presented a flag to Lane. Never known for his oratorical skills, the band saved Lane by prematurely striking up a rendition of "Dixie." The general took the opportunity to gracefully excuse himself from any formal address. "If it were not for that infernal band I had a splendid speech made up."[17]

As with most anniversaries, the semi-centennial inspired Texans to reflect about the past and draw meaning from the stories that the veterans told. Several historians had already started this discourse, and Lane actively contributed. Between 1876 and 1887, John Henry Brown, James T. DeShields, Victor M. Rose, and Homer S. Thrall published eight books on Texas history, emphasizing its heroic past. Brown and DeShields corresponded with Lane about his participation in the Surveyors' Fight. Although he claimed, "[I]t has been so long ago I have forgotten most of the incidents," he provided both historians with extended accounts of the 1838 clash with the Kickapoos. The general provided Rose with details about the Civil War battle of Chustenahlah, and he was also the subject of several biographical sketches written by Brown and Rose. At the 1886 reunion in Dallas, John S. Ford took subscriptions for a prospective autobiography, while the association sought ways to complete and publish the history of Texas, on which their late president, Francis Johnson, was working when he died in Mexico. In 1886, William H. Huddle completed his painting *The Surrender of Santa Anna*, while another artist, Henry McArdle, approached the veterans as early as 1885, seeking information to complete a painting depicting the battle of San Jacinto. Lane provided him with his own account.[18]

As a former Confederate general and president of the Texas Veteran Association, Lane was a visible figure in this discussion. An admirer claimed, "The history of Walter P. Lane is indissolubly entwined with the history and glo[r]y of Texas," and by 1886, he had already received his sobriquets. In 1878, Brown styled him the "Marshall Ney of Texas," and the Texas legislature called him the "hero of three wars," when that body invited him to a seat in 1885. As Texans looked to the past to help define who they were, Walter Lane and his military exploits epitomized the archetypes that they admired—the rugged westerner who rescued an aggrieved Texas from Mexican tyrants and savage Indians and the Southern gentleman defending the lost cause and white superiority to the last.[19]

In this context, Lane's friends and family, led by Mary Jane, encouraged him to write his memoirs. When his niece approached him, the general claimed that "he was better calculated to make history than to write it." She offered to write it for him, if he would provide the information. In late 1887, Lane and his niece began work, and in December, they produced a slim, 120-page volume. The title was nonetheless comprehensive—*The Adventures and Recollections of General Walter P. Lane, a San Jacinto Veteran, Containing Sketches of the Texian, Mexican, and Late Wars with Several Indian Fights Thrown in.* He claimed that he wrote his memoirs in order to provide his own perspective of his career, on which several historians had commented. "I am not writing a history of any of the three wars I have been engaged in, only my personal recollections of some of the events through which I passed." Although Mary Jane may have dictated for her uncle, the words in the memoirs were clearly the general's own.[20]

In January 1888, Lane sent copies of his "little book," as he described it, to some thirty towns throughout the state. He gave several away to friends, but he hoped to make some profit. He sent twenty-five to Brown and wanted eighty cents per copy but was willing to reduce the price to fifty cents if sales lagged. From the other towns, Lane "got from each a flattering encomium but not much sale." The general was also a little self-conscious. When Brown did not immediately respond to his first letter, Lane was concerned. "I fear your silance [*sic*] as to your *opinion* of the *book* is *ominous* and that the d—lish thing does not *jingle* but in any case write to me, and let me know the worst for I would rather have your opinion than any one in the state."[21]

The title, "Adventures and Recollections," was an apt description of the themes of the book. As "adventures" suggested, Lane presented an often romanticized and sometimes frank image of himself and Texas history. The term "recollections" testified to the book as a document of memory—although at times imperfect, distorted, and not even his own.

In his memoirs, Lane portrayed himself as an adventurer, with little concern for the causes and impact of the wars and movements in which he participated. He described being struck by "Texas fever," explained his leaving San Augustine for San Antonio in 1844 as a "search for adventure," and joined the Civil War because he wished "to have a finger in that pie."

Lane admitted that after San Jacinto, he returned home and "ventilated my laurels"—proudly offering tales of Mexican lancers and Texas alligators. His memoirs recorded moments of personal gratification, such as the time he defied Gen. Zachary Taylor in defense of John J. Glanton, momentarily commanding a brigade as lieutenant colonel at Pea Ridge, or receiving a commendation for valor after his stand at Farmington.

The general, however, was not too proud to describe those moments when he experienced fear. He admitted that during his scout with Erastus "Deaf" Smith, the Mexican bullets whizzed by him, "greatly to my demoralization," and when his horse plunged him into the midst of Santa Anna's soldiers, it did so "much to my disgust." Lane remembered that when Samuel Walker chose him for picket duty during the battle for Monterrey, "I would have cheerfully given the only three dollars I had in the world if he had dropped the mantle on some other officer's shoulders," and expressed similar misgivings when he recalled the moment James McIntosh selected him to lead the charge against the Creek Indians at Chustenahlah. Lane's self-image included those revealing moments that contradicted the archetype of the intrepid Texas hero, but on these occasions, he never failed to fulfill his duty as a proper soldier—at least as recorded in his memoirs.

Lane also revealed the cruel side of Texas history. He recalled the bloodlust, as Texas soldiers wantonly shot down Mexicans who were fleeing the battle of San Jacinto. When a fellow Texas Ranger became frustrated with capturing a wounded Comanche, he simply drew his pistol and "blew out the Indian's brains," as Lane remembered. These moments served to illustrate the violence of Texas's past, but they also served as foils against which Lane demonstrated his own moral grit. At the slaughter after San Jacinto, he assured his readers, "I never fired a shot," and during his flight from the Surveyors' Fight, he refused to follow Mr. Button's suggestion to kill their Kickapoo guide. "I told [Button], rather than betray his confidence, I would walk in on one leg." At several points in his memoirs, however, Lane admitted to his own acts of violence. During the U.S.-Mexican War, for example, he ordered the execution of Nicolás García and the beating of several Saltillo horse claimants. He certainly felt justified in these actions, but perhaps he could not recognize his own capacity for brutality. His Texas friends and readers in 1887 likely sympathized with him.[22]

By the time Lane produced his memoirs, some of his stories were well practiced. Storytelling was an important aspect of the expeditions and veteran reunions, and "ventilating" ones "laurels," as Lane occasionally admitted, no doubt involved an enthusiastic retelling of his adventures. While dining with U.S. Army officers in Camargo, Mexico, Lane recalled, "I warmed to my work, telling some exploits I had gone through, by flood and field." Jasper M. Hixson, who traveled with Lane across the continent to California, regarded the Texan as a "professional Indian fighter," and could not have obtained that notion without hearing of Lane's stories.[23] Lane's scout with Deaf Smith, the cavalry skirmish before San Jacinto, the Surveyors' Fight, and the battle of Chustenahlah were the subjects of the general's surviving correspondence before he wrote his memoirs. The details he related then were similar in both content and style with the ones he provided in *The Adventures and Recollections,* suggesting that he often retold his stories.[24]

Although many of his stories were well-practiced, Lane's memory suffered as much from intentional as unintentional imperfection. As expected in a document of memory, the autobiography often contained incomplete or misspelled names of people and places, and Lane also experienced a problem with recalling chronology. These lapses, however, did not alter the tenor or content of Lane's *Adventures and Recollections.* The places where Lane deliberately omitted parts of his life served to reinforce his image as an adventurer and soldier. He framed his memoirs with his leaving Ohio for Texas in 1835 and the rallying of his troops in 1865, at the end of the Civil War. He provided no comment on his childhood, or the twenty years of his life between the Confederate surrender and the writing of his book. He glossed over the more sedentary moments of his life and omitted any military service that did not result in action.[25] Lane offered only a single sentence regarding the assault on the Federal works at Donaldsonville, passing on an opportunity to explain why his regiment failed to join the disastrous attack. Whether he mishandled the maneuver, or defied orders to spare the lives of his men, the general's omission suggested that he did not want to tarnish his image as a dutiful soldier.[26]

Some of the memories contained within Lane's *Adventures and Recollections* did not belong to the general. While writing his autobiography, he was actively engaged in conversation with his friends across the state, as well as his old comrades still living in Marshall—characters who populated Lane's memoirs.[27] While Lane wrote his account of the affair at Farmington, Dr. Eugene B. Blocker was a ready source for details. In his memoirs, the general revealed, "The doctor told me, the other day. . . ."[28] He also used his friends' romantic misadventures—perhaps because he had none of his own, and felt compelled by the conventions of the adventure story to include them. Nevertheless, Lane's use of others' memories did not subsume or diminish the authenticity of his own. The conversations with former comrades not only jogged Lane's recollections but also reestablished ties of masculine friendship.

In one extraordinary case, however, Lane not only borrowed the memories of another but also fabricated details to make it appear as his own. In May 1848, while stationed at Mazapil during the U.S.-Mexican War, Lane gave his unofficial consent for Lt. William H. Francis and eight other rangers to ride for Salado and exhume the bodies of the Mier prisoners executed there five years earlier. They succeeded in retrieving the remains and sent them back to Texas for burial.[29]

Walter Lane played only a small role in this affair, but in 1878, a story circulated that credited him with leading the exhumation. In early April, when the general arrived in Dallas to investigate the Sam Bass train robberies, a writer in the *Morning Call* wrote a biographical notice. In it, he traced Lane's military exploits, including his March 1848 scout toward Matehuala during the U.S.-Mexican War. The writer added, "Returning, he shot across the mountain to the hacienda of Salado, where reposed the remains of the 17 decimated Mier prisoners. . . . Impressing men to dig and mules to pack, he forced the disinterment of the remains and brought them triumphantly to Gen. Taylor." The article contained several mistakes in regard to Lane's experience, but in his defense, the author admitted, "We write this hurried sketch from memory, not having seen the gallant old hero for quite a time."[30]

The Marshall *Messenger* reprinted the notice and expressed surprise about Lane's participation in the exhumation of the Texans. "The General is so modest that although we were raised in Texas, and have lived the greater portion of our time in this city, where he has also resided, we have never heard of his action in regard to the Mier prisoners." As the authors in both the *Morning Call* and the *Messenger* stated, the story did not originate from Lane. The writer of the original essay claimed to have been working from memory, while the *Messenger* noted, "It is only through his old army friends and the press of the State that the people are informed of his noble and daring deeds."[31] Lane, however, never made an effort to correct the misunderstanding. He left Dallas before the *Morning Call* could consult with him, but the writer in the *Messenger* certainly had access to the general. In September 1881, for example, a New Orleans newspaper published an account of the skirmish the day before San Jacinto, crediting Lane with rescuing Mirabeau B. Lamar. The *Tri-Weekly Herald* in Marshall reprinted the article after consulting with Lane, who corrected the story. "The boot is on the other foot," the general declared, "It was Lamar who saved my life."[32] If Lane ever informed his hometown newspaper about the truth of the Mier prisoners, it never printed a retraction.

Lane, nevertheless, let the mistake continue. In 1881, John Henry Brown reprinted the 1874 essay that he wrote about the general in his *Encyclopedia of the New West*. The original notice did not include the exhumation, but Brown appended a lengthy treatment on the subject in his book and provided new details about the affair. "Few know even to this day that to General Walter P. Lane Texas is indebted for the possession of these mementos of a heroism never surpassed." Lane and Brown had been in contact, but the general did not inform his friend of the mistake. Victor M. Rose reprinted the account in the 1884–1885 proceedings of the Texas Veteran Association for all of Lane's comrades to read and comment, as they had with other controversies, but no discussion emerged regarding the Mier prisoners. John Dusenberry, who supplied the alternative account, which the La Grange *Texas Monument* printed in 1850, died in 1874 and could not challenge this new version.[33]

In 1887, when Lane set out to complete his *Adventures and Recollections,* he had the opportunity to correct the misunderstanding. He claimed, "I may appear egotistical, but, whether so or not, I wish to reproduce in this what Texas historians have written in regard to my services. Whether they have either overrated or lied about them, the blame should fall upon their heads, and not mine."[34] If he did not want to embarrass those who wrote about him—such as his friend John Henry Brown—or quietly accept the honor in some strange sense of duty to Texas myth, Lane could have simply omitted any comment about the exhumation, as he had for several other episodes of his career. Instead, he accepted the honor that was not his and further embellished the story to support his claim.

In his memoirs, Lane spun the tale that on the return leg of his scout toward Matehuala, he decided to detour through Salado, following the *Morning Call* account. Capt. John Pope of the U.S Corps of Engineers accompanied Lane and, according to the story, balked at the idea. Lane claimed, "I told him it could not be expected that he would have the same feeling on the subject as I had—as a Texan—but those bones I was going to have, all the same." He continued, supplying details of how he surprised Salado at dawn, forced the alcalde to show him the grave site, and impressed men and horses for digging and transportation.[35]

Lane never revealed why he assumed this honor for himself. Elder storytellers such as Lane could often convince themselves of personal memories that never occurred, but as his autobiography illustrated, his other recollections were accurate, even episodes of apparent exaggeration.[36] Perhaps he felt ashamed for not taking the opportunity to exhume the remains when he scouted near Salado two months before, or perhaps he felt that he deserved credit as the commander of those who actually performed the deed. Whatever his reasons, Lane did not convince himself through years of practiced storytelling. Instead, he deliberately fabricated the details.

Protecting his friends from embarrassment, duty to myth, or other reasons might have motivated Lane to embellish the yarn, but the exhumation of the Mier prisoners also offered the general an opportunity to lay claim to a renown that had long eluded him. It was a dramatic story of chivalry, in the reclamation of martyrs from the clutches of the enemy—tied to the romanticized notion of Texas honor. Brown claimed that it was the "[o]ne episode . . ." that would "embalm his memory forever in the hearts of Texans."[37] Lane was only one of several hundred San Jacinto veterans. His surviving the Kickapoo attack was an accident—or at least an act of self-preservation, not heroism. During the U.S.-Mexican War, he commanded a battalion of Texas Rangers—but in a theater that saw little action. His comrades, such as Jack Hays, Sam Walker, and Ben McCulloch, attained lasting fame for their services. Throughout his career in the Confederate Army, Lane chafed at his lack of promotion, and when he did finally receive his long-sought-for brigadier stars, they came on the last day the Confederate Congress met—two months before the surrender at Appomattox Court House. He did not make the ultimate sacrifice, or lead the decisive campaigns that would legitimize his long career as an adventurer. Even in retirement, he experienced disappointments with business and politics.[38] The exhumation of the Mier prisoners offered Lane the renown that could validate his adventurous career.

In his last years, Lane tended to the business of the Texas Veteran Association and the county tax collector's office. At the 1887 Corsicana reunion, Lane offered to step down as president, but the membership refused. Two years later, Lane convened the meeting in the hall of the Texas House of Representatives, in the recently completed capitol building. In 1890, three hundred members participated in the reunion at Fort Worth, and in 1891 at Brenham, Lane and other veterans signed a letter, testifying to the "absolute historical truth" of Henry McArdle's painting, "Battle of San Jacinto." As tax collector, Lane continued to publish straightforward warnings to Harrison County taxpayers, imploring them to settle with his office before he had to publicize their delinquency in the local newspapers. Lane also lived in a home opened to his family and friends, and it served as a personal museum, filled with relics that he captured from his Mexican, Indian, and Yankee enemies. Over his bed, he placed banners, weapons, and pictures of his comrades.[39]

On April 19, 1889, just before he departed for the reunion in Austin, Lane filed his last will and testament. He acknowledged "the uncertency [*sic*] of Life and the certency [*sic*] of Death," and bequeathed all of his possessions to his niece, Mary Jane Lane. In the following year, the deaths of three officers of the Texas Veteran Association—Stephen W. Blount, Jerome B. Robertson, and Joel W. Robinson—offered somber testimony to Lane's recognition that he, too, was nearing the end of his earthly expedition.[40]

EPILOGUE

In the course of his long career, Gen. Walter P. Lane had suffered wounds inflicted by a Mexican lancer, Kickapoo warriors, and Yankee infantry, and survived them all, but defeating old age was a battle that no soldier could win. In October 1890, he suffered a lapse in his health. The Marshall *Messenger* diligently monitored his status, noting on the 18th that he was improving, "able to be on the streets again but is quite feeble." By November 7, the newspaper reported that he was "growing stronger daily." Unknown to the public, the general's liver was slowly failing.[1]

Liquor was the likely culprit. Social drinking was a favorite pastime among many nineteenth-century men, but for Lane, it had special significance. In his memoirs, he often commented on his fondness for alcoholic beverages. During the U.S.-Mexican War, dining with his fellow officers at Camargo, Lane recalled the pleasant feeling of "having my skin well filled with champagne." As the U.S. troops withdrew from Mexico, Gen. John E. Wool invited the Texan into his tent for a glass of wine. Lane recalled, "I went in, but took whiskey *in mine,* as wine was deleterious to my constitution." He sipped Pike County whiskey with several Missourians while mining in California, and during the closing moments of the battle of Pea Ridge, Gen. Sterling Price offered Lane a swig from his canteen. "I acquiesced with great alacrity, being very dry and very thirsty, and expecting to get a straight drink." Lane was disappointed when he took a hit of sugar water instead. No one recorded any episode where the general might have been improperly drunk, but his imbibing was well known. A rather unflattering notice in an 1882 issue of the Galveston *News* described the general as red-faced, adding sardonically, "though we hear it whispered that he is a prohibitionist."[2] By

1890, decades of hard drink had weakened his liver and complicated his physical condition.

In March 1891, concerned about his failing health, the general repaired to Hot Springs, Arkansas, hoping that the mineral baths would soothe his ailments. When he returned to Marshall after a week and a half, he claimed to feel "somewhat improved." In April, Lane felt capable of traveling to Brenham, to preside over the nineteenth annual reunion of the Texas Veteran Association. By December, however, his conditioned worsened, and he was confined to bed during the week of the 11th. The *Messenger* maintained vigil. On January 20, 1892, the newspaper noted that Lane "is no better today," but the next day found the old general "being able to walk around his apartments." The 23rd and 25th found him unimproved, and on the 26th, his situation turned grave. "It was reported about 11 o'clock to-day that Gen. Lane was dying," the *Messenger* informed its concerned readers, "but he rallied, and is resting well as we go to press, though he may die at any moment."[3]

The General lingered, resting on his mahogany-framed bed. On January 25, he jotted off a defiant notice to the tax payers of Harrison County. "I will positively close the tax rolls this week, and all who do not come up and settle, will have to pay cost of collecting." Lane would not be able to deliver on his promise. At six in the morning on January 28, the old veteran quietly surrendered to his disease, a month shy of his seventy-fifth birthday. The attending physician pronounced his cause of death as cirrhosis of the liver.[4]

A hush fell over the community of Marshall. "In every groupe [sic], where his death was announced, silence reigned for a few moments," the local newspaper reported, "and after deep drawn sighs, such expressions of regret as each individual could command followed." A mass meeting convened that afternoon and selected a committee—headed by Lane's former partner, Charles H. McGill—to arrange for the general's funeral. That evening, the *Messenger* released its regular issue, with its entire front page devoted to Lane's life, death, and the plans for his funeral. "Truthfully can it be said, that no man ever lived and died in Harrison county who was more universally admired," the *Messenger* observed.[5]

At nine in the morning on January 30, a bell rang out over the town, and the mourners—3,500 strong—gathered at the courthouse. The funeral was probably the largest in Marshall, before or since. The procession—which included veterans of the Texas Revolution, U.S.-Mexican War, and both Confederate and Union soldiers—traveled several blocks north, along Wellington Street to Lane's home, where the pallbearers took up the general's remains and carried them to the Methodist Church. Six of the eight pallbearers had served with Lane during the Civil War. After Reverend J. S.

Mathias offered prayers, Franklin B. Sexton, a former Confederate congressman, delivered the eulogy, and then the procession escorted Lane's body to the Marshall City Cemetery, where they placed him alongside the gravesite of his brother George.[6]

Newspapers across the state also marked the occasion of General Lane's death. Usually reprinting information from the *Messenger,* major dailies, such as the Austin *Statesman,* Galveston *News,* and the San Antonio *Express,* described Lane as the hero of three wars and credited him with the exhumation of the Mier prisoners. The Fort Worth *Gazette* proclaimed, "Gen. Lane was a soldier, a man and a hero in every sense of the word." Gov. James S. Hogg ordered the flag over the capitol to fly at half-mast and offered to bury Lane in the State Cemetery in Austin. During its extra session, the state legislature passed a joint resolution stating, "[T]he state has lost a citizen whose life was devoted to her welfare. In war he was the incomparable soldier and in peace the modest and dutiful citizen. . . . [T]he services he rendered Texas will be ever cherished by patriotic people, and his glorious character will always be a splendid example for the coming generations of our state." The Texas Veteran Association met at Lampasas a few months after Lane's death. Mary Jane represented her uncle and listened to Guy M. Bryan's memorial. "Brethren, since our last meeting, death has been busy in our midst, he has cut down many—among them our lamented president General Walter P. Lane. No more will we see his martial face and step among us." Although they paused to pay their respects to the fallen leader, the old veterans were accustomed to deaths and elected Bryan to replace the general as president.[7]

In Marshall, memories of the general endured. A year after his death, a citizens' committee raised enough funds to erect a large, handsome marker at Lane's grave site. The inscription announced, "The Citizen Soldier . . . From Youth to the End of His Life, He Served His Country Well." The local members of the United Confederate Veterans named their camp in Lane's honor, and the Marshall chapter of the United Daughters of the Confederacy—which Mary Jane organized in 1900—annually celebrated the general's birthday into the 1920s. The chapter also commissioned two oil portraits of the general. In 1906, Houston artist L. L. Cohen completed the paintings, and the Daughters sent them to the capitol in Austin and the "Confederate White House" in Richmond, Virginia, for display. In 1904, as one of the more bizarre memorials, the Hicks Company of Marshall named a cigar in the general's honor, encouraging their patrons, "Smoke the Gen'l. Walter P. Lane 5c cigar." Mary Jane Lane planned to reissue *The Adventures and Recollections,* but she died before she could complete it. Her sister and the

In 1893, a year after Lane's death, the citizens of Marshall erected this marker over his grave in the Marshall City Cemetery. Author's photograph, Walter P. Lane Grave Site, Marshall, Tex.

general's namesake, Louisa Paye Lane, finished the project, publishing the second edition in 1928.[8]

Lane's home on Wellington Street stood as a visible and active memorial. Mary Jane inherited the place upon her uncle's death and often conducted meetings of the United Daughters of the Confederacy and other organizations. Unfortunately, in November or December 1905, while Mary Jane attended the national convention in St. Louis, fire destroyed the Lane home. She managed to salvage a few trinkets, but most of the general's relics and papers were lost. At some point, an effort was made to restore the home, but the city eventually razed the building in 1947 to make way for an automobile dealership.[9]

Two modern journalists—both natives of Marshall—offered differing views of Walter Lane's legacy. In 1984, Bill Moyers launched his award-winning, PBS documentary series on the twentieth century with a personal look at his home town. Entitled "Marshall, Texas," the episode traced the social transformation of the small, East Texas town. After he nostalgically reminisced with old friends, Moyers strolled through the city cemetery and encountered the grave site of General Walter P. Lane. As a local historian recited the general's exploits, the camera panned down the monument to its base, where a later generation added the initials "C.S.A." Here, Moyers revealed the darker side of Marshall history. "What was it that John Reb had fought for? You knew that there was something terribly wrong about it," he concluded. For Moyers, Lane represented the memory of the Old South that the white community in Marshall used to maintain the segregation and second-class citizenship of their black neighbors.[10]

In 1992, Max S. Lale delivered the annual presidential address to the Texas State Historical Association, announcing, "[T]onight I want to remember with you one old soldier many of you may never have heard of." He used General Lane's experience to celebrate the idea of the Texas military hero. Himself a decorated World War II veteran, Lale told the audience, "His [Lane's] deeds reflect the valor which we like to regard as purely Texan." For Lale, General Lane embodied the idealized virtues of honor, courage, and manhood.[11]

Although the state legislature passed a joint resolution expressing sorrow over Lane's death, the body never named a county in the general's honor, as it had done for many of his contemporaries. The timing of his death explains the omission. Lane did not make the ultimate sacrifice, as had many of the veterans for whom counties were named during the 1870s. The legislature named the counties created after Lane's death to honor those veterans with local or political connections. During the 1936 centennial, the commission on celebration erected monuments and markers across the state and remembered Lane in several places. They inscribed Lane's name, along with his fellow veterans, on the wall of honor beneath the 570-foot shaft at the San Jacinto battlefield. The commission erected a local marker to his memory at the courthouse in Marshall and at Monument Hill, outside of La Grange, the commission placed a forty-eight-foot, frescoed shaft over the grave of the Mier prisoners. On one side, a plaque dedicated to Lane's memory declares that he had reclaimed the bodies through his "personal initiative." Mounted onto the enduring Texas shell stone, the inscription perpetuates Lane's fabrication, but it also serves to remind his fellow Texans of his contribution to the history and lore of their state.[12]

Walter Lane's life was one of movement. The trans-Atlantic voyage that he experienced as a four-year-old in 1821 was but a dim memory to him, yet it foretold of the restlessness that would seize him throughout much of his life. In 1835, at age eighteen, a romantic fire, stoked by images of Indians and warfare, consumed and compelled him to Texas, where he soon experienced the brutal realities of U.S. expansionism. The expedition and the lure of far-off vistas, provided Lane with the opportunity to define his sense of manhood and took him to the sandy beaches of the Campeche Banks, the hostile walls of Monterrey, the alpine reaches of the Sierra Nevada, and to the inhospitable wastes of the Sonoran Desert. The masculine camaraderie transformed him into a strict, yet caring, paternal figure, as he led younger men into Yankee guns. Lane also made his compromise with domesticity, by setting up house with his niece Mary Jane. His business and political ventures frustrated his goal of financial security, but he worked with the white elite of Harrison County, overcoming the black majority in order to re-establish conservative rule. Lane also embraced the life of the retired adventurer, attending reunions and telling stories. Although he died a bachelor, he did not die alone. Mary Jane attended his needs, while his other nieces and nephews, their children, and his friends and associates in Marshall and across the state provided the general with the sustenance that only close families and friends could provide.

The native of County Cork participated in and embraced many of the major movements, events, and ideas that swept through the nineteenth-century United States—the romantic movement, U.S. expansion, adventurism, the Gold Rush, Reconstruction, and warfare with Mexicans, Native Americans, and Yankees. Lane's experiences illustrated the impact of these episodes on the lives of individuals, especially those who did not directly have an impact on the course of events, but who nonetheless made their own choices about how they would confront the challenges arrayed before them.

NOTES

Abbreviations Used in Endnotes

AMC	Republic of Texas Audited Military Claims, TSL
BFP	Barton Family Papers, University of Texas at Arlington
CAH	Center for American History, University of Texas at Austin
CDL	Centre Division Letterbook, John Ellis Wool Papers, NYSL
CGT	*Guernsey Times* (Cambridge, Ohio)
CPW	*Panola Watchman* (Carthage, Tex.)
CSR-CGS	Compiled Service Records of Confederate General Staff Officers . . . , USNA
CSR-MW	Compiled Service Records . . . Mexican War . . . Texas, USNA
CSR-TX	Compiled Service Records of Confederate Soldiers . . . Texas, USNA
DH	*Dallas Herald*
DMN	*Dallas Morning News*
EMR	*El Monitor Republicano* (Mexico City)
ETHJ	*East Texas Historical Journal*
ETRC	East Texas Research Center, Stephen F. Austin State University, Nacogdoches, Tex.
FWG	*Fort Worth Gazette*
GLO	General Land Office, Austin, Tex.
HCCM	Court Minutes, Harrison County Clerk's Office
HCDR	Deed Records, Harrison County Clerk's Office
HCHM	Harrison County Historical Museum, Marshall, Tex.
HED No. 56	30th Congress, 1st Session. House Executive Document No. 56
HED No. 60	30th Congress, 1st Session. House Executive Document No. 60
JEWP	John Ellis Wool Papers, NYSL

JHBFP	John Henry Brown Family Papers, CAH
JMH	Jasper Morris Hixson Diary, Bancroft Library, Berkeley, Calif.
Lane, AR	Lane, *Adventures and Recollections* (1887 edition)
Lane, AR (1928)	Lane, *Adventures and Recollections* (1928 edition)
Lane, AR (2000)	Lane, *Adventures and Recollections* (2000 edition)
LDJ	*Louisville Daily Journal*
LWT	*Weekly Tribune* (Liberty, Mo.)
MAB	Moses Austin Bryan Papers, CAH
RTMR	Republic of Texas Muster Rolls, TSL
MDG	*Diario del Gobierno* (Mexico City)
MHF	*The Harrison Flag* (Marshall, Tex.)
MM	*Marshall Messenger*
MTR	*Texas Republican* (Marshall, Tex.)
MTWH	*Tri-Weekly Herald* (Marshall, Tex.)
NHT	Tyler, ed., *The New Handbook of Texas*
NOB	*New Orleans Bee*
NOCB	*Commercial Bulletin* (New Orleans)
NOD	*The Daily Delta* (New Orleans)
NOP	*The Daily Picayune* (New Orleans)
NOTA	*True American* (New Orleans)
NYSL	New York State Library, Albany, NY
OR	*War of the Rebellion: Official Records of the Union and Confederate Armies* (Citations of the *Official Records* follow this format: "OR1, 10.1:724–25" refers to *Official Records,* series 1, volume 10, part 1, pages 724 through 725)
PMBL	Gulick, ed., *Papers of Mirabeau B. Lamar*
PTR	Jenkins, ed., *Papers of the Texas Revolution*
RTNP	Texas Navy Papers, Rosenburg Library, Galveston
QTSHA	*Quarterly of the Texas State Historical Association*
RTP	Republic of Texas Pension Applications, TSL
SCG	*St. Clairsville Gazette*
SED No. 896	62nd Congress, 2nd Session. Senate Executive Document No. 896
SHQ	*Southwestern Historical Quarterly*
TLR	Texas Local Records, TSL
TNP	Texas Navy Papers, TSL
TSL	Archives Division, Texas State Library, Austin, Tex
TTR	*Telegraph and Texas Register* (Houston and Columbia, Tex.)
TVA	Texas Veteran Association Papers, CAH
USNA	United States National Archives, Washington, D.C.

UTA	Special Collections Division, University of Texas at Arlington, Arlington, Tex.
WSH	Williams and Barker, ed., *Writings of Sam Houston*
WTB 1846	William J. Worth to W. W. S. Bliss, September 28, 1846, TTR, January 4, 1847

Introduction

1. Lane, AR, 47. As a rule throughout this biography, all emphases in quotes are original.

2. For a discussion of this episode, see Chapter 5.

3. Gary G. Hamilton views the Gold Rush of 1849 as an example of early American capitalist adventurism. Hamilton, "The Structural Sources of Adventurism: The Case of the California Gold Rush," *American Journal of Sociology* 83 (May 1978), 1466–90. Amy S. Greenberg shows that Manifest Destiny was a gendered ideology by exploring the world of American filibusters of the 1850s. She argues that "aggressive expansionists" and "martial manhood" fueled the movement, and that it contrasted with a powerful domestic counter-impulse. Greenberg, *Manifest Manhood and the Antebellum American Empire,* 1–17. Lane's experiences demonstrate that adventurism offered more than economic gain, and that by the 1850s, his ardor had waned. For a study of romantic adventurism of the early nineteenth-century United States, see Jimmy L. Bryan Jr., "The American Elsewhere: Adventurism and Manliness in the Age of Expansion, 1815–1848" (Ph.D. diss., Southern Methodist University, 2006).

4. Patricia Limerick, for example, describes adventure as "quaint" and irrelevant to the study of the American West, past and present. *The Legacy of Conquest: The Unbroken Past of the American West,* 19. Arguing for the seriousness of the U.S. exploration of North America, William H. Goetzmann notes that it was "something more than adventure," and that adventurers were "mere curosity seekers." *Exploration and Empire: The Explorer and the Scientist in Winning of the American West,* xi, 4.

5. Michael Nerlich, *Ideology of Adventure: Studies in Modern Consciousness, 1100–1750,* 3–30; Martin Green, *Dreams of Adventure, Deeds of Empire,* 3, 76–80, 118–21, 155–63. For the connection between adventure and U.S. literature, see Green, *The Great American Adventure* (1984), William E. Lenz, "Narratives of Exploration, Sea Fiction, Mariners' Chronicles, and the Rise of American Nationalism: 'To Cast Anchor on that Point Where All Meridians Terminate,'" *American Studies* 32 (Summer 1991), 41–61; Brady Harrison, "The Young Americans: Emerson, Walker, and the Early Literature of American Empire," *American Studies* 40 (Fall 1999), 75–97; and Greenberg, *Manifest Manhood* (2005).

6. E. Anthony Rotundo, *American Manhood: Transformations in Masculinity from the Revolution to the Modern Era,* 20–25, 75–91, 168–69, 178–85; Michael Kimmel, *Manhood in America: A Cultural History,* 7–8, 26, 61–60, 365–66.

7. Green, *Great American,* 13–15, 23–38; Henry Nash Smith, *Virgin Land: The American West as Symbol and Myth,* 59–70. Green argues that the gentleman adventurer was an American phenomenon, but Walter Scott's characters, such as Wilfred Ivanhoe and Edward Waverley, certainly exemplified this archetype.

8. W. P. Lane to E. Greer, March 18, 1862, OR1, 8:300.

9. Gerald F. Linderman argues that by 1864, the realities of war disillusioned many Civil War soldiers. Linderman, *Embattled Courage: The Experience of Combat in the American Civil War* (1987). James M. McPherson counters that ideology sustained soldiers even through the most trying times. McPherson, *For Cause and Comrades: Why Men Fought in the Civil War* (1997).

10. Lilian R. Furst, *Romanticism,* 1–14; Osterweis, *Romanticism and Nationalism in the Old South,* 8–9, 235–39; Green, *Dreams of Adventure,* 3, 76–80, 118–21, 155–63. See also Jacques Barzun, John B. Halstead, and J. J. Saunders in Halstead, ed., *Romanticism,* vii–x, 1–3, 18–29.

11. Goetzmann, *Exploration and Empire,* 181–98; Robert W. Johannsen, *To the Halls of the Montezumas: The Mexican War in the American Imagination,* 68–107; Roderick Nash, *Wilderness and the American Mind,* 44–67; Richard Slotkin, *Regeneration through Violence: The Mythology of the American Frontier, 1600–1860,* 394–465; Bryan, "The American Elsewhere," 103–106.

12. Sam W. Haynes, "Anglophobia and the Annexation of Texas: The Quest for National Security" in Haynes and Christopher Morris, ed., *Manifest Destiny and Empire: American Antebellum Expansionism,* 115–45; Reginald Horsman, *Race and Manifest Destiny: The Origins of American Racial Anglo-Saxonism* (1981) and Thomas R. Hietala, *Manifest Design: Anxious Aggrandizement in Late Jacksonian America* (1985). These build on Norman A. Graebner's *Empire on the Pacific: A Study in American Continental Expansion* (1955), and Frederick Merk's *Manifest Destiny and Mission in American History* (1963). They argue that anxieties over slavery, industrialization, urbanization, a racially charged separatist policy, and British ambitions fueled the U.S. drive to the Pacific.

13. In the 1940s or 1950s, Barnes F. Lathrop wrote an 80-page manuscript that focused on Lane's Civil War career. He based his work almost exclusively on Lane's memoirs and documents from the *Official Records* of the Civil War. Lathrop, "Walter Paye Lane: Biography," CAH. In 1992, Max S. Lale used Lane as the subject of his presidential address to the Texas State Historical Association. Lale, "Walter P. Lane: An Appreciation," Texas State Historical Association 96th Annual Meeting, 1992.

14. Louella Styles Vincent to Mary Jane Lane, December 8, 1905, and Lane to Vincent, January [1906], in Lane, AR (1928), 131, 132.

Chapter 1

1. Michael H. Tepper and Elizabeth P. Bently, *Passenger Arrivals at the Port of Baltimore,* 373; *American Commercial and Daily Advertiser* (Baltimore), August 11, 1821.

2. Eugene C. Barker, ed., "Journal of Stephen F. Austin on His First Trip to Texas, 1821," QTSHA 7 (Apr. 1904), 296; Gregg Cantrell, *Stephen F. Austin: Empresario of Texas,* 84–94.

3. Although known only to them, family members have forgotten how Walter Lane received the nickname "Nonny." William H. Lane to Jimmy Moore, December 9, 1994, and Margaret Pace to the author, September 24 and [November 15], 1995, author's file. Walter Lane claimed kinship with Denny Lane, Cork's representative in Parliament, and the Lady Hungerford, Duchess of County Cork. William S. Speer and John Henry Brown, *Encyclopedia of the New West,* 309; Mary Jane Lane to Louella Styles Vincent, January [1906], in Lane AR (1928), 142.

4. James S. Donnelly, *Land and the People of Nineteenth-Century Cork,* 18–19, 26, 45–46; John B. O'Brien, "Population, Politics, and Society in Cork, 1780–1900," in Patrick O'Flanagan and Cornelius G. Buttimer, ed. *Cork: History and Society,* 704–707; John King to Robert Nevin, September 1832, quoted from Kerby A. Miller, et al., "Emigrants and Exiles: Irish Cultures and Irish Emigration to North America, 1790–1922," *Irish Historical Studies* 82 (Sep. 1980), 116.

5. On December 25, 1833, William and Olivia sold their acreage. They might have resided in Wheeling, Virginia, before moving onto a town lot that they purchased on May 28, 1835, in Fairview, Ohio. 1828–1832 Tax Duplicate and Deed Records, G:37, I:116, O:391, Guernsey County Recorder's Office; MTWH, June 26, 1884; William Lane, "Gen. Walter P. Lane," East Texas Baptist University, Marshall, Tex.; Lane, AR, 5, 16.

6. Tepper and Bently, *Passenger Arrivals,* 373; Leonard Peacefull, ed., *A Geography of Ohio,* 6, 40; Cyrus P. B. Sarchet, *History of Guernsey County Ohio,* 25, 26; R. Douglas Hurt, *The Ohio Frontier,* 4, 152–55, 168; "Sketch of Guernsey County, Ohio," CGT, February 24, 1832.

7. F. A. Morgan, *Wagon Train to Oregon—also—Guernsey County's Texas Hero and Confederate General . . . ,* 21; SCG, September 17, 1825, June 24, July 29, 1826; William G. Wolfe, *Stories of Guernsey County, Ohio,* 216–17, 949; Norris F. Schneider, "The National Road: Main Street America," *Ohio History* 83 (Spring 1974), 123–24.

8. John S. Tyson, "Speech," *American and Daily Commercial Advertiser,* July 10, 1821. For the connections between expansionism and romanticism, see Robert W. Johannsen, *To the Halls of the Montezumas: The Mexican War in the American Imagination* (1985), and Richard V. Francaviglia and Jimmy L. Bryan Jr., "'Are we chimerical in this opinion?' Visions of the Pacific Railroad before 1845," *Pacific Historical Review* 71 (May 2002), 179–202.

9. For an expanded study of adventurism, expansionism, and romanticism, see Jimmy L. Bryan Jr., "The American Elsewhere: Adventurism and Manliness in the Age of Expansion, 1815–1848" (Ph.D. diss., Southern Methodist University, 2006). For the coupling of martial manhood with aggressive expansionism in the 1850s, see Amy S. Greenberg, *Manifest Manhood and the Antebellum American Empire* (2005).

10. Wolfe, *Stories of Guernsey,* 961–62.

11. Rollin G. Osterweis, *Romanticism and Nationalism in the Old South,* 41–53; Johannsen, *To the Halls,* 70; CGT, October 16, 1830, November 23, 1832. Bertram Wyatt-Brown argues that the South practiced an ancient code of honor inherited from their Celtic ancestors, contrary to Osterweis's interpretation that it was a recent cultural phenomenon. Brown, *Southern Honor: Ethics and Behavior in the Old South,* 25–61. Lane's experience supports Osterweis.

12. Walter Scott, *Ivanhoe,* 317.

13. CGT, July 20, 1833, September 20, October 18, 1834; *Guernsey Times, and Farmers' and Mechanics' Advocate* (Cambridge, Ohio), April 11, 1835. Further examples: CGT, January 29, 1831, June 22, October 19, 1832, October 19, 25, 1833. For Texas: SCG, October 7, 1826; CGT, April 20, 1832.

14. Lane, AR, 5.

15. SCG, September 17, 1825; CGT, February 2, 16, March 2, 30, 1827, November 29, 1834.

16. SCG, August 22, 1835; *Wheeling Tri-Weekly Gazette,* November 6, 18, 1835. Further examples from the Wheeling-Zanesville region include the *Guernsey Times* and *Farmers' and Mechanics' Advocate,* September 19, November 21, 28, December 12, 26, 1835; SCG, December 5, 8, 18, 24, 1835; *Wheeling Tri-Weekly Gazette,* September 14, 30, November 9–23, 1835; and *The Zanesville Gazette,* October 28, November 4, 25, December 2, 9, 1835.

17. *Wheeling Tri-Weekly Gazette,* November 4, 18, 1835; SCG, November 11, 1835.

18. For the best work: James E. Crisp, "Race, Revolution, and the Texas Republic: Toward a Reinterpretation," in Joseph G. Dawson, III, ed., *The Texas Military Experience: From the Revolution through World War II,* 36–48; Paul D. Lack, *The Texas Revolutionary Experience: A Political and Social History, 1835–1836,* 3; Lack, "In the Long Shadow of Eugene C. Barker," in Walter L. Buenger and Robert A. Calvert, eds., *Texas Through Time: Evolving Interpretations,* 139–49; and David J. Weber, *The Mexican Frontier, 1821–1846: The American Southwest under Mexico,* 165–67, 177.

19. Lane, AR, 5.

20. John C. Duval, *Early Times in Texas,* 8; Micajah Autry to wife, December 7, 1835, PTR, 3:105; John Sowers Brooks to sister, March 4, 1836, John Sowers Brooks Papers, CAH.

21. S. H. Walker to A. M. Walker, January 22, 1842, Samuel Hamilton Walker Papers, TSL.

22. Lane, AR, 5; W. M. Paxton, *The Marshall Family . . . ,* 184.

23. *Louisville Public Advertiser,* October 29, 1835, February 20, March 10, 1836; James E. Winston, "Kentucky and the Independence of Texas," SHQ 16 (Jul. 1912), 29, 33, 42–43, 62; Duval, *Early Times,* 8; Lane, AR, 5.

24. Lack, *Texas Revolutionary,* 53–74; Cantrell, *Stephen F. Austin,* 338–41.

25. Stephen F. Austin to James Perry, March 4, 1836, *The Austin Papers,* Eugene C. Barker, ed., 3:317–18.

26. *Louisville Public Advertiser,* March 10, 1836; "Austin's Address," Mary Austin Holley, *Texas,* 275, 279; Lane, AR, 5.

27. Lane, AR, 5–6.

28. William F. Gray, *From Virginia to Texas,* 88; Lane, AR, 6.

29. For the contradictions of forging a revolutionary identity among fierce individualists in both the Texas government and army, see Lack, *Texas Revolutionary,* 60–63, 97–108, 124–25, 137–55. For Texan individualism and its penchant for havoc, see William Ransom Hogan, *The Texas Republic: A Social and Economic History,* 267–90.

30. Lane attested to the service of veterans in both Kimbro and Chessher's companies. He does not appear on the two extant rolls for Chessher's company, and rolls for Kimbro's have not survived. Walter P. Lane and other files, RTP; *Muster Rolls of the Texas Revolution,* 132–33, 196–98; George Louis Crocket, *Two Centuries in East Texas: A History of San Augustine County and Surrounding Territory from 1685 to the Present Time,* 183; Hazel Miller Brittain, "Stories My Grandfather Told Me," ETHJ 8 (October 1970), 127; Walter P. Lane and other files, AMC; Stephen W. Blount to Thomas J. Rusk, April 1, 1836, PTR, 5:274.

31. Lane, AR, 6; Lack, *Texas Revolutionary,* 168–72; Diana Everett, *Texas Cherokees: A People between Two Fires, 1819–1840,* 71–73, 76–79; James Chessher and Ralph Chessher to Nacogdoches Committee of Vigilance and Safety, April 11, 1836, PTR, 5:429.

32. John A. Quitman to Felix Huston, [April] 15, 1836, in J. F. H. Claiborne, ed., *Life and Correspondence of John A. Quitman,* 1:149.

33. Lane, AR, 6–7. In a later letter, Lane recalled that he traveled with Dr. Lemuel Gustine during his journey to Groce's Retreat. Gustine later fought at San Jacinto in Henry Karnes's company. Walter P. Lane to Moses Austin Bryan, July 22, 1889, TVA.

34. Lane, AR, 7.

35. Lane, AR, 7.

36. Stephen L. Hardin, *Texian Iliad: A Military History of the Texas Revolution,* 185–91.

37. Lane, AR, 7; Lane file, RTP; Sam Houston Dixon and Louis Wiltz Kemp, *The Heroes of San Jacinto,* 305–22.

38. Frank X. Tolbert, *The Day of San Jacinto,* 94–97.

39. Lane, AR, 8; Lucy A. Erath, ed., *The Memoirs of George B. Erath,* 30–31; Hardin, *Texian Iliad,* 202–203.

40. Lane, AR, 9; Lane to Bryan, September 12, 1885, TVA. For an explanation of the timing of Smith's scout, see Lane, AR (2000), 132.

41. Lane, AR, 9–10; MTWH, September 10, 1881.

42. Lane, AR, 10; Hardin, *Texian Iliad,* 203–204.

43. Lane, AR, 10–11; Creed Taylor's memoirs as John W. Hunter Literary Effort, TSL, 41; Hardin, *Texian Iliad,* 208–209. At different times, Lane claimed to have served under William H. Patton and Isaac W. Burton. Lane file, RTP; File RV-238, GLO; R. K. Goodloe to [Bryan], July 3, 1875, TVA.

44. Lane to Bryan, September 12, 1885, TVA; Lane, AR, 11; Y. P. Alsbury Reminiscence, CAH; Hardin, *Texian Iliad,* 210–11.

45. Lane, AR, 11.

46. James Washington Winters, "An Account of the Battle of San Jacinto," QTSHA 6 (Oct. 1902) 143; Hardin, *Texian Iliad,* 213–15. Hardin provides a good review of Texan brutality at San Jacinto. For an apologetic account, see Tolbert, *San Jacinto,* 151–59.

47. Lane, AR, 11, 12; Winters, "An Account," 143; Taylor's memoirs, 42.

48. Deposition of Thomas F. Corry, December 12, 1859, and Deposition of Walter P. Lane, November 8, 1859, in John Forbes vs. Nicholas D. Labadie, Robert Bruce Blake Collection (typescript), ETRC, 36:127, 130, 134–37, 143–45; Report of Court of Enquiry, April 28, 1836, Andrew Jackson Houston Collection, TSL.

49. Sam'l A. Roberts to M. B. Lamar, September 4, 1839, PMBL, 3:116; Lane, AR, 12; Hardin, *Texian Iliad,* 215.

50. Moses Austin Bryan Reminiscence, MAB, 27; Isaac L. Hill in J. H. Kuykendall, ed., "Reminiscences of Early Texans," QTSHA 7 (Jul. 1903) 45.

51. Lane, AR, 13.

52. Lane, AR, 13–16; Thos. J. Rusk to the People of Texas, May 10, 1836, PTR 6:211–12.

53. Lane, AR, 16; Lane file, RTP.

Chapter 2

1. Stephen L. Hardin, *The Texian Iliad: A Military History of the Texas Revolution,* 246, 249–50; Jim Dan Hill, *The Texas Navy in Forgotten Battles and Shirtsleeve Diplomacy,* 56–66.

2. The volunteers were likely crewmen meant to serve on the *Thomas Toby.* William F. Gray, *From Virginia to Texas,* 210; John C. Duval, *Early Times in Texas,* 21; Lane, AR, 16; TTR, September 21, 1836; NOCB, September 10, 1836; Hill, *Texas Navy,* 93; Alex Dienst, "The Navy of the Republic of Texas," QTSHA 12 (Jan. 1909), 27–29.

3. Work Projects Administration, *Ship Registers and Enrollments of New Orleans,* 3:59; H. C. Thompson to Naval Department, August 29, 1837, TNP; NOB, April 30, May 16, 1836; NOTA, May 16, 1836. For descriptions of and comments about the *Thomas Toby,* see Toby to Burnet, July 12, September 1, 4, 1836, PTR, 7:435–36, 8:366, 391; A. G. Thurston to Editors, May 26, 1837, LDJ, June 6, 1837; NOCB, October 5, 1836; H. G. Heartt to A. G. M[?], April 4, 1874, undated Galveston clipping, TSL; Benjamin S. Grayson to Thurston, February 9, 1837, Thurston to S. Rhoads Fisher, April 4, 1837, and Francis B. Wright to Secretary of the Navy, September 20, 1837, TNP. James Reed & Company purchased the *DeKalb* on September 2, 1836, and re-fitted it for armaments. Once it arrived in Velasco, the merchants sold it to Benjamin S. Grayson and J. M. Shreve of Velasco, finalizing the transaction on November 30 for $1,757.63. Buchanan, "Notes and References," TNP; Receipt, November 30, 1836, undated note, and Shreve and Grayson to John Reed & Co., December 13, 1836,

Grayson Family Papers, CAH; David G. Burnet to Peter W. Grayson and James Collinsworth, May 26, 1836, and Collinsworth and Grayson to Burnet, July 15, 1836 in George P. Garrison, ed., *Diplomatic Correspondence of the Republic of Texas,* 1:89–91, 110–11.

4. Sam Houston to Collinsworth, March 17, 1836, PTR, 5:123; Richard V. Francaviglia, *From Sail to Steam: Four Centuries of Texas Maritime History, 1500–1900,* 105–108, 116; Hill, *Texas Navy,* 3–18.

5. James M. Denham, "New Orleans, Maritime Commerce, and the Texas War for Independence," SHQ 97 (Jan. 1994), 529; *Journal of the Proceedings of the General Council of the Republic of Texas held at San Felipe de Austin, November 14th, 1835,* 10; Hill, *Texas Navy,* 37–38; Dienst, "Navy of the Republic," 165–96; "An Ordinance and Decree for Granting Letters of Marque and Reprisal," November 25, 1835, PTR, 9:393–94; Richard E. Winslow, III, *"Wealth and Honor": Portsmouth During the Golden Age of Privateering, 1775–1815,* 1, 3; Ralph T. Ward, *Pirates in History,* 98–111.

6. Hill and Dienst have largely dismissed the Texas privateers as an ineffective sideshow to the national navy. Hill, *Texas Navy,* 36–40; Dienst, "Navy of the Republic," 169, 181–82. Recent Texas Navy chronicler Jonathan W. Jordan acknowledges the work of earlier privateers, but characterizes the cruises of the *Thomas Toby* as "frolicking." *Lone Star Navy: Texas, the Fight for the Gulf of Mexico, and the Shaping of the American West,* 25–35, 78–79.

7. Dienst identified six privateers: the *San Felipe, William Robbins, Flash, Ocean, Terrible,* and the *Thomas Toby.* Dienst, "Navy of the Republic," 165–70, 184–96. Another six active, irregularly commissioned vessels were the *Laura, Mary Jane, Comanche, Viper, David Crockett,* and the *Sam Houston;* and five that did not fulfill their commissions: the *Brutus* (served in the regular navy), *Bounty, Revenge, Benjamin R. Milam,* and the *Jim Bowie.* James Buchanan, "Notes and References taken from Documents on file in the office of the Navy Department," November 3, 1836, TNP; TTR, January 23, February 20, March 12, 1836; José Antonio Mexia to Gentlemen, October 29, 1835, T. F. McKinney to President, January 14, 1836, and J. D. Boylan to T. J. Rusk, June 22, 1836, PTR, 2:262–64, 4:12, 6:224; Charles E. Hawkins to James Morgan, May 9, 1836, RTNP; *Daily Commercial Register and Patriot* (Mobile, Ala.), July 22, 1836, June 5, 1837.

8. Buchanan, "Notes and References," TNP; Hill, *Texas Navy,* 27–28, 38–39; Dienst, "Navy of the Republic," 184–96; David G. Burnet Proclamation, March 25, 1836, and Burnet to Sam P. Carson, April 1, 1836, PTR, 5:188–89, 276; NOB, June 18, August 17, September 21, 23, 1836; NOCB, October 7, 13, 1836; TTR, August 16, 1836; NOTA, August 16, 17, September 22, 1836.

9. Population Schedules of the Seventh Census of the United States, 1850 (M432, roll 910), USNA; "Petition of Nathaniel Hoyt," [June 12, 1845], PMBL 6:5–6; Gray, *From Virginia,* 157; NOB, June 22, August 10, 1835, January 4, April 27, 1836; NOTA, August 10, 1835; MDG, September 7, 1835. As captain of the *Pennsylvania,* Hoyt transported volunteers

under William Ward and Amasa Turner, as well as the Twin Sisters, the artillery at San Jacinto. A. Houston to [?], April 1, 1836, William Bryan to [Burnet], March 31, 1836, Thomas Toby to Burnet, September 4, 1836, and Samuel G. Hardaway to Robert Collins, June 6, 1836, PTR, 5:251, 288, 391, 7:39.

10. Toby to Burnet, September 22, 1836, PTR, 8:515–17; Hoyt Petition, PMBL 6:6; Hill, *Texas Navy*, 64–66.

11. Hill, *Texas Navy*, 93; Dienst, "Navy of the Republic," 192; NOB, November 3, 1836; MDG, October 25, 1836; NOCB, November 8, 17, 1836; Lane, AR, 17; Hoyt Petition, PMBL 6:6.

12. Lane, AR, 17; TTR, November 12, 19, December 9, 1836; NOB, November 3, 1836; NOCB, November 3, 1836; LDJ, December 1, 1836.

13. NOB, November 3, 1836; NOCB, November 3, 8, 1836; LDJ, December 1, 1836; William H. Jack to Henry Smith, November 14, 1836, RTNP.

14. *Daily Commercial Record and Patriot*, November 29, 1836; *Morning Courier and New-York Enquirer*, November 21, 1836; TTR, November 30, 1836. For more examples of the alarm the *Toby* created, see: Lane, AR, 17; NOB, November 3, 11, 1836; TTR, November 9, 12, 1836.

15. Denham, "New Orleans," 529–31; Thomas Urquhart, et al., to A. J. Dallas, May 9, 1836, editorial [n.d.], and Dallas to Gentlemen, May 15, 1836, NOB, May 11, 19, 1836.

16. NOB, November 17, 1836, January 17, February 13, 1837; NOCB, November 17, 1836; LDJ, December 1, 1836; Lane, AR, 17–18.

17. Hoyt recalled that the mutiny occurred at Velasco, saved only by the loyal navigator, who piloted the schooner to New Orleans. The documentation supports Lane's version. Hoyt Petition, PMBL 6:6; TTR, March 2, 1837; Thurston to Fisher, February 10, 1837, TNP; Lane, AR, 18–21.

18. Thurston to Fisher, February 10, 1837, TNP; TTR, March 2, 1837; NOB, March 2, 1837; Lane, AR, 21.

19. Hill, *Texas Navy*, 74; Hoyt Petition, PMBL 6:6; Thurston to Hoyt, April 9, 1837, Thurston to Grayson, February 9, 1837, Thurston to Fisher, February 10, April 4, 1837, and Grayson to Thurston, February 9, 1837, TNP; Fisher to Thurston, January 31, February 26, March 28, 1837, and Fisher to Shreve and Grayson, March 1, 1837, RTNP.

20. Hill, *Texas Navy*, 68–74; NOTA, March 31, 1837; Moore Declaration, and Moore to Sirs, May 3, 1837, *Daily Commercial Record and Patriot*, June 5, 12, 1837.

21. Hill, *Texas Navy*, 75–80; Hoyt to Fisher, April 27, 1837, TNP; Anonymous, May 5, 1837, NOB, June 24, 1837; NOTA, April 24, 1837; S. W. Cushing, *Wild Oats Sowing, or the Autobiography of an Adventurer*, 226; Fisher to Thurston, February 26, 1837, RTNP.

22. Lane erroneously recalled this action as occurring during the *Toby*'s first cruise in 1836. Lane, AR, 16–17; MDG, June 10, 1837.

23. Lane, AR, 21–22.

24. MDG, June 11, 18, 1837.

25. MDG, June 18, 20, 1837; NYH, June 30, 1837.

26. Lane, AR, 22; Hoyt Petition, PMBL 6:6; Hill, *Texas Navy,* 93–96; Dienst, "Navy of the Republic," 192; NOB, June 13, 1837; NOP, June 11, 1837.

27. Hoyt Petition, PMBL 6:6; Thompson to Department, August 29, 1837, TNP; Hill, *Texas Navy,* 94, 96, 103.

28. Lane, AR, 22; Hoyt Petition, PMBL 6:6–7.

29. S. W. Geiser, "Racer's Storm (1837), with Notes on Other Texas Hurricanes in the Period 1818–1886," *Field and Laboratory* 12 (Jun. 1944), 59–61; Lane, AR, 22. Grayson and Shreve took possession of the *Fenix,* and renamed it the *Charles Edmonston.* NOB, October 25, 1837. On February 4, 1840, the Texas government later reimbursed the firm $2678.70 for expenses operating the *Tom Toby.* Grayson and Shreve file, AMC.

Chapter 3

1. Lane, AR, 24–25; Walter Lane to Moses Bryan, March 1, 1880, O. Hendrick file, TVA; William S. Speer and John Henry Brown, *Encyclopedia of the New West,* 268–71.

2. John S. Ford, *Rip Ford's Texas,* Stephen B. Oates, editor, 34.

3. Paul D. Lack views the revolt as a concerted policy of Tejanos battling against "their declining status" in the new republic. Lack, "The Córdova Revolt," in Gerald D. Poyo, ed., *Tejano Journey, 1770–1850,* 93–100; TTR, September 29, 1838.

4. Ford, *Rip Ford's,* 35; "A Muster and Final Roll of Capt. H. W. Augustine's Company of Mounted Volunteers in the August Campaign 1838 against the Mexicans," RTMR.

5. Córdova's declaration quoted from Lack, "Córdova Revolt," 97.

6. TTR, September 29, 1838; Thomas Rusk to Mirabeau Lamar, August 24, 1838, PMBL 2:207.

7. TTR, September 29, 1838; Ford, *Rip Ford's Texas,* 36; Rusk to Lamar, August 24, 1838, and Hugh McLeod to Lamar, August 20, 1838, PMBL 2:207, 209.

8. Ford, *Rip Ford's,* 35; "Roll of Capt. H. W. Augustine's Company," RTMR.

9. Lack, "Córdova Revolt," 101–108; Speer and Brown, *Encyclopedia,* 309; George Lane file, AMC. George Lane located at Milam, Sabine County, by May 1838, and he also served during the Córdova revolt in David Renfro's company. TTR, October 27, 1838; Kathryn Hooper Davis, *East Texas Militiamen,* 2:23.

10. Diana Everett, *Texas Cherokees: A People between Two Fires, 1819–1840,* 64–65; Ford, *Rip Ford's,* 36; *Report of George W. Bonnell, Commissioner Indian Affairs,* 1, 12.

11. Samuel Houston to the Congress, November 19, 1838, WSH 2:299, 301; Everett, *Texas Cherokees,* 14–15, 24–25.

12. *The Land Commissioners of Texas: 150 Years of the General Land Office,* 13; Thomas Lloyd Miller, *The Public Lands of Texas, 1519–1970,* 45, 48–49; Miller, *Bounty and Donation Land Grants of Texas, 1835–1888,* 801.

13. Miller, *Bounty and Donation,* 801; "Roll of Capt. H. W. Augustine's Company," RTMR; T. J. Allen to C. J. Allen, November 13, 1839, Samuel Tabor Allen Family Papers, CAH; San Augustine County Probate Minutes, A:50.

14. William M. Love to William R. Reding, March 2, 1838, in Walter Clay Dixson, *Richland Crossing: A Portrait of Texas Pioneers,* 126.

15. Portions of this account of the Surveyors' Fight first appeared as "'More Disastrous Than All:' The Surveyors' Fight, 1838," ETHJ 38 (Spring 2000), 3–14. For a discussion of the date, numbers and identities of surveyors, details of the battle and retreat, and the several accounts, see the ETHJ article. The primary accounts of the battle are: John Henry Brown, "Battle Creek," Corsicana *Navarro Express,* May 12, 1860; Lane to James T. DeShields, May 18, 1885, in DeShields, *Border Wars of Texas,* 247–55; Lane, AR, 25–34; and TTR, October 20, 1838. Unless otherwise stated, all quotations in the following section occur in Lane, AR, 26–34.

16. Lane to DeShields, May 18, 1885, *Border Wars,* 248.

17. Elizabeth and James R. Taylor to Joshua Barton, [November 1838], Barton Family Papers, UTA; W. H. Wagley to John Henry Brown, April 20, [1886], JHB.

18. Lane, AR, 35. On May 23, 1839, George Lane rented a lot on Columbia Street from Ebenezer Kellogg for two years. San Augustine County Deed Records, E:332.

19. A. M. Gibson, *The Kickapoos: Lords of the Middle Border,* 155–58.

20. Lamar, Message of the President, December 21, 1838, PMBL 2:352–53. For the failure of Houston's conciliatory Indian policy, see Gary Clayton Anderson, *The Conquest of Texas: Ethnic Cleansing in the Promised Land, 1820–1875,* 153–71.

21. Everett, *Texas Cherokees,* 102–108.

22. "Muster roll of William Kimbro's company," RTMR; Lane, AR, 34–35.

23. Lane, AR, 35–36; "J. E. Hamilton's company of mounted rangers, &c.," RTMR. Anderson views these Anglo-American campaigns against Native Americans in Texas as a deliberate policy of ethnic cleansing. *Conquest of Texas,* 7–8, 172–79. Lane's experience does not contradict this argument.

24. George Louis Crocket, *Two Centuries in East Texas,* 227–28, 235–37; William Ransom Hogan, *The Texas Republic,* 29–30; Ford, *Rip Ford's Texas,* 15–17. From the perspective of one of its leading families, the Cartwrights, Margaret Swett Henson and Deolece Parmelee trace the evolution of San Augustine, from frontier uncertainty to rural prosperity. *The Cartwrights of San Augustine: Three Generations of Agricultural Entrepreneurs in Nineteenth-Century Texas,* 41–190.

25. Lane, AR, 36; General Land Office, "Sabine County," *Maps of All Texas Counties;* Sam Houston, et al., "Constitution of the Company, of the Town of Hamilton," 1840, Thomas W. Streeter, *Bibliography of Texas, 1795–1845,* No. 318; Hogan, *Texas Republic,* 89–94; Frederick C. Chabot, ed., *McFarland Journal* 15, 61. Hamilton survived until the mid-twentieth century. It now lies under the Toledo Bend Reservoir, created in 1969.

26. Lane joined the Masons in 1843, but apparently was not an active member. Robert Bruce Blake Collection (typescript), ETRC, 35:233–43; "Celebration of the Battle of San Jacinto" (broadside), April 10, 1839, Lyne Taliaferro Barrett Papers, ETRC; Lane, AR, 25.

27. In his memoirs, Lane claimed that he left for San Antonio in 1843, but he still appeared on the tax rolls until 1844. Lane, AR, 36; San Augustine County Tax Rolls, TLR.

28. Lane, AR, 47; MM, October 8, 1886.

Chapter 4

1. Hays was born a month before Lane, in January 1817. Lane, AR, 36; James Kimmins Greer, *Colonel Jack Hays: Texas Frontier Leader and California Builder,* 15–125; Walter Prescott Webb, *The Texas Rangers: A Century of Frontier Defense,* 67–88; Frederick Wilkins, *The Highly Irregular Irregulars: Texas Rangers in the Mexican War,* 11–12; "J. C. Hays Company, 1844," RTMR.

2. For overviews of annexation and Polk's decision for war, see: Norman A. Graebner, *Empire on the Pacific: A Study in American Continental Expansion* (1955); Sam W. Haynes, *James K. Polk and the Expansionist Impulse* (3rd Ed., 2005); David M. Pletcher, *The Diplomacy of Annexation: Texas, Oregon, and the Mexican War* (1973).

3. Zachary Taylor to James P. Henderson, April 26, 1846, and Henderson, G.O. No. 1, May 2, 1846, TTR, May 13, 1846; Lane, AR, 36; Charles D. Spurlin, *Texas Veterans in the Mexican War,* 17–34.

4. Much later, Lane, Green, McCulloch, and Hamilton Bee would attain the rank of general in the Confederate army. Spurlin, *Texas Veterans,* 17–34; Samuel C. Reid, *The Scouting Expeditions of McCulloch's Texas Rangers, 11–23;* K. Jack Bauer, *The Mexican War, 1846–1848,* 19–20; [James L. Freaner] to Gentlemen, July 24, 1846, NOD, August 9, 1846. The black bean episode occurred after the Texas prisoners attempted to escape. As punishment, the Mexicans forced them to draw from a jar of beans, of which one in ten were black. Those who drew black were executed. Sam W. Haynes, *Soldiers of Misfortune: The Somervell and Mier Expeditions,* 123–27.

5. [Freaner] to Gentlemen, August 1 and 15, 1846, NOD, August 15, 1846; Bauer, *Mexican War,* 82, 87–88; Taylor to Adj. Gen., August 25, 1846, HED No. 60, 413.

6. Acklin file, CSR-MW; NYH, September 2, 1846; unsigned letter, August 6, 1846, NOD, August 15, 1846; (Austin) *Texas Democrat,* September 16, 1846.

7. Reid, *Scouting Expeditions,* 106–107; José María de Aguirre to Taylor, November 16, 1846, HED No. 60, 378; NYH, September 16, 1846; *Texas Democrat,* September 16, 1846; Wilkins, *Highly Irregular,* 78; and Spurlin, *Texas Veterans,* 30–31.

8. [Freaner] to Gentlemen, August 23, 1846, NOD, September 6, 1846.

9. Samuel Walker, Regimental Orders, August 27, 1846, Samuel Hamilton Walker Papers, TSL.

10. W. W. S. Bliss, Special Orders No. 129, August 27, 1846, HED No. 60, 526; Wilkins,

Highly Irregular, 76, 79; Spurlin, *Texas Veterans,* 19; James K. Holland, "Diary of a Texan Volunteer in the Mexican War," SHQ 30 (Jul. 1926), 22–23.

11. Lane, AR, 37; Reid, *Scouting Expeditions,* 141; Bauer, *Mexican War,* 89–92.

12. Lane AR, 37.

13. Bauer, *Mexican War,* 92–93.

14. Reid, *Scouting Expeditions,* 151, 154–55; WTB 1846; John C. Hays to Henderson, [September 1846], PMBL 4:139; A Pioneer, "Recollections of the Mexican War," *The Pioneer* 15 (Oct. 15, 1900), 152.

15. Reid, *Scouting Expeditions,* 158; WTB 1846.

16. Reid, *Scouting Expeditions,* 156–58; Lane, AR, 38–39; Hays to Henderson, [September 1846], PMBL 4:139; WTB 1846; Pioneer, "Recollections," 15 (Oct. 15, 1900), 153–54. Thomas W. Cutrer provides another perspective of the rangers at Monterrey. Cutrer, *Ben McCulloch and the Frontier Military Tradition,* 83–90.

17. Lane, AR 39; Spurlin, *Texas Veterans,* 18.

18. Lane, AR, 40; WTB 1846.

19. WTB 1846; Hays to Henderson, [September 1846], PMBL 4:139–40; Lane, AR, 40–41, 46–47; Justin H. Smith, *The War with Mexico,* 1:256–57; Pioneer, "Recollections," 15 (Oct. 14, 1900), 154.

20. Reid, *Scouting Expeditions,* 192.

21. *Cincinnati Daily Enquirer,* November 11, 1846.

22. Creed Taylor's Memoirs as John W. Hunter Literary Effort, TSL, 135.

23. *Cincinnati Daily Enquirer,* November 11, 1846.

24. Pioneer, "Recollections," 15 (Nov. 15, 1900), 169.

25. Lane, AR, 41; Reid, *Scouting Expeditions,* 191–95; WTB 1846; Pioneer, "Recollections," 15 (Nov. 15, 1900), 169; NYH, October 21, 1846; Smith, *War with Mexico,* 1:257–58, 501; Bauer, *Mexican War,* 97–99.

26. Lane, AR, 41; E. Anthony Rotundo, *American Manhood: Transformations in Masculinity from the Revolution to the Modern Era,* 82–85. Lane made special mention of this moment, when he slept next to Capt. John Pope, and to fellow officers of the Texas Veteran Association. Lane, AR, 59; Lane to Moses Bryan, April 12, 1885, Moses Austin Bryan Papers, CAH.

27. Lane, AR, 40–41; WTB 1846.

28. Lane, AR, 41.

29. Bauer, *Mexican War,* 99–101; Smith, *War with Mexico,* 1:260, 263, 503–506.

30. NYH, November 10, 1846; Reid, *Scouting Expeditions,* 204; Lane, AR, 41–42.

31. NYH, October 21, 1846, November 6, 1846; Cutrer, *Ben McCulloch,* 89–90.

32. [Luther Giddings], *Sketches of the Campaign in Northern Mexico in Eighteen Hundred Forty-Six and Seven,* 221; Holland, "Diary of a Texan," 27; Taylor to Adj. Gen., Octo-

ber 6, 1846, HED No. 60, 430; *Cincinnati Daily Enquirer,* November 11, 1846. The Cincinnati report might have been an exaggerated account of a ranger arrested by Colonel Hays for killing a Mexican soldier in the streets of Monterrey. Greer, *John C. Hays,* 154; Wilkins, *Highly Irregular,* 106–12; Reid, *Scouting Expeditions,* 61, 154; W. B. P. Gaines, statement, October 10, 1846, HED No. 60, 431–32.

33. Lane, AR, 12, 32, 41–43.

34. Taylor to Adj.Gen., October 6, 1846, and Bliss, Order No. 124, October 1, 1846, HED No. 60, 430, 508; Spurlin, *Texas Volunteers,* 19; [Giddings], *Sketches,* 221–22.

35. In 1857, S. Compton Smith remembered Lane, along with fellow rangers Hays, Walker, McCulloch, Chevallié, and Gillespie, but Lane was the only one that he included both his first and last name, suggesting that he was the least known of the rangers. Smith, *Chile Con Carne Or the Camp and the Field,* 268.

36. Hays to Henderson, [September 1846], PMBL 4:140; MM, December 8, 1890.

Chapter 5

1. Lane, AR, 41–42; *Texas Democrat* (Austin), December 16, 1846; John C. Hays to M. H. Chevallié, November 2, 1846, *Colorado Herald* (Matagorda, Tex.), November 28, 1846; W. W. S. Bliss, Orders No. 60, May 27, 1847, TTR, March 8, 1847; Frederick Wilkins, *The Highly Irregular Irregulars: Texas Rangers in the Mexican War,* 125; Bruce Winders, *Polk's Army: The American Military Experience in the Mexican War,* 70–71.

2. Lane, AR, 42; *Texas Democrat,* February 20, 1847; Charles D. Spurlin, *Texas Veterans in the Mexican War,* 150–61, 226–29.

3. Spurlin, *Texas Veterans,* 229–33; Lane, AR, 42; G. W. Conn to John Ellis Wool, October 11, 1847, JEWP.

4. Taylor to Polk, August 1, 1846, HED No. 60, 336; Taylor to Adj. Gen., June 16, 1847, HED No. 56, 368; "A Proclamation by the General Commanding," SED No. 896, 18–19. Scholars have not examined in depth the circumstances of the U.S. occupation of Mexico, but see K. Jack Bauer, *The Mexican War, 1846–1848,* 82, 202–204, 218–26; Paul Foos, *A Short, Offhand, Killing Affair: Soldiers and Social Conflict during the Mexican-American War,* 113–49; and Justin H. Smith, *The War with Mexico,* 2:210–32.

5. Creed Taylor's Memoirs as John W. Hunter Literary Effort, TSL, 17, 83–84. Although the Texans were not the only volunteers who troubled Mexican civilians, historians continue to emphasize their poor conduct. For example, Bauer, *Mexican War,* 221; James M. McCaffrey, *Army of Manifest Destiny: The American Soldier in the Mexican War, 1846–1848,* 209–10; Stephen B. Oates, *Visions of Glory: Texans on the Southwestern Frontier,* 25–52. Wilkins argues that observers have exaggerated ranger conduct. *Highly Irregular,* 109–11, 138, 142. Robert M. Utley charts a middle course with echoes of Wilkins. Utley, *Lone Star Justice: The First Century of the Texas Rangers,* 57–86.

6. [Luther Giddings], *Sketches of the Campaign in Northern Mexico in Eighteen Hundred Forty-Six and Seven,* 332. In February 1847, Arkansas volunteers killed twenty citizens in a cave near Patos, and in March, Texas Rangers, under Mabry "Mustang" Gray, killed an equal number at Guadalupe. Taylor to Adj. Gen., May 23, 1847, HED No. 56, 328; Creed Taylor Memoirs, 249–53, 256. Foos characterizes atrocities in Mexico as the "wages of Manifest Destiny," a class-based reaction against the failed promises of the elite-driven rhetoric of expansion. Foos, *A Short, Offhand,* 113–37.

7. Bauer, *Mexican War,* 218–19.

8. J. A. Magee, Returns of Chevallié's Battalion Texas Mounted Volunteers, CSR-MW.

9. Lane, AR, 42–45.

10. Anonymous, March 27, 1847, *Niles National Register,* April 17, 1847; DMN, April 22, 1894; Felix to Friend, March 25, 1847, NOD, April 6, 1847; Taylor to Adj. Gen., April 4 and 21, 1847, HED No. 56, 317, 321; Bliss to Wool, April 21, 1847, JEWP; Magee, Returns, CSR-MW; [Giddings], *Sketches,* 329.

11. Lane, AR, 45–48. For a discussion of the identity of Nicolás and Antonia García, see Lane, AR (2000), 154.

12. Those who found the proceedings justified: A. Wislizenus, *Memoir of a Tour to Northern Mexico Connected with Col. Doniphan's Expedition in 1846 and 1847,* 78; Jacob S. Robinson, *A Journal of the Santa Fe Expedition under Colonel Doniphan,* 88–89; John Taylor Hughes, *Doniphan's Expedition,* 184; [William H. Richardson], *Journal of William H. Richardson, a Private Soldier in the Campaign of New and Old Mexico, under the Command of Colonel Doniphan of Missouri,* 78. Those who criticized the execution: Frank S. Edwards, *A Campaign in New Mexico with Colonel Doniphan,* 110; Odon Guitar to Connelley, June 14, 1906, William Elsey Connelley, *Doniphan's Expedition and the Conquest of New Mexico and California,* 487–88.

13. Lane, AR, 47–48; Robinson, *Journal,* 89.

14. Lane, AR, 48–50; Guillermo Morales to José María Parás, June 8, 1847, Mexican War Collection, Huntington Library, San Marino, Calif.; Bliss to Wool, June 14, 1847, JEWP.

15. Lane, AR, 50.

16. Lane, AR, 50–51; Lane file, CSR-MW.

17. Lane, AR, 51–52. Glanton later transferred to Hays's new regiment on September 1. Spurlin, *Texas Veterans,* 152.

18. NHT 3:180, 5:517.

19. Bliss to Wool, June 14, 1847, JEWP.

20. Wool, Special Orders No. 512, June 16, 1847, JEWP; Irwin McDowell to Chevallié, June 17, 1847, to George Adams, July 11, 1847, and to Lane, July 18, 1847, CDL; JED to editors, July 13, 1847, NOP, August 9, 1847. About the middle of July, an inspector criticized Lane for keeping an unclean and disorderly camp. McDowell to Comg. Officer La Encantada, July 21, 1847, CDL.

21. McDowell to Comg. Officer La Encantada, July 23, 1847, CDL; Wool to Chevallié, August 1, 1847, JEWP; Wool, Orders No. 405, August 16, 1847, Order Book, JEWP.

22. Lane, AR, 45; NOP, October 4, 1847; Spurlin, *Texas Veterans,* 151; McDowell, "Return of Volunteer Officers discharged the service," March 13, 1848, JEWP. Lane received 108 votes. Capt. Henry Baylor received 10. Chevallié received 1. Lane file, CSR-MW.

23. W. B. Franklin to Lane, August 31, 1847, McDowell to [Robert H.] Taylor, October 1st, and McDowell to Lane, October 16, 1847, CDL; Wool to Lane, September 1, 1847, JEWP.

24. [Robert H.] Taylor to McDowell, October 16, 1847, JEWP; T[obin] to Eds., January 4, 1848, NOD, February 6, 1848; Spurlin, *Texas Veterans,* 151–67.

25. José Ignacio Arsave to [John F.] Hamtramck, December 1, 1847, *El Monitor Republicano,* December 25, 1847; T[obin] to Eds., January 4, 1848, NOD, February 6, 1848; [Wool] to Hamtramck, December 10, 1847, CDL.

26. Wool to Bliss, July 28 and October 18, 1847, CDL.

27. McDowell to Lane, October 20, 1847, and to Hamtramck, November 7, 1847, CDL.

28. NYH, August 23, 1846; W. L. Marcy to Taylor, July 27, 1846, and Taylor to Adj. Gen., August 3, 1846, HED No. 60, 395, 402; McDowell to Arsave, October 6, 1847, CDL; Vito Alessio Robles, *Coahuila y texas desde la consumacion de la independencia hasta el tratato de paz de guadalupe hidalgo,* 2:229–43. Brian Delay argues that not only did Indian raids influence the perceptions that Mexicans and U.S. citizens had of one another, but that by raiding, native groups such as Comanches enacted deliberate, self-interested policies informed by their understanding of the geopolitical environment of the U.S.-Mexican borderlands. "Independent Indians and the U.S.-Mexican War," *American Historical Review* 112 (Feb. 2007), 35–68.

29. Lane, AR, 52–53; McDowell to Hamtramck, November 22, 1847, CDL; [Wool] to R. Jones, November 29, 1847, and to Taylor, November 29, 1847, JEWP; Lane to G. H. Nelson, November 22, 1847, NOP, December 15, 1847.

30. Lane to Nelson, November 22, 1847, NOP, December 15, 1847; Lane, AR, 55–56; T[obin] to Eds., November 25, 1847, NOD, December 26, 1847.

31. Lane, AR, 56, 56–55; Lane to Nelson, November 22, 1847, NOP, December 15, 1847; Lane to Nelson, November 22, 1847, NOD, December 15, 1847.

32. *American Flag* (Matamoros), December 8, 1847; NOP, December 15, 1847; NOD, December 15, 1847; *Daily American Star* (Mexico City), January 12, 1848; *Northern Standard* (Clarksville, Tex.), January 15, 1848; *Cincinnati Daily Enquirer,* December 27, 1847; *Niles National Register,* January 16, 1848.

33. Lane, AR, 54–55.

34. Tobin to Eds. *Delta,* February 7, 1848, NOD, March 12, 1848.

35. Charles Clark to Wool, April 9, 1848, JEWP; *Daily American Star,* January 7, 25, 1848; A. J. Trussell to James M. Trussell, February 28, 1848, Trussell Family Papers, UTA; Smith, *War with Mexico,* 2:418; *Texas Monument* (La Grange), July 20, 1850; *Cincinnati Daily Enquirer,* April 4, 1848.

36. Lane to Wool, February 4, 20, and April 7, 1848, JEWP. The February 20 and April 7 letters not found—cited from index.

37. Lane, AR, 56. According to T. B. Tinnard, Lane volunteered to accompany Pope. Tinnard to Hamtramck, April 2, 1848, JEWP.

38. Pope to Tinnard, April 2, 1848, JEWP; Lane, AR, 56–58.

39. Pope to Tinnard, April 2, 1848, JEWP.

40. *Texas Monument,* July 20, 1850.

41. In his 1887 memoirs, Lane included a detailed account of his exhumation of the Mier prisoners, which was not true. For a discussion, see Chapter 11. Lane, AR, 58–60; *Texas Monument,* July 20, 1850; Pope to Wool, April 2, 1848, and Louis P. Cooke to Wool, May 9 and 10, 1848, JEWP.

42. Wool, Orders No. 156, June 12, 1848, Order Book 1847–1848, JEWP; Lane, AR, 60.

43. Lane, AR, 64–65.

44. A. G. Stakes, et al., to Lane, June 30, 1848, and Lane to H. Clay Davis, July 1, 1848, *American Flag,* July 22, 1848.

Chapter 6

1. Olivia Lane was not a party to the sale of William Lane's town lots in Fairview, suggesting that she had passed away by 1847. An Olivia Lane who died on October 20, 1846, was buried in the Fairview Methodist Cemetery, but an inscription recorded in 1993 shows that her husband was John Lane, not William. The author could not locate the grave site in 1998 to confirm the inscription. Deed Records, Guernsey County Recorder's Office, U:139; Kurt Tostenson, *Cemeteries of Guernsey County, Ohio, Oxford Twp.,* 8:39. By 1850, William Lane and a daughter, Mary, resided with his son, Wade, in Louisville. Population Schedules of the Seventh Census of the United States 1850 (M432), USNA, roll 206.

2. Anonymous, July 16, 1848, *Wheeling Times and Advertiser,* December 20, 1848; CGT, January 5 to March 23, 1849; Hugh H. Davis, "Gold Rush Vignettes from Middlebourne," *Manuscripts* 34 (Spring 1982), 110.

3. Lane, AR, 65. William H. Lane moved to Liberty about 1830. Nadine Hodges and Mrs. Howard Woodruff, *Genealogical Notes from the "Liberty Tribune,"* 6:109; Population Schedules 1850 (M432), USNA, roll 396. The diary that survives may well have been written by Hixson in later years, based on a journal he kept during the journey. He also wrote a number of letters to the Liberty *Weekly Tribune,* that testify to the reliability of the surviving diary. JMH, 1–5; J. M. Hixson to Robert Miller, May 20, 1849, LWT, June 8, 1849.

4. JMH, 2; Hixson to Miller, August 6, 1849, LWT, October 26, 1849. For adventurism as an economic strategy, see Gary G. Hamilton, "The Structural Sources of Adventurism: The Case of the California Gold Rush," *American Journal of Sociology* 83 (May 1978), 1466–90.

5. JMH, 1–4.

6. Hixson to Miller, December 1, 1849, LWT, March 1, 1850.

7. JMH, 5–44; Hixson to Miller, May 20, 1849, LWT, June 8, 1849.

8. JMH, 22, 39–40

9. JMH, 12, 32.

10. John D. Unruh Jr., *The Plains Across: The Overland Emigrants and the Trans-Mississippi West, 1840–1860,* 9–27, 141–49, 156–60, 208, 244–66, 379–416; Malcom J. Rohrbough, *Days of Gold: The California Gold Rush and the American Nation,* 55, 61–66.

11. JMH, 7–8.

12. JMH, 16–17.

13. JMH, 106.

14. Hixson to Miller, August 11, December 1, 1849, LWT, October 26, 1849, March 1, 1850; Rohrbough, *Days of Gold,* 75.

15. Rohrbough, *Days of Gold,* 127–34.

16. During this time, Lane traveled with James, brother of William S. McMurtry. Hixson to Miller, December 1, 1849, LWT, March 1, 1850; Lane, AR, 65–66; *Nevada Journal,* March 13, 1852.

17. Lane, AR, 66–68.

18. NHT, 2:66, 3:519, 4:384–85; "Biographies of Leading Texans," TSL, 1:1–3, 144–45; John Waters file, Mexican War Pensions, USNA; Ben McCulloch to Henry McCulloch, December 24, 1849, Garnet A. Dibrell Collection, TSL.

19. Lane, AR, 68.

20. Lane, AR, 68; Benjamin P. Avery to Edwin F. Bean, December 20, 1866, in Edwin F. Bean, *Bean's History and Directory of Nevada County, California,* 75.

21. Bean, *Bean's History,* 10, 81; Israel Shipman Peltron Lord, *"At the Extremity of Civilization": An Illinois Physician's Journey to California in 1849,* Necia Dixon Liles, ed., 342–43; *Nevada Journal,* January 3, 1852. In November 1850, the census listed Lane and Hargrove in a household, with Samuel Nesbitt and Henry Buck. Population Schedules 1850 (M432), USNA, roll 36.

22. Lord, *At the Extremity,* 343–44; Avery to Bean, December 20, 1866, in Bean, *Bean's History,* 76; Lane, AR, 68.

23. Rohrbough, *Days of Gold,* 97–105; Susan Lee Johnson, *Roaring Camp: The Social World of the California Gold Rush,* 138, 141–42; Albert L. Hurtado, *Intimate Frontiers: Sex Gender and Culture in Old California,* 75–114.

24. Johnson, *Roaring Camp,* 168–70; Rohrbough, *Days of Gold,* 35, 94–95, 139–40.

25. Examining the more diverse southern mines, Susan Lee Johnson finds that forty-niners of Mexican and Asian descent often suffered under various forms of discrimination and violence at the hands of European Americans. Johnson, *Roaring Camp,* 25–53, 141–234.

26. Rohrbough, *Days of Gold,* 13–14, 61–62; McCulloch to McCulloch, December 24, 1849, Dibrell Collection, TSL; Lord, *At the Extremity,* 271.

27. Rohrbough, *Days of Gold,* 70–71, 75; Johnson, *Roaring Camp,* 177.

28. Lane, AR, 68–69; Bean, *Bean's History,* 81.

29. Lane, AR, 69.

30. Lord, *At the Extremity,* 345; Lane, AR, 69.

31. Lane, AR, 69–70; Population Schedules 1850 (M432, roll 36), USNA; MTR, February 16, 1856.

32. William S. Speer and John Henry Brown, *Encyclopedia of the New West,* 309; NHT, 4:61–62, 520–21.

33. The firm of Lane and Ward included a minority partner, C. S. Sabine of Jefferson. MTR, February 16, 26, May 8, 10, 1856; Ward Family file, HCHM.

34. MTR, August 16, 1856; W. P. McCall, extract of letter, January 6, 1857, MTR, February 21, 1857; Lane, AR, 70–71.

35. MTR, August 30, September 6, October 4, 1856; V. V. Ward to W. R. D. Ward, December 31, 1856, MTR, February 14, 1857.

36. Ward to Ward, December 31, 1856, MTR, February 14, 1857.

37. McCall letter, January 6, 1857, MTR, February 21, 1857; Ward to Ward, December 31, 1856, MTR, February 14, 1857.

38. John C. Reid, *Reid's Tramp . . .*, 13–14, 26, 80–81, 125–31, 181; MTR, December 27, 1856.

39. Reid, *Reid's Tramp,* 182–93, 197; Lane, AR, 71.

40. Reid, *Reid's Tramp,* 198, 200; Robert H. Forbes, *Crabb's Filibustering Expedition into Sonora, 1857,* 49–50; W. P. Lane to George Lane, May 3, 1857, MTR, July 11, 1857.

41. Granville Oury was a brother of William S. Oury, with whom Lane fought in Mexico and encountered in California. The two may have met again in Arizona as they remained in contact with one another at least into the 1880s. NHT, 4:1184; Oury to Lane, in Cornelius G. Smith Jr., *William Sanders Oury,* 234.

42. Reid, *Reid's Tramp,* 201–202, 204–10; Forbes, *Crabb's Filibustering,* 50–51; Lane to Lane, May 3, 1857, MTR, July 11, 1857.

43. B. Sacks, "The Origins of Fort Buchanan Myth and Fact," *Arizona and the West* 8 (Autumn 1965), 200–22; Lane, AR, 71; MTR, November 7, 1857, January 30, 1858. Reid first traveled to San Francisco, where he took passage to New Orleans via Panama. During the Civil War, he fought for the South at Murfreesboro, Chickamauga, and at Missionary Ridge as colonel of the Twenty-eighth Alabama Infantry. He died in Selma about 1909. Reid, *Reid's Tramp,* 242–45; Clement A. Evans, ed., *Confederate Military History,* 8:768–69.

44. Lane, AR, 71.

45. File C-4746, GLO.

Chapter 7

1. *Texas Almanac and State Industrial Guide,* 134, 139–42.

2. JMH, 17; Virgil Ward to W. R. D. Ward, December 31, 1856, MTR, February 14, 1857.

3. Lane, AR, 15, 23–24, 33, 47, 60, 64, 96.

4. Lane, AR, 47.

5. Mexican War Survivors Pensions, USNA; Population Schedules of the Eighth Census of the United States 1860 (M653), USNA, Roll 1296; Howard P. Chudacoff, *The Age of the Bachelor: Creating an American Subculture,* 33–34, 79–84, 92–101. Randolph B. Campbell notes that the citizens of Harrison County considered themselves as a single community of which Marshall was an important, but smaller, part. *A Southern Community in Crisis: Harrison County, Texas, 1850–1880,* 7, 99.

6. Mary Jane Lane recalled that sometime before or during the Civil War, her uncle Walter Lane deeded the Ward home to her in case he did not return from the war. In late 1863, she purchased several town lots from Ward for ten thousand dollars. [Mary Jane Lane] to Louella Styles Vincent, January [1906], Lane, AR (1928), 132–33; HCDR, T:550, Z:310, 333, 335–36, 427.

7. "General Lane Home, Built by Col. Ward in 1847, Was a Landmark," newspaper clipping, Walter P. Lane file, HCHM; [Lane] to Vincent, January [1906], Lane, AR (1928), 132–33.

8. HCDR, book 1, 214–15, 383; MTWH, January 13, 1881, June 1, 1882, January 25, 1883, May 29, June 12, 1884.

9. MTWH, May 2, 1882, July 5, 1885.

10. MTR, April 8, 1859; MHF, April 8, 1859.

11. MTR, May 20, October 8, 1859, January 28, February 25, April 21, 28, 1860, September 21, 1861; MHF, April 8, May 20, September 30, October 8, 1859, March 2, 23, April 27 1860; HCDR, S:753, 771, V1:471–73.

12. Walter Lane reported $5,000 in personal property, slightly below the mean of Harrison County merchants. Population Schedules 1860 (M653, Roll 1296); Campbell, *Southern Community,* 31, 84–85, 94.

13. Campbell, *Southern Community,* 19, 119–28, 148, 156–57, 176–79, 183–97. Although the experience varied in the disparate sections of the state, pro-slavery politicians led the call for secession in Texas. With clear economic, cultural, and political ties to the Lower South, they were better organized than their Unionist adversaries and co-opted the concerns of non-slave-owning Texans. Campbell, *Southern Community,* 183–97; Walter L. Buenger, *Secession and Union in Texas,* 8–118. For a meticulous examination of voting patterns of the period, see Dale Baum, *The Shattering of Texas Unionism: Politics in the Lone Star State during the Civil War Era,* 42–81. Clayton E. Jewett argues that in Texas the democratic ethic, frontier security, and non-slave agricultural pursuits "transcended a desire to maintain the

institution of slavery." *Texas in the Confederacy: An Experiment in Nation Building,* 11–75. Walter Lane, who made his reputation on western frontiers and who likely never owned a slave, followed in the wake of the pro-South, slave-owning elite of Harrison County.

14. Gerald F. Linderman and Reid Mitchell both emphasize the importance of family and community in motivating and shaping soldier's experiences in the Civil War. Linderman, *Embattled Courage: The Experience of Combat in the American Civil War,* 80–110; Mitchell, *Civil War Soldiers: Their Expectations and Their Experiences,* 56–89.

15. Lane, AR, 73; MHF, September 29, 1860; Population Schedules 1860, Harrison County, Slave Schedules (M653), USNA, Rolls 403, 661, 1310; Harrison County Tax Rolls, Texas Local Records, TSL. William Lane served in Sterling Price's Missouri State Guard. His son, Walter Jr., came to Texas and served in the Marshall company named for his uncle–the W. P. Lane Rangers–and later transferred to his uncle's regiment—the First Texas Partisan Rangers. R. S. Bevier, *History of the First and Second Missouri Confederate Brigades, 1861–1865: And from Wakarusa to Appomattox,* appendix, 18; W. W. Heartsill, *Fourteen Hundred and 91 Days in the Confederate Army,* Bell I. Wiley, ed., 83; W. P. Lane [Jr.], file, CSR-TX, Roll 192.

16. MTR, August 18, 1860; W. P. Lane to E. Greer, March 18, 1862, OR1, 8:300; Campbell, *Southern Community,* 99, 150.

17. MTR, June 2, 23, November 24, December 1, 8, 15 1860, January 5, February 23, 1861; Campbell, *Southern Community,* 183–90.

18. MTR, December 8, 1860; William W. Heartsill, *Fourteen Hundred,* 2–3; Campbell, *Southern Community,* 200; Ernest William Winkler, ed., *Journal of the Secession Convention of Texas 1861,* 200–202.

19. MTR, May 4, 1861; Campbell, *Southern Community,* 200–202; W. T. Scott to Edward Clark, April 19, 1861, Records of Edward Clark, Texas Office of the Governor, TSL.

20. MTR, May 18, 1861; Earl Van Dorn to H. E. McCulloch, May 25, 1861, and A. Pope, et al., May 7, 1861, OR1, 1:575–76, 53:679; W. T. Patton to *Dallas Herald,* May 5, 1861, DH, May 8, 1861; Campbell, *Southern Community,* 200–201. See also Wm. C. Young to Clark, May 2, 1861, Records of Clark, TSL.

21. MTR, May 18, June 15, 1861; T. A. Harris to "Dear Sir," December 9, 1861, Sixth Brigade, Brigade Correspondence, TSL; Population Schedules 1860 (M653), USNA, Roll 1296.

Chapter 8

1. Lane, AR, 73.

2. Gerald F. Linderman argues that Victorian ideas of courage left Civil War soldiers unprepared to meet the cruelty of war. By 1864, disillusionment replaced their superficial enthusiasm. Their experiences, furthermore, created a gulf between themselves and civilians who maintained the old ideas. James M. McPherson counters that enduring ideological convictions sustained soldiers, North and South, throughout the war. Although he

acknowledges that for some, adventure played a role, he emphasizes a sincere adherence to duty as the over-arching impulse. Lane's experience falls somewhere in between these interpretations. As a field officer, he did not represent the rank-and-file who populate these studies, nor did he experience the ghastly battlefields in the East on which Linderman focuses. Linderman, *Embattled Courage: The Experience of Combat in the American Civil War* (1987), and McPherson, *For Cause and Comrades: Why Men Fought in the Civil War* (1997). For a thoughtful review of the debate, see Mark Grimsley, "In Not So Dubious Battle: The Motivations of American Civil War Soldiers," *Journal of Military History,* 62 (1998), 175–88.

3. MTR, September 27, 1856, June 1, 1861; Douglas Hale, *The Third Texas Cavalry in the Civil War,* 26–27; Alvin M. Josephy Jr., *The Civil War in the American West,* 324–27.

4. A. B. Blocker Reminiscences (typescript), CAH, 3–4; Lane, AR, 73; MTR, June 1, 1861.

5. DH, June 19, 1861; Blocker Reminiscences, 4–6; Hale, *Third Texas,* 33–41.

6. DH, June 19, July 3, 1861.

7. DH, July 3, 1861.

8. S. B. Barron, *The Lone Star Defenders: A Chronicle of the Third Texas Cavalry, Ross' Brigade,* 27.

9. DH, June 26, July 3, 1861; Hale, *Third Texas,* 48–49, 55–56.

10. *Fort Smith Daily Times and Herald,* July 29, August 3, 1861; Hale, *Third Texas,* 50–57.

11. Barron, *Lone Star,* 40, 40–42; Blocker Reminiscences, 12–13.

12. Lane, AR, 73; M. D. Ector to Editor, August 12, 1861, MTR, August 31, 1861; Barron, *Lone Star,* 43; William Garrett Piston and Richard W. Hatcher III, *Wilson's Creek: The Second Battle of the Civil War and the Men Who Fought It,* 108–10, 146–48, 161, 187–286.

13. A. B. Blocker and historians Hale, Piston, and Hatcher placed Lane with the companies that remained behind. Lane, Greer, and Mills placed him with the companies at the ford, while Ector, in command of the separated elements, did not mention Lane in his report, suggesting that Lane did not serve with him. Blocker Reminiscences, 15, 19–20; Hale, *Third Texas,* 58–64; Piston and Hatcher, *Wilson's Creek,* 224–26; Ector to Editor, August 12, 1861, and Roger Q. Mills to C. R. Pryor, August 22, 1861, MTR, August 31, September 7, 1861; Lane, AR, 73–74; Barron, *Lone Star,* 43, 49; Greer to Ben McCulloch, August 12, 1861, OR1, 3:120.

14. Greer to McCulloch, August 12, 1861, OR1, 3:73–75, 118–20; Mills to Pryor, August 22, 1861, MTR, September 7, 1861; Lane, AR, 73–74. Totten's scathing report appeared in at least one Texas newspaper. *McKinney Messenger,* October 18, 1861; Piston and Hatcher, *Wilson's Creek,* 270–72.

15. Hale, *Third Texas,* 67–68.

16. John J. Good to Sue Good, August 26, 29, September 6, 20, October 7, 21, and November 29, 1861, in Lester Newton Fitzhugh, ed., *Cannon Smoke: The Letters of Captain John J. Good, Good-Douglas Texas Battery, C.S.A.*, 55–56, 62, 66, 74, 93, 100–101, 133; Hale, *Third Texas,* 73–76; Lane, AR, 75.

17. Hale, *Third Texas,* 78–79; McIntosh to General, January 1, 1862, OR1, 8:22; Blocker, Reminiscences, 36–37; Lane, AR, 76; MTR, January 11, 1862.

18. Lane, AR, 76. Linderman argues that Civil War soldiers were unwilling to express fear—that they defined courage as "heroic action undertaken without fear." *Embattled Courage,* 17–20. Lane's experience counters this observation. He often admitted fear throughout his Civil War and earlier career. He expressed those feelings, however, in his memoirs much later in life.

19. Lane, AR, 76–78; A. W. Sparks, *The War between the States as I Saw It: Reminiscent, Historical and Personal,* 160; McIntosh to General, January 1, 1862, and Lane to McIntosh, December 26, 1861, OR1, 8:23, 29; MTR, January 11, 1862; Blocker Reminiscences, 37–40; Hale, *Third Texas,* 80–82. See also, Lane to Victor M. Rose, February 4, 1881, in Sparks, *As I Saw It,* 338; Lane to Ector, December 27, 1861, MTR, January 11, 1862.

20. Lane, AR, 79; James J. Diamond to W. W. Diamond, December 26, 1861, and C. R. P[ryor] to *Herald,* January 13, 1862, DH, January 5, 29, 1862 ; MTR, January 11, February 11, 22, 1862.

21. Lane, AR, 79; Hale, *Third Texas,* 86–90; William L. Shea and Earl J. Hess, *Pea Ridge: Civil War Campaign in the West,* 2–59; Josephy, *War in the West,* 335–43.

22. Lane, AR, 79–80; Hugo Wangelin to Colonel, [n.d.], and E. Greer to D. H. Maury, March 1862, OR1, 8:228, 297; B. P. Hollinsworth, "Battle of Elkhorn (Arkansas)," *The New Texas School Reader,* 134–35; Barron, *Lone Star,* 65–66; Blocker Reminiscences (typescript), 47, 1; Shea and Hess, *Pea Ridge,* 76–77; Hale, *Third Texas,* 91–92.

23. Douglas John Cater, *As It Was: Reminiscences of a Soldier of the Third Texas Cavalry and the Nineteenth Louisiana Infantry,* 115; Blocker Reminiscences, 47; Stephen Hale quoted from Rose, *Ross' Texas Brigade,* 57.

24. Shea and Hess, *Pea Ridge,* 79–99; Hale, *Third Texas,* 93–94; Lane, AR, 80; P. J. Osterhaus to T. I. McKinney, March 14, 1862, Cyrus Bussey to Samuel R. Curtis, March 14, 1862, and Earl Van Dorn to Braxton Bragg, March 27, 1862, OR1, 8:216–21, 232, 283; Henry Dysart Diary (typescript), Pea Ridge National Military Park, 34.

25. Lane, AR, 80; Hale, *Third Texas,* 95; Theodrick Jones Logwood Diary (typescript), Harold B. Simpson History Complex, 9; Sparks, *As I Saw It,* 176; Barron, *Lone Star,* 68; Greer to Maury, March 1862, OR1, 8:298.

26. Some confusion exists concerning the composition of the cavalry charge at Pea Ridge. Hale and Josephy, for example, place Albert Pike's Indian regiments in the action, but they participated in a separate affair with a portion of the Ninth Texas Cavalry, during which they captured one piece of artillery protected by detachments of the Third Iowa

Cavalry. Bussey to Curtis, March 14, 1862, and Albert Pike to Maury, March 14, 1862, OR,1, 8:233, 288; Hale, *Third Texas,* 95; Josephy, *War in the West,* 342–43; Shea and Hess, *Pea Ridge,* 101.

27. Lane, AR, 80; Barron, *Lone Star,* 68; W. K. to *News,* March 16, 1862, *Shreveport News,* April 8, 1862.

28. Osterhaus to McKinney, March 14, 1862, OR1, 8:217–18; Dysart Diary, 35; Shea and Hess, *Pea Ridge,* 102–103.

29. Bussey to Curtis, March 14, 1862, and Greer to Maury, March 19, 1862, OR1, 8: 234, 293; Lane, AR, 80–81. According to Grady McWhiney and Perry D. Jamieson, the cavalry charge fascinated Civil War commanders but was largely ineffective, especially when facing infantry armed with rifles. McWhiney and Jameison, *Attack and Die: Civil War Military Tactics and the Southern Heritage,* 126–39.

30. Hale, *Third Texas,* 95–98; Lane, AR, 81–84; W. P. Lane to Greer, March 18, 1862, OR1, 8:300.

31. Lane, AR, 81–82; Cater, *As It Was,* 119.

32. Lane, AR, 82; Shea and Hess, *Pea Ridge,* 251–52.

33. Barron, *Lone Star,* 71–73; Lane to Greer, March 18, 1862, OR1, 8:300; D. R. Garrett to Wm. Gibbard, March 20, 1862, Hobart Key Jr. and Max S. Lale, eds., *The Civil War Letters of David R. Garrett, Detailing the Adventures of the 6th Texas Cavalry, 1861–1865,* 49; Lane, AR, 83; Hollinsworth, "Battle of Elkhorn," 137–38; Shea and Hess, *Pea Ridge,* 313.

34. Maury to Greer, March 19, 1862, Trans-Mississippi District Letters, Special Collections Division, University of Arkansas Libraries; Hale, *Third Texas,* 101–104.

35. Rose, *Ross' Brigade,* 64; Lane, AR, 84. See also, Blocker Reminiscences, 59; Barron, *Lone Star,* 79.

36. Homer L. Kerr, ed., *Fighting with Ross' Texas Cavalry Brigade, C.S.A: The Diary of George L. Griscom, Adjutant, 9th Texas Cavalry,* 35; Hale, *Third Texas,* 106–107; Lane, General Orders, April 17, 1862, John A. Bryan Papers, CAH.

37. J. L. Hogg to Gen. Beauregard, April 26, 1862, Lane to Hogg, April 27, 1862, and Hogg to J. B. Slaughter, April 27, 1862, in Joseph L. Hogg file, CSR-CGS, roll 129; Blocker Reminiscences, 63–65; Lane, AR, 84–85; Barron, *Lone Star,* 82; Hale, *Third Texas,* 108.

38. Lane, AR, 85; Blocker Reminiscences, 65; Lane to Hogg, April 27, 1862, Hogg file, CSR-CGS, roll 129; A. A. Slaughter to C. S. Williams, April 25, 1862, Lane file, CSR-CGS, roll 152.

39. Hogg to J. B. Slaughter, April 27, 1862, Hogg file, CSR-CGS, roll 129; Lane, AR, 85–86.

40. Barron, *Lone Star,* 93; J. W. Whitfield to Thomas L. Snead, June 3, 1862, John W. Whitfield file, CSR-CGS; Hale, *Third Texas,* 112–16; Lane, AR, 86.

41. Cumby would resign his colonel's commission before the end of summer, 1862. Hale, *Third Texas,* 110–16, 121; Lane, AR, 86–87.

42. Schuyler Hamilton to General Elliott, June 17, 1862, Beauregard to S. Cooper, [n.d.], and John E. Murray to General Cleburne, May 4, 1862, OR1, 10.1:724–25, 762–65, 10.2:485–86; Lane, AR, 87, 89; Lane to Colonel, June 2, 1862, MTR, July 12, 1862; Robert C. Cotner, ed., "Reminiscences of the War: The Last Days at Corinth," ETHJ 20 (No. 1, 1982), 48–49.

43. Lane to Colonel, June 2, 1862, MTR, July 12, 1862; Barron, *Lone Star,* 94; Cotner, ed., "Reminiscences," 49.

44. Cater, *As It Was,* 135; Lane, AR, 89; Lane to Colonel, June 2, 1862, MTR, July 12, 1862.

45. Cater, *As It Was,* 135; Whitfield to Snead, June 3, 1862, Whitfield file, CSR-CGS; Lane, AR, 90; George Wm. Brent, G. O. No. 62, June 4, 1862, OR1, 10.2:583–84. The memory of Farmington would linger with Lane and the men with whom he fought. For his action there, an early Texas historian, John Henry Brown, would attach to Lane the sobriquet, "the Marshal Ney of Texas," comparing him to Michel Ney, the general who in 1812 defended Napoleon's retreat from Russia. William S. Speer and John Henry Brown, *Encyclopedia of the New West,* 311.

46. Lane, AR, 90–91; Hale, *Third Texas,* 120–266.

Chapter 9

1. A. B. Blocker Reminiscences (typescript), CAH, 65; Lane, AR, 85.

2. Thos. Cellum to Victor M. Rose, June 30, 1881, Victor Marion Rose Papers, CAH.

3. Lane, AR, 90–91.

4. Lane, AR, 90; W. P. Lane to R. W. Loughery, September 6, 1861, MTR, September 28, 1861; Lane, General Orders, April 17, 1862, John A. Bryan Papers, CAH; S. B. Barron, *The Lone Star Defenders,* 27, 29–30.

5. S. Cooper, G. O. No. 30, April 28, 1862, OR4, 1:1094–95.

6. Lane, AR, 92; A. M. Burnham file, CSR-CGS, roll 41; MTR, June 21, 28, and July 19, 1862; Jno. T. Mills to J. Y. Dashiell, April 3, 1862, Sixth Brigade, Brigade Correspondence, TSL; Various files, CSR-TX, roll 192.

7. All files, CSR-TX, roll 192; various files, Confederate Pension Applications, TSL; MTR, March 15, August 9, 1862, June 29, 1876.

8. Lane, AR, 92; J. P. Johnson, "My War Experience," (typescript), Harold B. Simpson History Complex, 2; MTR, July 19, 1862.

9. R. C. Newton, G. O. No. 26, July 27, 1862, clipping of Tyler *Reporter,* Garnet A. Dibrell Collection, TSL; A. Neill to Agnes Neill, August 3, 1862, Andrew Neill Papers, TSL.

10. Charles DeMorse to Clarksville *Standard,* August 24, 1862, DH, September 20, 1862; Neill, "Attention, Partizan Rancers!" [*sic*], August 15, 1862, T. Michael Parrish and Robert M. Willingham Jr., *Confederate Imprints: A Bibliography of Southern Publications from Secession to Surrender,* No 4976.

11. H. McKay, orders, August 4, 1862, MTR, August 9, 1863. In addition to Wilcox, the signers included: Malcolm D. Graham, Peter W. Gray, Claiborne C. Herbert, William S. Oldham, Frank B. Sexton, Louis T. Wigfall, and William B. Wright. W. Wright, et al., to Jefferson Davis, August 23, 1862, Lane file, CSR-CGS, roll 152.

12. Marcus J. Wright, comp., *Texas in the War, 1861–1865*, 4, 6, 14–16, 77, 80, 89, 92–93; Wright, et al., to Davis, August 23, 1862, Lane file, CSR-CGS, roll 152.

13. James M. McPherson, for example, takes a dim view of political generals. McPherson, *Battle Cry of Freedom: The Civil War Era*, 328–29. Ralph A. Wooster evaluated the Texas generals, ranking Ector and Gregg as "outstanding commanders," Scurry as "above average," and Steele as "probably the most disappointing of any Texas general." Wooster, *Lone Star Generals in Gray*, 233, 235, 238.

14. Neill to Neill, August 3 and September 19, 1862, Neill Papers, TSL; Wm. H. Barnes to Lizzie, October 25, 1862, William H. Barnes Papers, CAH.

15. Lane, AR, 92; MTR, October 11, 1862; McKay file, CSR-TX, roll 192.

16. Lane, AR, 92; T. H. Holmes to F. R. Lubbock, November 26, 1862, OR1, 53:836. Holmes replaced the weapons by May 1863. Dashiell to T. A. Harris, May 11, 1863, Adjutant General Letterbook, TSL.

17. Lane, AR, 92–93; A. P. Cartwright to Lon Cartwright, December 16, 1862, Cartwright Family Papers, CAH.

18. T. C. Hindman to S. S. Anderson, February 15, 1863, OR1, 22.1:171; MTR, February 22, 1863; Alexander Earp file, CSR-TX, roll 192.

19. MTR, February 22, 1863; Lane, Notice, January 15, 1863, MTR, January 22, 1863; Wm. Steele to Anderson, February 15, 1864, and J. F. Crosby to Crump, January 19, 1863, OR1, 22.1:28, 22.2:775–76.

20. Crosby to Crump, January 19, 1863, OR1, 22.2:776; W. P. Lane, General Orders, February 21, 1863, MTR, February 26, 1863. Earp later transferred to the Tenth Texas Cavalry. Earp file, CSR-TX, roll 192.

21. MTR, March 26, 1863; Lane, General Orders, February 21, 1863, MTR, February 26, 1863; R. F. Mitchell file, CSR-TX, roll 192. The staff that Lane appointed in 1863 included Adolphus Powell (assistant adjutant general), Thomas Poland (assistant quartermaster), John C. McKay (assistant commissary), and William D. Powell (inspector general). Emmett Carrington would later join as aide de camp. Form completed by Lane for Marcus J. Wright, n.d., Eldridge Collection, Huntington Library.

22. A. R. Chandler and Z. M. P. Motley files, CSR-TX, roll 192.

23. Harris to E. A. Blanch, April 28, 1863, Sixth Brigade, Brigade Correspondence, TSL; Dashiell to Harris, May 11, 1863, Adjutant General Letterbook, TSL; Steele to Lane, April 22, 1863, and W. R. Boggs to Holmes, May 11, 1863, OR1, 22.2:830, 837.

24. Steele to Lane, April 18, 22, 1863, and Steele to Anderson, May 1, 1863, OR1, 22.2:827, 830, 834; MTR, April 25, 1863.

25. John D. Winters, *The Civil War in Louisiana,* 221–83; T. Michael Parrish, *Richard Taylor: Soldier Prince of Dixie,* 264–92; Donald S. Frazier, "Texans on the Teche: The Texas Brigade at the Battles of Bisland and Irish Bend," *Louisiana History* 32 (Fall 1991), 417–35; MTR, May 2, 1863; E. K. Smith to Richard Taylor, OR1, 15:1081.

26. S. A. Bean to Godfrey Weitzel, May 14, 1863, Weitzel to Richard B. Irwin, May 18, 19, and 20, 1863, OR1, 15:346, 26.1:36, 38, 39; C. G. Forshby to Eds. *News,* May 24, 1863, and J. B. Manning, letter, May 28, 1863, *Galveston Tri-Weekly News,* June 10, 20, 1863; H. H. Boone to Lane, May 26, 1863, *Bellville Countryman,* August 8, 1863; Smith letter dated, May 24, 1863, DH, June 10, 1863.

27. Richard Taylor, *Destruction and Reconstruction,* 137–39; Jas. P. Major to Louis Bush, June 30, 1863, and Boggs to Taylor, May 19, 1863, OR1, 26.1:217, 26.2:10–11.

28. Lane, AR, 92–94; Winters, *Civil War in Louisiana,* 284–89; L. Boyd Finch, "Surprise at Brashear City: Sherod Hunter's Sugar Cooler Cavalry," *Louisiana History* 25 (Fall 1984), 407–408; W. H. Emory to Irwin, June 30, OR1, 26.1:188.

29. Albert Stickney to W. D. Smith, July 9, 1863, and Major to Bush, June 30, 1863, OR1, 26.1:193, 218; Barnes to Lizzie, June 26, 1863, Barnes Papers, CAH; DH, June 22, 1863.

30. Cartwright to Parents, June 30, 1863, Cartwright Papers, CAH; B. F. Price to Sister, July 1, 1863, Mary Martha Hackney Papers, UTA; Barnes to Lizzie, June 26, 1863, Barnes Papers, CAH; Stickney to Smith, July 9, 1863, and Major to Bush, June 30, 1863, OR1, 26.1:193, 218.

31. Lane, AR, 93.

32. Lane, AR, 93–94; DH, June 22, 1863; Major to Bush, June 30, 1863, OR1, 26.1: 219.

33. Taylor to Boggs, June 23 and 24, 1863, OR1, 26.1:210–11.

34. Green to Bush, July 3, 1863, OR1, 26.1:227–29.

35. Price to Sister, July 1, 1863, Hackney Papers, UTA; Green to Bush, July 3, 1863, OR1, 26.1:228.

36. N. A. M. Dudley to W. W. Carruth, July 15, 1863, and Green to Bush, July 14, 1863, OR1, 26.1:207, 230; Lane, AR, 94.

37. Dudley to Carruth, July 15, 1863, and Green to Bush, July 14, 1863, OR1, 26.1:207, 230; John W. Lane to [*Herald*], July 14, 1863, DH, August 5, 1863; J. E. Hart to Editor, July 13, 1863, and CDB to Editor, July 14, 1863, Houston *Tri-Weekly Telegraph,* July 16, August 10, 1863; Lane, AR, 94–95; Winters, *Civil War in Louisiana,* 292–93.

38. C. Grover to Irwin, July 14, 1863, and G. Norman Lieber, G. O. No. 67, September 10, 1863, OR1, 26.1: 204, 205–206.

39. Green to Bush, July 14, 1863, OR1, 26.1: 231–32.

40. Mamie Yeary, *Reminiscences of the Boys in Gray,* 781; Smith to Taylor, July 12, 1863, OR1, 26.2:109.

41. McAdoo to [Pendleton] Murrah, January 4, 1864, Pendleton Murrah Papers, Office of the Governor, TSL; Murrah letter, February 20, 1864, and Lane to J. B. Slaughter, February 25, 1864, W. P. Lane file, CSR-CGS, roll 152; Rebecca W. Smith and Marion Mullins, ed.,

"The Diary of H. C. Medford, Confederate Soldier, 1864" SHQ 34 (Oct. 1930 and Jan. 1931), 106–40, 203–30.

42. Ludwell H. Johnson, *Red River Campaign: Politics and Cotton in the Civil War,* 5–99, 112–13, 124–25; Gary D. Joiner, *Through the Howling Wilderness: The 1864 Red River Campaign and Union Failure in the West,* 1–108; Winters, *Civil War in Louisiana,* 317–39, 427; Parrish, *Richard Taylor,* 322–44; Smith to Jefferson Davis, June 11, 1864, and S. S. Anderson to Magruder, March 7, 1864, OR1, 34.1:479, 579.

43. Yeary, *Reminiscences,* 781; Smith and Mullins, ed., "Diary of Medford," 211.

44. R. Taylor to Boggs, March 24, 1864, Geo. Wyth Baylor to Captain Ogden, April 18, 1864, and "Organization of Troops," January 1864, OR1, 34.1:507, 618, 34.2:932.

45. Taylor to Anderson, April 18, 1864, OR1, 34.1:561.

46. A. L. Lee to George B. Drake, April 13 and 29, 1864, and Taylor to Boggs, April 2, 1864, OR1, 34.1:450, 454, 518.

47. Lee to Drake, April 13, 1864, Lee to W. B. Franklin, April 7, 1864, and Baylor to Ogden, April 18, 1864, OR1, 34.1:450, 454, 616; Lane, AR, 95.

48. Lane, AR, 95–96.

49. Theo. Noel, *A Campaign from Santa Fe to the Mississippi . . . ,* 116–17; Smith and Mullins, ed., "Diary of Medford," 213, 214; N. P. Banks to E. M. Stanton, April 6, 1865, OR1, 34.1:199; Joiner, *Howling Wilderness,* 82–84.

50. Johnson, *Red River,* 127–28, 132–69, 206–76; Winters, *Civil War in Louisiana,* 341–39. Lee quoted from Johnson, *Red River Campaign,* 134.

51. Taylor to Anderson, April 18, 1864, OR1, 34.1, 563; George Wythe Baylor, *Into the Far, Wild Country: True Tales of the Old Southwest,* Jerry D. Thompson, ed., 233; Smith and Mullins, ed., "Diary of Medford," 218; James K. Ewer, *The Third Massachusetts in the War for the Union,* 148; Lane, AR, 96–97.

52. Lane, AR, 97; J. O. Crutchfield letter [n.d.], DH, April 11, 1874; Taylor to Anderson, April 18, 1864, and Baylor to Ogden, April 18, 1864, OR1, 34.1:564, 617.

53. Yeary, *Reminiscences,* 421.

54. Lane, AR, 98; Mary Jane Lane to Louella Styles Vincent, January [1906], Lane, AR (1928), 136; Walter P. Lane Jr., file, CSR-TX, roll 192.

55. Major to Smith, July 20, 1864, Lane file, CSR-CGS, roll 152. After fire destroyed Lane's home in 1905, Mary Jane salvaged a letter that Major wrote to the colonel. She reported that the letter thanked Lane "in unreserved terms for the gallant manner in which he had always commanded the Brigade. . . . This noble acknowledgment was highly prized and very gratifying to my uncle." Lane to Vincent, January [1906], Lane, AR (1928), 135.

56. Smith, endorsement of Major to Smith, July 20, 1864, Lane file, CSR-CGS, roll 152; Smith to Cooper, October 28, 1864, Memoranda to Smith's letter dated October 28, 1864, and Cooper to Smith, December 23, 1864, OR1, 41.4:1017, 1019, 1122.

57. Lane to Vincent, January [1906], Lane, AR (1928), 136; Smith to J. G. Walker, August 7,

1864, OR1, 41.2:1045; G. to Jno. W. Swindell, August 12, 1864, DH, September 7, 1864; MTR, December 2, 1864; R. M. Caddell to Father and Mother, January 8, 1865, Third Texas Cavalry file, vertical files, Simpson History Complex.

58. Robert J. Townes, "Joint Resolutions Concerning Peace, Reconstruction, and Independence," November 15, 1864, Parrish and Willingham, *Confederate Imprints,* No. 4188; DH, January 12, 1865; MTR, January 27, February 3, 1865; *Henderson Times* (Athens, Tex.), December 17, 1864; Randolph B. Campbell, *A Southern Community: Harrison County, Texas, 1850–1880,* 217–18.

59. Smith to John A. Wharton, January 30, 1865, Boggs to Wharton, February 17, 1865, and Organization of Wharton's Command, March 1865, OR1, 48.1:1351–52, 1392, 1458.

60. Thomas L. Snead to Cooper, February 11, 1865, and brigadier general commission, March 18, 1865, Lane file, CSR-CGS, roll 152. Texas generals Richard M. Gano, William P. Hardeman, and Richard Waterhouse received their confirmations on the same day as Lane. Ezra J. Warner, *Generals in Gray: Lives of the Confederate Commanders,* 96, 125, 174, 327, 351–52.

61. MTR, March 24, April 21, 1865; Smith to Soldiers, April 21, 1865, OR1, 48.1: 1284; William Physick Zuber, *My Eighty Years in Texas,* Janis Boyle Mayfield, ed., 226; Lane, AR, 113–14.

62. Zuber, *My Eighty Years,* 226–27.

63. Joseph B. Mims file No. 01076, Confederate Pension Applications, TSL; Zuber, *My Eighty Years,* 228. Gerald Linderman argues that by 1864, soldiers on both sides suffered a pervasive disillusionment. Lane, and the Texans under his command, apparently did not suffer from this despondency until after Lee surrendered. They, however, had not endured the ghastly conditions in the East, as did those soldiers who populate Linderman's sampling. Linderman, *Embattled Courage: The Experience of Combat in the American Civil War,* 240–65. Brad R. Clampitt notes that the army in Texas equated Lee's surrender with the end of the war, and that many looted public supplies on their way home. Clampitt, "The Breakup: The Collapse of the Confederate Trans-Mississippi Army in Texas, 1865," SHQ 108 (Apr. 2005), 498–534.

64. MTR, May 26, 1865. Linderman and Reid Mitchell agree that many soldiers resented civilians like Loughery, who adhered to the quaint, pre-war notions of courage and cause without having experienced the horrors of combat. Linderman, *Embattled Courage,* 216–29; Mitchell, *Civil War Soldiers: Their Expectations and Their Experiences,* 56–89.

65. Smith to Allen, et al., May 9, 1865, and Military convention, [n.d.], OR1, 48.1:190–91, 48.2:600–602.

Chapter 10

1. Lloyd Wheaton, G. O. No. 1, June 20, 1865, and public meeting, MTR, June 23, 1865; Eric Foner, *Reconstruction: America's Unfinished Revolution, 1863–1877,* 124–227;

Randolph B. Campbell, *A Southern Community in Crisis: Harrison County, Texas, 1850–1880,* 217; Campbell, *An Empire for Slavery: The Peculiar Institution in Texas,* 248–50; Campbell, *Grass-Roots Reconstruction in Texas, 1865–1880,* 99–142; Max Lale, "The Military Occupation of Marshall, Texas, by the 8th Illinois Volunteer Infantry, U.S.A.," *Military History of Texas and the Southwest* 13 (No. 13, 1976), 39–48.

2. Walter P. Lane, signed parole, June 24, 1865, Lane file, CSR-CGS, roll 152.

3. Lane, signed oath, August 18, 1865, Lane to Andrew J. Hamilton (cover letter and petition), September 20, 1865, Pardon Petitions and Related Papers Submitted in Response to President Johnson's Amnesty Proclamation, 1865 (M1003), USNA, roll 53; Lane, AR, 73.

4. J. B. Williams and Davis B. Bonfoey endorsements of Lane's cover letter and petition to Hamilton, September 20, 1865, and Wm. Evans and A. R. Woodall to Hamilton, September 21, 1865, Pardon Petitions, roll 53; Campbell, *Southern Community,* 79, 87, 249, 255. Brad R. Clampitt lists Lane as one of twenty-seven Texans whose applications President Johnson rejected. This might refer to Lane's first application, which Governor Hamilton returned for lacking the necessary endorsements. The ultimate disposition of the application might have been lost in the backlog that Clampitt describes at the pardon clerk's office. Clampitt, "Two Degrees of Rebellion: Amnesty and Texans after the Civil War," *Civil War History* 52 (Sep. 2006), 255–81.

5. MTR, August 18 23, 25, November 10, 1866, March 28, 30, June 1, 1867, April 11, May 11, 15, 1868; MHF, August 23, September 13, October 25, 1866; Ward Family and Turney Family files, HCHM; Campbell, *Southern Community,* 86, 88–93, 260, 281–83. Virgil V. Ward, Lane's former partner and son of W. R. D. Ward, died in 1864 at his father's home while a member of the Seventh Texas Infantry. Ward Family file, HCHM.

6. MTR, July 24, 1868. Foner, *Reconstruction,* 228–80; Campbell, *Southern Community,* 276–88, 305. Kenneth M. Hamilton, "White Wealth and Black Repression in Harrison County, Texas: 1865–1868," *Journal of Negro History* 84 (Fall 1999), 340–59.

7. Lawrence D. Rice, *The Negro in Texas, 1874–1900,* 162–69; Campbell, *Southern Community,* 293–95.

8. HCDR, book V1, 744–50, book W, 493, 509, book X, 73–74, 459–65, 520, book Y, 224–28, 246–54, 293–94, 444–47, 451–54, 494, 524, 596, book Z, 552–55, book 1, 263–71, 401–405, 526–27; Population Schedules of the Ninth Census of the United States 1870 (M593), USNA, roll 1590; List of Registered Voters, 1867–1869, TSL.

9. MTR, October 18, 1868; Jefferson *Times and Republican,* July 29, 1869; HCDR, book W, 364; book Z, 333, 335–36; Ninth Census, USNA, roll 1590; Campbell, *Southern Community,* 301.

10. HCDR, book Z, 552–55, book 1, 213–15, 263–71, 383, 401–404, 526–27, book 2, 152, 349–51. Lane did not record his feelings about assistance from these women, but his attitudes toward females during this time receives discussion in Chapter 7.

11. CPW, October 1, 8, 29, 1873; William Steadman, Raguet and Fry, Matthew D. Ector,

and Lane to Richardson, Belo and Company, October 1, 1873, Galveston *News,* October 2, 1873; Margaret Humphreys, *Yellow Fever and the South,* 3–9, 21–25, 77–111; Margaret Johnson, "The Great Yellow Fever Epidemic of 1873 in Shreveport," *North Louisiana History* 30 (Fall 1999), 96–108.

12. Mary Jane Lane to Louella Styles Vincent, January [1906], Lane, AR (1928), 137–38; CPW, October 29, 1873; Humphreys, *Yellow Fever,* 34–35.

13. *Iron Age* article, CPW, December 10, 1873; Lane to Vincent, January [1906], Lane, AR (1928), 140; Jonathan D. Rudd obituary, *Confederate Veteran* 28 (1920), 346; Campbell, *Southern Community,* 184, 305–13, 338–39; Ezra J. Warner, *Generals in Gray: Lives of the Confederate Commanders,* 129–30.

14. [John Henry Brown], "Old Heroes of Texas—General Walter P. Lane of Marshall," DH, April 1, 1874; Lane, AR (2000), 117–19, 183–84.

15. Amory R. Starr, et al. to Lane, June 25, 1874, and Lane to Starr, et al., June 27, 1874, CPW, July 1, 1874.

16. NHT, 2:164–65, 436, 591–92; *Iron Age* article and other notices, CPW, August 5, 12, 1874; Lane, AR, 113.

17. *Iron Age* article, CPW, August 12, 1874; HFC to Editor, August 25, 1874, DH, September 5, 1874.

18. DH, September 5, 1874.

19. Jefferson *Times and Republican,* July 29, 1869; MTWH, May 29, 1875, March 22, 31, November 3, 1877, April 23, 1878. See also running advertisement, MTWH, September 16, 1876–January 6, 1877. In August 1876, Lane, McGill, and John T. Pierce formed the Harrison County Land and Immigration Company. The *Herald* viewed it as an opportunity to attract white farmers, but it apparently did not survive a year. MTWH, August 10, 1876.

20. MTWH, January 25, August 19, September 5, 12, 1876; Campbell, *Southern Community,* 314–15.

21. MTWH, February 27, 1877, March 30, April 18, 1878; MM, January 12, March 5, 23, 30, 1878; Campbell, *Southern Community,* 308–309, 333.

22. DH, April 12, 1878; MM, April 13, 1878; Stillwell H. Russell to Charles Devens, April 11, 1878, Letters Received by the Department of Justice from the State of Texas, 1871–1884 (M1449), USNA, roll 6; Thomas E. Hogg to Lane, April 11, 1878, MTWH, April 25, 1878.

23. MM, April 16, 20, 1878; Hogg to Lane, April 11, 1878, MTWH, April 25, 1878; Jno. B. Jones to W. F. Egan, April 28, 1878, Adjutant General Correspondence, TSL.

24. MTWH, April 23, June 6, 8, 1878; MM, May 11, 18, 1878; Register of Letters Received by the Department of Justice from the State of Texas (M701), USNA, roll 8.

25. MTWH, September 17, 1878; MM, November 22, 1878. Fraud, and perhaps intimidation, played a role in narrowing the voting margin. Campbell, including *Southern Community,* 334–56, and *Grass-Roots,* 134; Rice, *Negro in Texas,* 114–16.

26. Carl H. Moneyhon, *Texas after the Civil War: The Struggle of Reconstruction,* 188–205; Foner, *Reconstruction,* 587–601.

27. A Democratic court later cleared the defendants. MTWH, December 5, 1878, October 25, 1879.

28. MTWH, December 14, 21, 28, 1878, January 25, 28, 1879; MM, December 13, 1878.

29. Oran M. Roberts to Lane, May 17, 1879, and other notices, MM, May 23, 24, June 10, 1879; Lane to Roberts, May 30, 1879, Oran M. Roberts Papers, Texas Office of the Governor, TSL; Register of Elected and Appointed State and County Officials, 1878–1880, TSL; W. H. King to Lane, January 6, [1883], Letters Sent, Adjutant General Correspondence, TSL.

30. Lane to Roberts, July 12, 1879, and Lane to Francis R. Lubbock, July 12, 1879, Roberts Papers, TSL. In 1883, the adjutant general requested that Lane return the arms he borrowed. King to Lane, January 6, [1883], Letters Sent, Adjutant Generals Correspondence, TSL.

31. MTWH, December 16, 1879, March 18, May 18, 1880; MM, December 12, 1879, May 21, 1880; Campbell, *Southern Community,* 356–57.

32. MTWH, May 25, August 12, 24, September 16, 21, 1880.

33. Federal authorities charged sixty-five Harrison County citizens with voter fraud and obstruction. Forty-five pleaded guilty, and received light fines and no jail time. Rice, *Negro in Texas,* 116–17.

34. MTWH, November 6, 18, 1880, January 13, 18, 25, 29, March 26, 1881, June 20, July 11, October 10, 12, November 23, 1882; Lane to Editor, n.d., MTWH, March 5, 1881; HCDR, book 1, 338; Rice, *Negro in Texas,* 117–18.

35. MTWH, August 18, September 1, 4, 6, 12, 18, 1883; Lane to Vincent, January [1906], Lane, AR (1928), 136–37; Lane, et al., to John Ireland and Wilburn H. King, September 2, 1883, Adjutant General Correspondence, TSL; W. H. King, Report of the Adjutant General, December 15, 1883, *Texas Military History* 1 (Nov. 1961), 42–47. Reacting to their own racial anxieties, Anglo Texans often used the specter of Texas blacks organizing and arming themselves as justifications for violent action. For an enumeration of white crimes committed against Texas blacks, see Barry A. Crouch, "A Spirit of Lawlessness: White Violence, Texas Blacks, 1865–1868," *Journal of Social History* 18 (Dec. 1984): 217–32.

36. Population Schedules 1870 (M593), USNA, roll 1590; Population Schedules 1880 (T9), USNA, roll 1309; Lane to Vincent, January [1906], Lane, AR (1928), 140.

37. Lane, AR, 114; Lane, et al., to Ireland and King, September 2, 1883, Adjutant General Correspondence, TSL; Lane to Vincent, January [1906], Lane, AR (1928), 139–40; MTWH, September 4, 1883.

38. Lane to Vincent, January [1906], Lane, AR (1928), 136–37, 140; MTR, July 24, 1868; MTWH, August 10, 1876; CPW, December 10, 1873.

39. For Jim Crow Texas, see Alwyn Barr, *Black Texans: A History of African Americans in Texas, 1528–1995* (rev. ed., 1996), 173–229.

40. MTWH, June 12, July 5, August 26, 30, September 16, 23, November 4, 13, 1884.

41. MTWH, March 26, June 11, August 15, November 7, 1885; MM, June 4, 1886.

42. MM, September 6, October 8, November 5, 12, 1886.

43. DMN, July 20, 1886, January 15, February 18, 1887; John Ireland, "Message of the Governor," January 11, 1887, John Ireland Papers, Texas Office of the Governor, TSL; *General Laws of the State of Texas Passed at the Regular Session of the Twentieth Legislature*, 2–4; *Journal of the Senate of Texas Being the Regular Session, Twentieth Legislature*, 155–56; C. Richard King, *Wagons East: The Great Drouth of 1886—An Episode in Natural Disaster, Human Relations, and Press Leadership*, 1–8, 19–23; W. C. Holden, "West Texas Drouths," SHQ 32 (Oct. 1928), 103, 106–107, 116; Shirley W. Caldwell, "'God Help Them All and So Must We': Clara Barton, Reverend John Brown, and Drought Relief Efforts, 1886–1887," SHQ 106 (Apr. 2003), 506–30.

44. Lane to A. H. Belo & Co., February 20, 1887, DMN, February 21, 1887; Lane to Editor, n.d., FWG, March 1, 1887; Abilene *Taylor County News*, March 11, 1887. The *Dallas Morning News* and the Fort Worth *Gazette* carefully followed the movements and activities of the relief committee. DMN, February 7 to March 8, 1887; FWG, February 15 to March 6, 1887. The core of the drought-stricken region created a triangle from Dallas, Abilene, and Lawton in the Indian Territory. The area received only fifteen percent of its normal rainfall during the course of the dry spell. J. W. Williams, "A Statistical Study of the Drouth of 1886," *West Texas Historical Association Year Book* 21 (Oct. 1945), 85–109.

45. Lane, Teague, and Ferguson to Senate and House, March 15, 1887, *Journal of the Senate*, 492–94.

Chapter 11

1. Lane's letter dated September 25, 1877, and the adjutant general's response, dated October 25, have not survived. Registers of Letters, Received, Adjutant General Correspondence, TSL.

2. William Physick Zuber, *My Eighty Years in Texas*, 241–42, 244; *Proceedings of the Convention of Texian Veterans Held at Houston . . .*, 1–2.

3. *Proceedings . . . Houston*, 83–84.

4. Lane obtained his pension, and testified on behalf of a number of former comrades. Lane and various files, RTP; *Proceedings . . . Houston*, 83.

5. *Proceedings . . . Houston*, 84; Lane and R. K. Goodloe to President, May 21, 1874, TVA; DMN, April 22, 1886. Although he focuses on race and reconciliation, David W. Blight notes that reunions of Civil War veterans also celebrated the "former strenuous life" and "a time of authentic, romantic experience." Blight, *Race and Reunion: The Civil War in American Memory*, 172, 199, 208–209.

6. Mary Jane Lane to Brown, January 4, 1881, JHBFP.

7. Lane's extant correspondence with Bryan dates from May 1874 to January 1886. Lane

to Moses A. Bryan, April 2 and 12, 1885, MAB; Mary Jane Lane to Brown, January 4, 1881, JHBFP; Lane, AR (2000), 127, 135, 136. Lane also befriended Guy M. Bryan and Anthony Deffenbaugh, officers of the association.

8. Lane to Moses Bryan, April 12, 1885, MAB; Lane to Brown, March 23, 1886, JHBFP; Lane, AR, 40; MTWH, June 29, 1876, June 24, 1878, October 1, 1881; DH, April 20, 1882.

9. CPW, October 15, 1873; DH, January 3, 1874, August 7, 14, 1884; MTWH, March 11, 1879, October 11, 1881, October 12, 1882, July 14, August 7, 1883, August 5, 1884; Walter P. Lane Camp U.C.V. file, HCHM. Lane also attended reunions of U.S.-Mexican War veterans. Frank S. Bond to Lane and J. M. Curtis, May 17, 1876, MTWH, May 23, 1876. Furthermore, Lane was active in local, patriotic celebrations, and a supporter of the Irish Land League movement. MTWH, June 13, July 3, 8, 1876, October 15, 18, 20, 1881, May 2, June 1, 1882; MM, March 26, 1880.

10. MTWH, including, June 25, 1878, April 21, 26, 1881, April 20, May 2, 1882, April 25, 1883; *Proceedings, Constitution, By-Laws and Address of the Old Texas Veterans Held at San Antonio,* 6; Brown to Lane, April 18, 1885, *Proceedings, Constitution, By-Laws and Addresses of the Texas Veterans Held at Paris and Sherman;* Lane to Vincent, [1906], and Mary Jane Lane, "The Passing of the Texas Veterans' Association," Lane, AR (1928), 132, 150–51.

11. J. B. Robertson to Guy M. Bryan, March 9, 1884, Guy Morrison Bryan Papers, CAH; *Proceedings . . . Paris and Sherman,* 1.

12. A. Deffenbaugh to Moses Bryan, February 15, 1885, and Lane to Moses Bryan, February 17 and 19, 1885, MAB.

13. Austin *Statesman* and Sherman newspaper clippings, attached to William Neal Ramey to Moses Bryan, March 17, 1885, MAB.

14. C. N. Buckler to Lane, March 20, 1885, and Lane to Bryan, March 23, 1885, MAB; *Proceedings . . . Paris and Sherman,* 22.

15. Brown to Lane, April 18, 1885, Jackson Crouch to Lane, April 18, 1885, W. H. Wilkes to Lane, April 20, 1885, and W. L. [Cabell] to Lane, April 20, 1885, *Proceedings . . . Paris and Sherman,* 42; Lane to Brown, January 15, March 6, and 11, 1886, JHBFP.

16. DMN, April 19, 21, 22, 1886.

17. Alwyn Barr, "The Semicentennial of Texas Independence in 1886," SHQ 91 (Jan. 1988), 349–59; DMN, April 20, 21, 22, 1886.

18. Lane to James T. DeShields, May 18, 1885, in James T. DeShields, *Border Wars of Texas,* 247–50; DeShields to Brown, February 12, 1886, JHBFP; Lane to Moses Bryan, September 12, 1885, TVA; Sam DeShong Ratcliffe, *Painting Texas History to 1900,* 43–44.

19. MM, April 20, 1878; William S. Speer and John Henry Brown, *Encyclopedia of the New West,* 311; DH, January 15, 1885. Beginning in 1880, a renaissance of reminiscences and reunions flourished, as many Civil War veterans began grappling with the meanings of their experiences. Gerald F. Linderman, *Embattled Courage: The Experience of Combat in the American Civil War,* 275–97; Blight, *Race and Reunion,* 170–209. Laura Lyons McLemore

argues that Texas lore-makers of the late nineteenth century emphasized the pioneer heroism of the revolution and republic era over the Civil War, disconnecting Texas from the failures and stigma of the lost cause. McLemore, *Inventing Texas: Early Historians of the Lone Star State,* 71–80. Lane's experience suggests that Texans celebrated both ideas in his time, supporting the views of Walter L. Buenger and Gregg Cantrell, who argue that this disconnection from the Civil War occurred in the early twentieth century. Buenger, "Texas and the South," SHQ 103 (Jan. 2000), 308–24; Cantrell, "The Bones of Stephen F. Austin: History and Memory in Progressive-Era Texas," SHQ 108 (Oct. 2004), 144–78.

20. Lane, AR, 101; Lane, AR (1928), 131. Lane's peculiar use of italics in both his correspondence and the book, and the similarities to earlier versions of the stories, demonstrate that the words in his memoirs were his own.

21. Lane to Guy Bryan, April 4, 1888, Guy Bryan Papers; Lane to Brown, January [16], 26, and February 10, 1888, JHBFP.

22. Lane, AR, passim.

23. JMH, 3.

24. Compare Lane to Victor M. Rose, February 4, 1881, in Rose, *Ross' Texas Brigade: Being a Narrative of Events Connected with Its Service in the Late War between the States,* 127–28; Lane to Moses Bryan, September 12, 1885, TVA; Lane to DeShields, May 18, 1885, *Border Wars,* 247–50; and MTWH, September 10, 1881, to Lane, AR, 9–10, 25–34, 75–78.

25. These included Lane's tour during the 1838 Córdova Revolt and the 1861 Washita expedition.

26. Lane, AR, 13–15, 64, 94–95.

27. Includes Joseph H. Bell, Eugene B. Blocker, Andrew E. Clemmons, John N. Coleman, and others.

28. Lane, AR, 89.

29. Louis P. Cook to [John E.] Wool, May 10, 1848, JEWP; La Grange, *Texas Monument,* July 20, 1850.

30. Dallas *Morning Call* reprinted in MM, April 20, 1878.

31. MM, April 20, 1878.

32. MTWH, September 10, 1881.

33. Speer and Brown, *Encyclopedia,* 311; Mary Jane Lane to Brown, January 4, 1881, JHBFP; *Proceedings . . . Paris and Sherman,* 50–54; John E. Dusenberry file, Mexican War Pensions, USNA. A similar, but more open controversy, occurred at the 1882 meeting in Waco. Joel W. Robinson had claimed the distinction of capturing Santa Anna after San Jacinto, contradicting the honor given to James A. Sylvester. A number of veterans came forward to denounce or support Robinson's claim. After several rounds of discussion, the veterans concluded that Robinson and Sylvester should share the credit. Galveston *News,* April 22, 1882.

34. Lane, AR, 101.

35. Lane, AR, 58–60. Lane's account was very similar to Dusenberry's, one of the actual participants with Lieutenant Francis. Apparently Lane could recall the details related to him after the rangers' return. *Texas Monument,* July 20, 1850; James M. Day, *Black Beans and Goose Quills: Literature of the Texan Mier Expedition,* 146–47.

36. For an insightful study of personal memory, see Richard White, *Remembering Ahanagran: Storytelling in a Family's Past* (1998).

37. Speer and Brown, *Encyclopedia,* 311.

38. Linderman observes that the spate of Civil War reminiscences after 1880 represented the authors' search for relevancy amidst Gilded Age disappointments and urban emasculation. Linderman, *Embattled Courage,* 280. Lane's experience seems to follow this pattern.

39. Lane to Guy Bryan, April 4, 1888, Guy Bryan Papers; FWG, April 19, 1890, January 29, 1892; Lane, et al., statement, April 21, 1891, battle of San Jacinto, Henry A. McArdle Notebooks, TSL. Lane published notices in delinquencies in the following issues: MM, February 26, 1886, March 15, 1889, December 11, 1890, January 15, December 19, 1891, January 16, 25, 28, 1892.

40. Lane file, Harrison County Probate Minutes, book J, 62; FWG, April 20, 1890.

Epilogue

1. MM, October 6, 18, November 7, 1890.

2. E. Anthony Rotundo, *American Manhood: Transformations in Masculinity from the Revolution to the Modern Era,* 48–50; Lane, AR, 45, 60–61, 67, 81; Galveston *News* reprinted in MTWH, May 2, 1882. The *News* reporter made this comment because a statewide prohibitionist convention met in Waco the same day as the Texas veterans.

3. MM, March 19, 30, December 11, 1891, January 20, 21, 23, 25, 26, 1892; *Proceedings of the Texas Veterans Association at the Annual Re-Union Held at Lampasas,* 1.

4. MM, January 28, 1892.

5. MM, January 28, 1892; Mary Jane Lane to Louella Styles Vincent, January [1906], Lane (1928), AR, 133; DMN, January 29, 1892.

6. The pallbearers were Joseph H. Bell, Eugene B. Blocker, Thomas H. Cellum, Edmund J. Fry, Endymion B. Gregg, and J. F. Godbolt. DMN, January 31, 1892; [Lane] to Vincent, January 1905, Lane, AR (1928), 143; William S. Speer and John Henry Brown, *Encyclopedia of the New West,* 342; Lane, AR, 78, 88–89, 90–91.

7. *Austin Statesman,* January 29, 1892; *Galveston News,* January 29, 30, 1892; *San Antonio Express,* January 29, 1892; FWG, January 29, 1892; Lane to Vincent, January [1906], Lane, AR (1928), 143; *Journal of the House of Representatives of the Twenty-Second Legislature, Extra Session,* 46; *Proceedings . . . Lampasas,* 8.

8. Lane to Vincent, January [1906], and miscellaneous clippings, Lane, AR (1928), 131, 132, 144–45, 155–57; MM, May 1, 1904, September 16, 1906; Mary Jane Lane died in 1922. Lane, AR (2000), 182.

9. Miscellaneous clippings, Lane, AR (1928), 155; newspaper clipping, Walter P. Lane file, HCHM.

10. David Grubin, dir., "Marshall, Texas; Marshall, Texas," *A Walk through the 20th Century with Bill Moyers,* episode 1.

11. Max S. Lale, "Walter Paye Lane, An Appreciation," Texas State Historical Association 96th Annual Meeting, February 1992.

12. Harold Schoen, comp., *Monuments Erected by the State of Texas to Commemorate the Centenary of Texas Independence,* 82, 91, 161.

BIBLIOGRAPHY

Manuscripts

Adjutant General Letterbook. Adjutant General Correspondence. Texas State Library, Archives Division, Austin.

Allen, Samuel Tabor, Family Papers. University of Texas, Center for American History, Austin.

Alsbury, Y. P., Reminiscences. University of Texas, Center for American History, Austin.

Barnes, William H., Papers. University of Texas, Center for American History, Austin.

Barrett, Lyne Taliaferro, Papers. Stephen F. Austin State University, East Texas Research Center, Nacogdoches.

Barton Family Papers. University of Texas at Arlington, Special Collections, Arlington.

"Biographies of Leading Texans." 4 vols. Typescript. Texas State Library, Archives Division, Austin.

Blocker, A. B., Reminiscences (typescript). University of Texas, Center for American History, Austin.

Brigade Correspondence. Texas State Library, Archives Division, Austin.

Brooks, John Sowers, Papers. University of Texas, Center for American History, Austin.

Brown, John Henry, Family Papers. University of Texas, Center for American History, Austin.

Bryan, Guy Morrison, Papers. University of Texas, Center for American History, Austin.

Bryan, John A., Papers. University of Texas, Center for American History, Austin.

Bryan, Moses Austin, Papers. University of Texas, Center for American History, Austin.

Cartwright Family Papers. University of Texas, Center for American History, Austin.

Compiled Service Records of Confederate General and Staff Officers and Non-Regimental Enlisted Men. 275 Rolls. Microcopy M331. U.S. National Archives, microfilm publications.

Compiled Service Records of Confederate Soldiers Who Served in Organizations from the State of Texas. 445 rolls. Microcopy M323. U.S. National Archives, microfilm publications.

Compiled Service Records of Volunteer Soldiers Who Served during the Mexican War in Organizations from the State of Texas. 19 rolls. Microcopy M278. U.S. National Archives, microfilm publications.

Confederate Pension Applications. Texas State Library, Archives Division, Austin.

County Court Minutes. Harrison County Clerk's Office, Marshall.

Deed Records. Guernsey County Recorder's Office, Cambridge, Ohio.

Deed Records. Harrison County Clerk's Office, Marshall. County Court Minutes.

Deed Records. San Augustine County Clerk's Office, San Augustine.

Dibrell, Garnet A., Collection. Texas State Library, Archives Division, Austin.

Dysart, Henry M., Diary (typescript). Pea Ridge National Military Park.

Eldridge Collection. Huntington Library, San Marino, Cal.

Grayson Family Papers. University of Texas, Center for American History, Austin.

Hackney, Mary Martha, Papers. University of Texas at Arlington, Special Collections, Arlington.

Hixson, Jasper M., Diary (typescript). University of California at Berkeley, Bancroft Library, Berkeley.

Houston, Andrew Jackson, Collection. Texas State Library, Archives Division, Austin.

Hunter, John W., Literary Effort. Texas State Library, Archives Division, Austin.

Johnson, J. P. "My War Experience" (typescript), First Texas Partisan Rangers file. Harold B. Simpson History Complex, Hillsboro, Texas.

Kuykendall, James Hampton, and William Kuykendall Papers. Stephen F. Austin State University, East Texas Research Center, Nacogdoches.

Land Claim Files. General Land Office, Austin.

Lane, Walter P. file. Harrison County Historical Museum, Marshall.

Lane, William. "Gen. Walter P. Lane," mss. April 30, 1925. Walter P. Lane file. East Texas Baptist University, Rare Book Collection, Marshall.

Lathrop, Barnes F., Narratives. University of Texas, Center for American History, Austin.

Letters Received by the Department of Justice from the State of Texas, 1871–1884. Microcopy M1449. U.S. National Archives, microfilm publications.

List of Registered Voters, 1867–1869. Texas State Library, Archives Division, Austin.

Logwood, Theodrick Jones, Diary (typescript), Third Texas Cavalry file. Harold B. Simpson History Complex, Hillsboro, Texas.

Marriage Records, Probate Division. Belmont County Court of Common Pleas, St. Clairsville, Ohio.

McArdle, Henry A., Notebooks. Texas State Library, Archives Division, Austin.

Mexican War Collection. Huntington Library, San Marino, Cal.

Mexican War Pensions. U.S. National Archives, manuscripts.

Neill, Andrew, Papers. Texas State Library, Archives Division, Austin.

Pardon Petitions and Related Papers Submitted in Response to President Johnson's Amnesty Proclamation, 1865. 72 rolls. Microcopy M1003. U.S. National Archives, microfilm publications.

Population Schedules of the Eighth Census of the United States 1860. 1438 rolls. Microcopy M653. U.S. National Archives, microfilm publications.

Population Schedules of the Fifth Census of the United States 1830. 201 rolls. Microcopy M19. U.S. National Archives, microfilm publications.

Population Schedules of the Ninth Census of the United States 1870. 1748 rolls. Microcopy M593. U.S. National Archives, microfilm publications.

Population Schedules of the Seventh Census of the United States 1850. 1009 rolls. Microcopy M432. U.S. National Archives, microfilm publications.

Population Schedules of the Tenth Census of the United States 1880. 1454 rolls. Microcopy T9. U.S. National Archives, microfilm publications.

Probate Minutes. Harrison County Clerk's Office, Marshall.

Probate Minutes. San Augustine County Clerk's Office, San Augustine.

Register of Elected and Appointed State and County Officials, 1878–1880. Texas State Library, Archives Division, Austin.

Register of Letters Received by the Department of Justice from the State of Texas. Microcopy M701. U.S. National Archives, microfilm publications.

Republic of Texas Audited Military Claims. Texas State Library, Archives Division, Austin.

Republic of Texas Muster Rolls. Texas State Library, Archives Division, Austin.

Republic of Texas Pension Applications. Texas State Library, Archives Division, Austin.

Robert Bruce Blake Collection (typescript, 93 vols.). Stephen F. Austin State University, East Texas Research Center, Nacogdoches.

Rose, Victor Marion, Papers. University of Texas, Center for American History, Austin.

Tax Duplicate Records. Guernsey County Recorder's Office, Cambridge, Ohio.

Texas Collection. Rosenberg Public Library, Galveston.

Texas Local Records. Texas State Library, Archives Division, Austin.

Texas Navy Papers. Rosenberg Public Library, Galveston

Texas Navy Papers. Texas State Library, Archives Division, Austin.

Texas Office of the Governor. Texas State Library, Archives Division, Austin.

Texas Veteran Association Papers. University of Texas, Center for American History, Austin.

Trans-Mississippi District Letters. University of Arkansas, Special Collections Division, Fayetteville.

Trussell, Andrew J., Papers. University of Texas at Arlington, Special Collections, Arlington.

Turney Family file. Harrison County Historical Museum, Marshall.

Walker, Samuel Hamilton, Papers. Texas State Library, Archives Division, Austin.

Walter P. Lane Camp U.C.V. file. Harrison County Historical Museum, Marshall.

Ward Family file. Harrison County Historical Museum, Marshall.

Wool, John Ellis, Papers. New York State Library, Special Collections, Albany.

Government Publications

[Bonnell, George W.], Report of G. W. Bonnell, Commissioner, Indian Affairs. (Houston: Telegraph Power Press, 1838).

General Laws of the State of Texas Passed at the Regular Session of the Twentieth Legislature (1887).

Journal of the House of Representatives of the Twenty-Second Legislature, Extra Session (Austin: Henry Hutchins, State Printer, 1892).

Journal of the Proceedings of the General Council of the Republic of Texas

Held at San Felipe de Austin, November 14th, 1835 (Houston: [n.p.], 1839).

Journal of the Senate of Texas, Regular Session, Twentieth Legislature (Austin: Triplett and Hutchins, 1887).

U.S. Congress. *Correspondence between the Secretary of War and Generals Scott and Taylor and between General Scott and Mr. Trist.* 30th Cong., 1st Sess., 1848. House Executive Document No. 56.

U.S. Congress. *Mexican War Correspondence.* 30th Cong., 1st Sess., 1848. House Executive Document No. 60.

U.S. Congress. *Occupation of Mexican Territory.* 62nd Cong., 2nd Sess., 1912. Senate Executive Document No. 896.

Published Primary Sources

Barker, Eugene C., ed. "Journal of Stephen F. Austin on His First Trip to Texas, 1821," *Quarterly of the Texas State Historical Association* 7 (Apr. 1904), 286–307.

———, ed. *The Austin Papers.* 3 vols. Washington, D.C.: American Historical Association, 1924–1928; Austin: The University of Texas, 1926.

Barron, S. B. *The Lone Star Defenders: A Chronicle of the Third Texas Cavalry, Ross' Brigade.* New York: Neale Publishing Company, 1908.

Baylor, George Wythe. *Into the Far, Wild Country: True Tales of the Old Southwest.* Jerry D. Thompson, ed. El Paso: Texas Western Press, 1996.

Bevier, R. S. *History of the First and Second Missouri Confederate Brigades, 1861–1865, and from Wakasura to Appomattox: A Military Anagraph.* St. Louis: Bryan, Brand & Co., 1879.

Cater, Douglas John. *As It Was: Reminiscences of a Soldier of the Third Texas Cavalry and the Nineteenth Louisiana Infantry.* Austin: State House Press, 1990.

Chabot, Frederick C., ed. *McFarland Journal.* San Antonio: Yanaguana Society, 1942.

Claiborne, J. F. H., ed. *Life and Correspondence of John A. Quitman.* 2 vols. New York: Harper & Bros., 1860.

Cotner, Robert C., ed. "Reminiscences of the War: The Last Days at Corinth," *East Texas Historical Journal* 20 (No. 1, 1982), 48–53.

Cushing, S. W. *Wild Oats Sowing, or the Autobiography of an Adventurer.* New York: [n.p.], 1857.

Davis, Hugh H., ed. "Gold Rush Vignettes from Middlebourne: Letters of Anna E. Brown and Sibs," *Manuscripts* 34 (Spring 1982), 109–20.

Davis, Kathryn Hooper. *East Texas Militiamen.* 2 vols. Nacogdoches: Ericson Books, [1992].

Duval, J. C. *Early Times in Texas.* 1892 reprint. Austin: Steck Company, 1935.

Edwards, Frank S. *A Campaign in New Mexico with Colonel Doniphan.* 1847 reprint. Albuquerque: University of New Mexico Press, 1996.

Erath, Lucy A., ed. *The Memoirs of George B. Erath.* 1923 reprint. [Waco]: The Heritage Society of Waco, 1956.

Ewer, James K. *The Third Massachusetts Cavalry in the War for the Union.* [Maplewood, Mass.]: Historical Committee of the Regimental Association, 1903.

Ferrell, Robert H., ed. *Monterrey Is Ours! The Mexican War Letters of Lieutenant Dana, 1845–1847.* Lexington: University of Kentucky Press, 1990.

Fitzhugh, Lester Newton, comp., ed. *Cannon Smoke: The Letters of Captain John J. Good, Good-Douglas Texas Battery, C. S. A.* Hillsboro: Hill Junior College Press, 1971.

Ford, John Salmon. *Rip Ford's Texas.* Stephen B. Oates, ed. Austin: University of Texas Press, 1987.

Garrison, George P., ed. *Diplomatic Correspondence of the Republic of Texas.* 3 vols. Washington: 1908–11.

General Land Office. "Sabine County," *Maps of All Texas Counties.* Tulsa: Wolf & Bennett, 1920.

[Giddings, Luther]. *Sketches of the Campaign in Northern Mexico in Eighteen Hundred Forty-Six and Seven.* New York: George P. Putnam & Co., 1853.

Gray, William F. *From Virginia to Texas, 1835: Diary of Col. Wm. F. Gray Giving Details of His Journey to Texas and Return in 1835–1836 and Second Journey to Texas in 1837.* 1909 reprint. Houston: Fletcher Young Pub. Co., 1965.

Gulick, Charles Adams, et al., ed. *The Papers of Mirabeau Buonaparte Lamar.* 6 vols. Austin: Texas State Library, [1920]–1924.

Heartsill, W. W. *Fourteen Hundred and 91 Days in the Confederate Army.* Bell I. Wiley, ed. 1876 reprint. Jackson, Tenn.: McCowat-Mercer Press, 1953.

Holland, James K. "Diary of a Texan Volunteer in the Mexican War," *Southwestern Historical Quarterly* 30 (Jul. 1926), 1–33.

Holley, Mary Austin. *Texas.* 1836 reprint. Austin: Texas State Historical Association, 1985.

Hollinsworth, B. P. "Battle of Elkhorn (Arkansas)," *The New Texas School Reader.* 1864 reprint. Austin: Steck Company, 1962.

Hughes, John Taylor. *Doniphan's Expedition.* 1847 reprint. College Station: Texas A&M University Press, 1997.

Jenkins, John H., ed. *The Papers of the Texas Revolution.* 10 vols. Austin: Presidial Press, 1973.

Kerr, Homer L., ed. *Fighting with Ross' Texas Cavalry Brigade, C.S.A: The Diary of George L. Griscom, Adjutant, 9th Texas Cavalry.* Hillsboro: Hill Junior College Press, 1976.

Key, Hobart, Jr., and Max S. Lale, eds. *The Civil War Letters of David R. Garrett: Detailing the Adventures of the 6th Texas Cavalry, 1861–1865.* Marshall: Port Caddo Press, 1963.

King, W. H. Report of the Adjutant General, December 15, 1883, *Texas Military History* 1 (Nov. 1961), 42–47.

Kuykendall, J. H., ed. "Reminiscences of Early Texans," *Quarterly of the Texas State Historical Association* 7 (Jul. 1903), 29–64.

Lane, Walter P. *The Adventures and Recollections of General Walter P. Lane, a San Jacinto Veteran, Containing Sketches of the Texian, Mexican, and Late Wars with Several Indian Fights Thrown In.* Marshall: Tri-Weekly Job Print, 1887.

———. *The Adventures and Recollections. . . .* 1887 reprint. Marshall: Messenger, 1928.

———. *The Adventures and Recollections. . . .* 1887 reprint. Jimmy L. Bryan Jr., ed. Dallas: DeGolyer Library and William P. Clements Center for Southwestern Studies, 2000.

Lord, Israel Shipman Pelton. *"At the Extremity of Civilization": An Illinois Physician's Journey to California in 1849.* Necia Dixon Liles, ed. Jefferson, N.C.: McFarland & Company, Inc., Publishers, 1995.

Miller, Thomas Lloyd. *Bounty and Donation Land Grants of Texas, 1835–1888.* Austin: University of Texas Press, 1967.

Muster Rolls of the Texas Revolution. Austin: Daughters of the Texas Revolution, 1986.

Noel, Theo. *A Campaign from Santa Fe to the Mississippi . . .* 1865 reprint. Martin Hardwick Hall and Edwin Adams Davis, eds. Houston: Stagecoach Press, 1961.

Parrish, T. Michael, and Robert M. Willingham, Jr. *Confederate Imprints: A Bibliography of Southern Publications from Secession to Surrender.* Austin: Jenkins Publishing Co., [1987].

Pioneer, A. "Recollections of the Mexican War," *The Pioneer* (San Jose, Ca.) 15 (Feb. 15 to Nov. 15, 1900), 20–21, 36–39, 52–55, 88–91, 120–26, 152–54, 169–71.

Proceedings, Constitution, By-Laws and Address of the Old Texas Veterans Held at San Antonio. San Antonio: M. M. Mooney, 1880.

Proceedings, Constitution, By-Laws and Addresses of the Texas Veterans Held at Paris and Sherman. Austin: A. Deffenbaugh, 1885.

Proceedings of the Convention of Texian Veterans Held at Houston. . . . Galveston: [n.d.], 1873.

Proceedings of the Texas Veterans Association at the Annual Re-Union Held at Lampasas. Austin: Eugene Von Boeckman, 1892.

Reid, John C. *Reid's Tramp. . . .* 1858 reprint. Austin: The Steck Company, 1935.

Reid, Samuel C. *Scouting Expeditions of McCulloch's Texas Rangers. . . .* 1847 reprint. Freeport: NY: Books for Libraries Press, 1970.

[Richardson, William H.] *Journal of William H. Richardson, a Private Soldier in the Campaign of New and Old Mexico, under the Command of Colonel Doniphan of Missouri.* New York: William H. Richardson, 1848.

Robinson, Jacob S. *A Journal of the Santa Fe Expedition under Colonel Doniphan.* Carl L. Cannon, ed. Princeton: Princeton University Press, 1932.

Rose, Victor M. *Ross' Texas Brigade: Being a Narrative of Events Connected with Its Service in the Late War between the States.* 1881 reprint. Kennesaw, Ga.: Continental Book Co., 1960.

Schoen, Harold, comp. *Monuments Commemorating the Centenary of Texas Independence.* Austin: Commission of Control for Texas Centennial Celebrations, 1938.

Scott, Sir Walter. *Ivanhoe.* 1819 reprint. New York: Penguin Books, 1994.

Smith, Rebecca W., and Marion Mullins, eds. "The Diary of H. C. Medford, Confederate Soldier, 1864," *Southwestern Historical Quarterly* 34 (Oct. 1930 and Jan.1931), 106–40, 203–30.

Smith, S. Compton. *Chile con Carne: Or the Camp and the Field.* New York: Miller & Curtis, 1857.

Sparks, A. W. *The War between the States As I Saw It: Reminiscent, Historical and Personal.* Tyler, Tex.: [n.p.], 1901.

Taylor, Richard. *Destruction and Reconstruction.* 1879 reprint. Princeton, N.J.: Collectors Reprints, Inc., 1997.

Tepper, Michael H., and Elizabeth P. Bently. *Passenger Arrivals at the Port of Baltimore, 1820–1834: From Customs Passenger Lists.* Baltimore: Genealogical Publishing Company, 1982.

Texas Almanac and State Industrial Guide, the: The Encyclopedia of Texas. Texas Centennial Edition. Dallas: A. H. Belo Corporation, 1936.

Tostenson, Kurt. *Cemeteries of Guernsey County, Ohio, Oxford Twp., Volume 8.* Cambridge: Guernsey County Genealogical Society, 1993.

War of the Rebellion: A Compilation of the Official Records of the Union and Confederate Armies. 1880–1901 reprint. 128 vols. Harrisburg, Pa.: National Historical Society, 1985.

Williams, Amelia, and Eugene C. Barker, eds. *The Writings of Sam Houston, 1813–1863.* 8 vols. Austin: University of Texas Press, 1938–43.

Winkler, Ernest William. *Journal of the Secession Convention of Texas, 1861.* Austin: State Library, 1912.

Winters, James Washington, "An Account of the Battle of San Jacinto," *Quarterly of the Texas State Historical Association* 6 (Oct. 1902), 139–44.

Wislizenus, [Frederick] A. *Memoir of a Tour to Northern Mexico Connected with Col. Doniphan's Expedition in 1846 and 1847.* 1848 reprint. Albuquerque: Calvin House Publisher, n.d.

Works Progress Administration. *Ship Registers and Enrollments of New Orleans.* 6 vols. Baton Rouge: Louisiana State University, 1942.

Yeary, Mamie. *Reminiscences of the Boys in Gray, 1861–1865.* Dallas: Smith and Lamar, 1912.

Zuber, William Physick. *My Eighty Years in Texas.* Janis Boyle Mayfield, ed. Austin: University of Texas Press, 1971.

Secondary Sources

Alessio Robles, Vito. *Coahuila y texas desde la consumacion de la independencia hasta el tratato de paz de guadalupe hidalgo.* 2 vols. Mexico, 1945, 1946

Anderson, Gary Clayton. *The Conquest of Texas: Ethnic Cleansing in the Promised Land, 1820–1875.* Norman: University of Oklahoma Press, 2005.

Armstrong, Mary K. "The Recovery of the Remains of the Mier Prisoners," *Naylor's Epic-Century,* (1935), 10–12.

Bauer, K. Jack. *The Mexican War, 1846–1848.* New York: Macmillan, 1974.

Baum, Dale. *The Shattering of Texas Unionism: Politics in the Lone Star State during the Civil War Era.* Baton Rouge: Louisiana State University Press, 1998.

Barr, Alwyn. *Black Texans: A History of African Americans in Texas, 1528–1995.* Revised Edition. Norman: University of Oklahoma Press, 1996.

———. "The Semicentennial of Texas Independence in 1886," *Southwestern Historical Quarterly* 91 (Jan. 1988), 349–59.

Bean, Edwin F. *Bean's History and Directory of Nevada County, California.* Nevada: Daily Gazette Book and Job Office, 1867.

Blight, David W. *Race and Reunion: The Civil War in American Memory.* Cambridge, Mass.: The Belknap Press of Harvard University Press, 2001.

Brittain, Hazel Miller. "Stories My Grandfather Told Me," *East Texas Historical Journal* 8 (1970), 125–62.

Bryan, Jimmy L., Jr. "The American Elsewhere: Adventurism and Manliness in the Age of Expansion, 1815–1848." PhD. Dallas: Southern Methodist University, 2006.

———. "'More Disastrous Than All': The Surveyors' Fight, 1838," *East Texas Historical Journal* 38 (Spring 2000), 3–14.

Bryan, Jimmy L., Jr., and Robert A. Calvert, eds. *Texas through Time: Evolving Interpretations.* College Station: Texas A&M Press, 1991.

Buenger, Walter L. *Secession and the Union in Texas.* Austin: University of Texas Press, 1984.

———. "Texas and the South," *Southwestern Historical Quarterly* 103 (Jan. 2000), 308–24.

Caldwell, Shirley W. "'God Help Them All and So Must We': Clara Barton, Reverend John Brown, and Drought Relief Efforts, 1886–1887." *Southwestern Historical Quarterly* 106 (Apr. 2003), 506–30.

Campbell, Randolph B. *A Southern Community in Crisis: Harrison County, Texas, 1850–1880.* Austin: Texas State Historical Association, 1983.

———. *An Empire for Slavery: The Peculiar Institution in Texas.* Baton Rouge: Louisiana State University Press, 1989.

———. *Grass-Roots Reconstruction in Texas, 1865–1880.* Baton Rouge: Louisiana State University Press, 1997.

Cantrell, Gregg. *Stephen F. Austin: Empresario of Texas.* New Haven: Yale University Press, 1999.

———. "The Bones of Stephen F. Austin: History and Memory in Progressive-Era Texas," *Southwestern Historical Quarterly* 108 (Oct. 2004), 144–78.

Chudacoff, Howard P. *The Age of the Bachelor: Creating an American Subculure.* Princeton, N.J.: Princeton University Press, 1999.

Clampitt, Brad R. "The Breakup: The Collapse of the Confederate Trans-Mississippi Army in Texas, 1865." *Southwestern Historical Quarterly* 108 (Apr. 2005), 498–534.

———. "Two Degrees of Rebellion: Amnesty and Texans after the Civil War," *Civil War History* 52 (Sep. 2006), 255–81.

Connelley, William E. *Doniphan's Expedition and the Conquest of Mexico and California.* Topeka: n.p., 1907.

Crocket, George Louis. *Two Centuries in East Texas: A History of San*

Augustine County and Surrounding Territory from 1685 to the Present Time. Dallas: The Southwest Press, 1932.

Cutrer, Thomas W. *Ben McCulloch and the Frontier Military Tradition.* Chapel Hill: University of North Carolina Press, 1993.

Dawson, Joseph G., III. *The Texas Military Experience: From the Revolution through World War II.* College Station: Texas A&M University Press, 1995.

Day, James M. *Black Beans and Goose Quills: Literature of the Texan Mier Expedition.* Waco: Texian Press, 1970.

Delay, Brian. "Independent Indians and the U.S.-Mexican War," *American Historical Review* 112 (Feb. 2007), 35–68.

Denham, James M. "New Orleans, Maritime Commerce, and the Texas War for Independence, 1836," *Southwestern Historical Quarterly* 97 (Jan. 1994), 511–34.

DeShields, James T. *Border Wars of Texas. . . .* Matt Bradley, ed. Tioga, Tx: Herald Company, 1912.

Dienst, Alex. "The Navy of the Republic of Texas," *Quarterly of the Texas State Historical Association* 12 (Jan. 1909), 165–203.

Diner, Hasia R. *Erin's Daughters in America: Irish Immigrant Women in the Nineteenth Century.* Baltimore: The Johns Hopkins University Press, 1983.

Dixon, Sam Houston, and Louis Wiltz Kemp. *The Heroes of San Jacinto.* Houston: Anson Jones Press, 1932.

Dixon, Walter Clay. *Richland Crossing: A Portrait of Texas Pioneers.* Everman: Peppermill Publishing Company, 1994.

Donnelly, James S., Jr. *The Land and the People of Nineteenth-Century Cork: The Rural Economy and the Land Question.* London: Routledge & Kegan Paul, 1975.

Evans, Clement A., ed. *Confederate Military History.* 1899 reprint. 17 vols. Wilmington, N.C.: Broadfoot Publishing Company, 1987–1989.

Everett, Diana. *The Texas Cherokees: A People between Two Fires, 1819–1840.* Norman: Oklahoma University Press, 1990.

Finch, L. Boyd. "Surprise at Brashear City: Sherod Hunter's Sugar Cooler Cavalry," *Louisiana History* 25 (Fall 1984), 403–35.

Foner, Eric. *Reconstruction: America's Unfinished Revolution, 1863–1877.* New York: Harper & Row, 1988.

Foos, Paul. *A Short, Offhand, Killing Affair: Soldiers and Social Conflict during the Mexican-American War.* Chapel Hill: University of North Carolina Press, 2002.

Forbes, Robert H. *Crabb's Filibustering Expedition into Sonora, 1857.* [Tucson]: Arizona Silhouettes, 1952.

Francaviglia, Richard V. *From Sail to Steam: Four Centuries of Texas Maritime History, 1500–1900.* Austin: University of Texas Press, 1998.

Francaviglia, Richard V., and Jimmy L. Bryan Jr., "'Are we chimerical in this opinion?' Visions of the Pacific Railroad before 1845," *Pacific Historical Review* 71 (May 2002), 179–202.

Frazier, Donald S., ed. *The United States and Mexico at War: Nineteenth-Century Expansionism and Conflict.* New York: Macmillan, 1998.

———. "Texans on the Teche: The Texas Brigade at the Battles of Bisland and Irish Bend," *Louisiana History* 32 (Fall 1991), 417–35.

———. "'The Battles of Texas Will Be Fought in Louisiana': The Assault on Fort Butler, June 28, 1863," *Southwestern Historical Quarterly* 104 (Jan. 2001), 333–64.

Furst, Lilian R. *Romanticism.* New York: Methuen, 1969.

Geiser, S. W. "Racer's Storm (1837), with Notes on Other Texas Hurricanes in the Period 1818–1886," *Field and Laboratory* 12 (Jun. 1944), 59–65.

Gibson, A. M. *The Kickapoos: Lords of the Middle Border.* Norman: University of Oklahoma Press, 1963.

Goetzmann, William H. *Exploration and Empire: The Explorer and the Scientist in the Winning of the American West.* 1966 reprint. New York: W. W. Norton and Company, 1978.

Graebner, Norman A. *Empire on the Pacific: A Study in American Continental Expansion.* 1955 reprint. Claremont, CA: Regina Books, 1983.

Green, Martin. *Dreams of Adventure, Deeds of Empire.* New York: Basic Books, Inc., 1979.

———. *The Great American Adventure.* Boston: Beacon Press, 1984.

Greenberg, Amy S. *Manifest Manhood and the Antebellum American Empire.* New York: Cambridge University Press, 2005.

Greer, James Kimmins. *Colonel Jack Hays: Texas Frontier Leader and California Builder.* New York: E. P. Dutton & Company, Inc., 1952.

Grimsley, Mark. "In Not So Dubious Battle: The Motivations of American Civil War Soldiers," *Journal of Military History* 62 (1998), 175–88.

Grubin, David, dir. "Marshall, Texas; Marshall, Texas," *A Walk through the 20th Century with Bill Moyers,* Episode 1. VHS tape. Alexandria, Va.: PBS Video, 1988.

Guinnane, Timothy W. *The Vanishing Irish: Households, Migration, and the Rural Economy in Ireland, 1850–1914.* Princeton, N.J.: Princeton University Press, 1997.

Hale, Douglas. *The Third Texas Cavalry in the Civil War.* Norman: University of Oklahoma Press, 1993.

Halsted, John B. *Romanticism: Problems of Definition, Explanation, and Evaluation.* Boston: D. C. Heath and Company, 1965.

Hamilton, Gary G. "The Structural Sources of Adventurism: The Case of the California Gold Rush," *American Journal of Sociology* 83 (May 1978), 1466–90.

Hamilton, Kenneth M. "White Wealth and Black Repression in Harrison County, Texas: 1865–1868," *Journal of Negro History* 84 (Fall 1999), 340–59.

Hardin, Stephen L. *Texian Iliad: A Military History of the Texas Revolution.* Austin: University of Texas Press, 1994.

Harrison, Brady. "The Young Americans: Emerson, Walker, and the Early Literature of American Empire," *American Studies* 40 (Fall 1999), 75–97.

Haynes, Sam W. *Soldiers of Misfortune: The Somervell and Mier Expeditions.* Austin: University of Texas Press, 1990.

———. *James K. Polk and the Expansionist Impulse.* New York: Longman, 1997.

Haynes, Sam W., and Christopher Morris, eds. *Manifest Destiny and Empire: American Antebellum Expansionism.* College Station: Texas A&M University Press, 1997.

Henson, Margaret Swett, and Deolece Parmelee. *The Cartwrights of San Augustine: Three Generations of Agrarian Entrepreneurs in Nineteenth-Century Texas.* Austin: Texas State Historical Association, 1993.

Hietala, Thomas R. *Manifest Design: Anxious Aggrandizement in Late Jacksonian America.* Ithaca, NY: Cornell University Press, 1985.

Hill, Jim Dan. *The Texas Navy in Forgotten Battles and Shirtsleeve Diplomacy.* 1937 reprint. Austin: State House Press, 1987.

Hodges, Nadine, and Mrs. Howard Woodruff. *Genealogical Notes from the "Liberty Tribune."* 7 vols. Independence, Mo.: Hodges & Woodruff, 1967–1982.

Hogan, William Ransom. *The Texas Republic: A Social and Economic History.* Norman: University of Oklahoma Press, 1946.

Holden, W. C. "West Texas Drouths," *Southwestern Historical Quarterly* 32 (Oct. 1928), 103–23.

Horsman, Reginald. *Race and Manifest Destiny: The Origins of American Racial Anglo-Saxonism.* Cambridge, MA: Harvard University Press, 1981.

Humphreys, Margaret. *Yellow Fever and the South.* Baltimore: John Hopkins University Press, 1992.

Hurt, R. Douglas. *The Ohio Frontier: Crucible of the Old Northwest, 1720–1830.* Bloomington: Indiana University Press, 1996.

Hurtado, Albert L. *Intimate Frontiers: Sex, Gender, and Culture in Old California.* Albuquerque: University of New Mexico Press, 1999.

Jewett, Clayton E. *Texas in the Confederacy: An Experiment in Nation Building.* Columbia: University of Missouri Press, 2002.

Johannsen, Robert W. *To the Halls of the Montezumas: The Mexican War in the American Imagination.* New York: Oxford University Press, 1985.

Johnson, Ludwell H. *Red River Campaign: Politics and Cotton in the Civil War.* Baltimore: John Hopkins University Press, 1958.

Johnson, Margaret. "The Great Yellow Fever Epidemic of 1873 in Shreveport," *North Louisiana History* 30 (Fall 1999), 96–108.

Johnson, Susan Lee. *Roaring Camp: The Social World of the California Gold Rush.* New York: W. W. Norton and Company, 2000.

Joiner, Gary D. *Through the Howling Wilderness: The 1864 Red River Campaign and Union Failure in the West.* Knoxville: University of Tennessee Press, 2006.

Jordan, Jonathan W. *Lone Star Navy: Texas, the Fight for the Gulf of Mexico, and the Shaping of the American West.* Washington, D.C.: Potomac Books, 2006.

Josephy, Alvin M., Jr. *The Civil War in the American West.* N.Y.: Alfred A. Knopf, 1992.

Kennedy, Robert E., Jr. *The Irish: Emigration, Marriage, and Fertility.* Berkeley: University of California Press, 1973.

Kimmel, Michael. *Manhood in America: A Cultural History.* New York: The Free Press, 1996.

King, C. Richard. *Wagons East: The Great Drouth of 1886—An Episode in Natural Disaster, Human Relations, and Press Leadership.* Austin: School of Journalism Development Program, University of Texas, 1965.

Lack, Paul D. *The Texas Revolutionary Experience: A Political and Social History, 1835–1836.* College Station: Texas A&M University Press, 1992.

Lale, Max S. "The Military Occupation of Marshall, Texas, by the 8th Illinois Volunteer Infantry, U.S.A.," *Military History of Texas and the Southwest* 13 (1976), 39–48.

———. "Walter P. Lane: An Appreciation." Texas State Historical Association 96th Annual Meeting, February 1992.

Land Commissioners of Texas: 150 Years of the General Land Office, the. Austin: General Land Office, 1986.

Limerick, Patricia. *The Legacy of Conquest: The Unbroken Past of the American West.* New York: W. W. Norton, 1987.

Linderman, Gerald F. *Embattled Courage: The Experience of Combat in the American Civil War.* New York: Free Press, 1987.

McCaffrey, James. *Army of Manifest Destiny: The American Soldier in the Mexican War, 1846–1848.* New York: New York University Press, 1992.

McLemore, Laura Lyons. *Inventing Texas: Early Historians of the Lone Star State.* College Station: Texas A&M University Press, 2004.

McPherson, James M. *Battle Cry of Freedom: The Civil War Era.* New York: Oxford University Press, 1988.

———. *For Cause and Comrades: Why Men Fought in the Civil War.* New York: Oxford University Press, 1997.

McWhiney, Grady, and Perry D. Jamieson. *Attack and Die: Civil War Military Tactics and the Southern Heritage.* Tuscaloosa: University of Alabama Press, 1982.

Merk, Frederick. *Manifest Destiny and Mission in American History.* 1963 reprint. Cambridge, Mass.: Harvard University Press, 1995.

Miller, Kerby, with Bruce Bolling and David N. Doyle. "Emigrants and Exiles: Irish Cultures and Irish Emigration to North America, 1790–1922," *Irish Historical Studies* 82 (Sep. 1980), 97–125.

Miller, Rick. *Sam Bass and Gang.* Austin: State House Press, 1999.

Miller, Thomas Lloyd. *The Public Lands of Texas, 1519–1970.* Norman: University of Oklahoma Press, 1972.

Mitchell, Reid. *Civil War Soldiers: Their Expectations and Their Experiences.* New York: Viking, 1988.

Moneyhon, Carl H. *Texas after the Civil War: The Struggle of Reconstruction.* College Station: Texas A&M University Press, 2004.

Morgan, F. A. *Wagon Train to Oregon—also—Guernsey County's Texas Hero and Confederate General. . . .* Quaker City, Oh.: Home Towner Publishing, 1987.

Nash, Roderick. *Wilderness and the American Mind.* Third Edition. New Haven: Yale University Press, 1982.

Nerlich, Michael. *Ideology of Adventure: Studies in Modern Consciousness, 1100–1750.* Ruth Crowley, trans. In two parts. Minneapolis: University of Minnesota Press, 1987.

Oates, Stephen B. *Visions of Glory: Texans on the Southwestern Frontier.* Norman: University of Oklahoma Press, 1970.

O'Flanagan, Patrick, and Cornelius G. Buttimer, ed. *Cork: History and Society, Interdisciplinary Essays on the History of an Irish County.* Dublin: Geography Publication, 1993.

Osterweis, Rollin G. *Romanticism and Nationalism in the Old South.* New Haven: Yale University Press, 1949.

Parrish, T. Michael. *Richard Taylor: Soldier Prince of Dixie.* Chapel Hill: University of North Carolina Press, 1992.

Paxton, W. M. *The Marshall Family. . . .* Cincinnati: Robert Clarke & Co., 1885.

Peacefull, Leonard, ed. *A Geography of Ohio.* Kent: Kent State University Press, 1996.

Piston, William Garrett, and Richard W. Hatcher III. *Wilson's Creek: The Second Battle of the Civil War and the Men Who Fought It.* Chapel Hill: University of North Carolina Press, 2000.

Pletcher, David M. *The Diplomacy of Annexation: Texas, Oregon, and the Mexican War.* Columbia: University of Missouri Press, 1973.

Poyo, Gerald E., ed. *Tejano Journey, 1770–1850.* Austin: University of Texas Press, 1996.

Ratcliff, Sam DeShong. *Painting Texas History to 1900.* Austin: University of Texas Press, 1992.

Rice, Lawrence D. *The Negro in Texas, 1874–1900.* Baton Rouge: Louisiana State University Press, 1971.

Rohrbough, Malcolm J. *Days of Gold: The California Gold Rush and the American Nation.* Berkeley: University of California Press, 1997.

Rotundo, E. Anthony. *American Manhood: Transformations in Masculinity from the Revolution to the Modern Era.* New York: Basic Books, 1993.

Sacks, B. "The Origins of Fort Buchanan Myth and Fact," *Arizona and the West* 7 (Autumn 1965), 207–26.

Sarchet, Cyrus P. B. *History of Guernsey County Ohio.* 1911 reprint. Columbus: Walsworth Publishing Company, [1983].

Schneider, Norris F. "The National Road: Main Street America," *Ohio History* 83 (Spring 1974), 114–45.

Shea, William L., and Earl J. Hess. *Pea Ridge: Civil War Campaign in the West.* Chapel Hill: University of North Carolina Press, 1992.

Slotkin, Richard. *Regeneration through Violence: The Mythology of the American Frontier, 1600–1860.* Middletown, Conn.: Wesleyan University Press, 1973.

Smith, Cornelius G., Jr. *William Sanders Oury.* Tucson: University of Arizona Press, 1967.

Smith, Henry Nash. *Virgin Land: The American West as Symbol and Myth.* 1950 reprint. Cambridge, Mass.: Harvard University Press, 1970.

Smith, Justin H. *The War with Mexico.* 2 vols. New York: Macmillan Company, 1919.

Speer, William S., and John Henry Brown, ed. *Encyclopedia of the New West.* 1881 reprint. Easely, SC: Southern Historical Press, 1978.

Spurlin, Charles D. *Texas Volunteers in the Mexican War.* Austin: Eakin Press, 1998.

Streeter, Thomas W. *Bibliography of Texas, 1795–1845.* Cambridge, Mass.: Harvard University Press, 1955–60.

Tolbert, Frank X. *The Day of San Jacinto.* New York: McGraw Hill Book Co., 1959.

Tyler, Ron, ed. *The New Handbook of Texas.* 6 vols. Austin: Texas State Historical Association, 1996.

Unruh, John D., Jr. *The Plains Across: The Overland Emigrants and the Trans-Mississippi West, 1840–1860.* Urbana: University of Illinois Press, 1979.

Utley, Robert M. *Lone Star Justice: The First Century of the Texas Rangers.* New York: Oxford University Press, 2002.

Ward, Ralph T. *Pirates in History.* Baltimore: York Press, 1974.

Warner, Ezra J. *Generals in Gray: Lives of the Confederate Commanders.* Baton Rouge: Louisiana State University Press, 1959.

Webb, Walter P. *The Texas Rangers: A Century of Frontier Defense.* Second Edition. Austin: University of Texas Press, 1965.

Weber, David J. *The Mexican Frontier, 1821–1846: The American Southwest Under Mexico.* Albuquerque: University of New Mexico Press, 1982.

White, Richard. *Remembering Ahanagran: Storytelling in a Family's Past.* New York: Hill and Wang, 1998.

Wilkins, Frederick. *The Highly Irregular Irregulars: Texas Rangers in the Mexican War.* Austin: Eakin Press, 1990.

Williams, J. W. "A Statistical Study of the Drouth of 1886," *West Texas Historical Association Year Book* 21 (Oct. 1945), 85–109.

Wilson, Steve. "Indians and Treasure Don't Mix," *Frontier Times,* December–January 1974, 8–13, 40.

Winslow, Richard E., III. *Wealth and Honor: Portsmouth During the Golden Age of Privateering, 1775–1815.* Portsmouth, NH: Portsmouth Marine Society, 1988.

Winders, Bruce. *Polk's Army: The American Military Experience in the Mexican War.* College Station: Texas A&M University Press, 1997.

Winston, James E. "Kentucky and the Independence of Texas," *Southwestern Historical Quarterly* 16 (Jul. 1912), 27–62.

Winters, John D. *The Civil War in Louisiana.* 1963 reprint. Baton Rouge: Louisiana State University Press, 1993.

Wolfe, William G. *Stories of Guernsey County, Ohio: History of an Average Ohio County.* 1943 reprint. Evansville, Ind: 1976.

Wooster, Ralph A. *Lone Star Generals in Gray.* Austin: Eakin Press, 2000.

Wright, Marcus J., comp. *Texas in the War, 1861–1865.* Harold B. Simpson, ed. Hillisboro, Tex.: Hill Junior College Press, 1965.

Wyatt-Brown, Bertram. *Southern Honor: Ethics and Behavior in the Old South.* New York: Oxford University Press, 1982.

Zweig, Paul. *The Adventurers.* New York: Basic Books, 1974.

INDEX

ISBN-13: 978-1-60344-070-7
ISBN-10: 1-60344-070-4